Collector's Encyclopedia of American
COMPOSITION DOLLS
1900 – 1950
VOLUME II

Identification and Values

Ursula R. Mertz

COLLECTOR BOOKS
A Division of Schroeder Publishing Co., Inc.

Front cover, L to R: 20" Nancy Lee, R & B; 14" Puss 'n Boots; 17"
Georgine Baby, Averill; 14" Hoo Choy; 17" Pinocchio, Knickerbocker

Back cover, L to R: 20" Nancy Lee, R & B; 19" Sonja Henie. MME.
Alexander; 11" Patsy Jr., Effanbee.

Photographs by Otto J. Mertz (unless otherwise noted)

Cover design by Beth Summers
Book design by Heather Warren

COLLECTOR BOOKS
P.O. Box 3009
Paducah, Kentucky 42002-3009

www.collectorbooks.com

Copyright © 2004 Ursula R. Mertz

The current values in this book should be used only as a guide. They are not intended to set prices, which vary from one section of the country to another. Auction prices as well as dealer prices vary greatly and are affected by condition as well as demand. Neither the author nor the publisher assumes responsibility for any losses that might be incurred as a result of consulting this guide.

Searching For A Publisher?

We are always looking for people knowledgeable within their fields. If you feel that there is a real need for a book on your collectible subject and have a large comprehensive collection, contact Collector Books.

Contents

Dedication

This book is dedicated to all those enthusiastic and persistent individuals who collect dolls, carrying them home one by one. Without the effort of these tireless gatherers, there would be no doll collections for us to admire and learn from.

Acknowledgments

No effort of this scope could ever be accomplished by one individual alone. Appreciation and many thanks are extended to all those who helped with pictures, information, or other support and encouragement.

Introduction

This book is intended to make American composition dolls more accessible and enjoyable for collectors and researchers by providing more in-depth, verified information. Wherever relevant, explanatory comments and references are listed with each individual doll.

New Discoveries

Many more dolls have come to light that have never been identified and studied before. It is particularly gratifying to be able to present so many new "finds" from the early decade (1910 – 1920). Ideal's Sanitary Baby (Peggy, Baby Talc), for example, though regularly featured in full-page illustrated ads in contemporary trade journals for at least four years, was heretofore unknown. Due to this lack of visibility, this vital, early period of American dollmaking has been greatly under appreciated.

Twelve of the rare Madame Alexander Portrait Dolls can now be studied.

Puppets and marionettes from the 1930s and 1940s have also been included, most notably those by Madame Alexander and Effanbee.

Assisting with Identification

Frequently, collectors have expressed the wish to know more about dolls without any identification marks. A special effort has been made to record unmarked examples in original clothes with original identification tags. If these dolls feature molded hair, close-up illustrations of the heads are provided, which will help identify unmarked dolls by comparing the configuration of molded curls. This should be particularly helpful with dolls from the 1940s, when companies shared molds for doll heads, and many dolls have come to us without embossed marks.

Collectors may also want to refer to the introductory chapters in *Collector's Encyclopedia of American Composition Dolls, Volume I*. In the sections on the manufacture of composition dolls, basic information can be found that would be helpful with identification. For example, if an unmarked doll has individually rocking eyes, the researcher should read the section on Ideal's winking, blinking eyes. Ideal had an exclusive patent on these, and thus, any dolls with these eyes were made by Ideal.

Another tool that can assist in identifying an unmarked doll can be the knowledge of trends and facts in manufacturing. A report on the American doll industry, published in *Fortune Magazine* in 1936, pointed out that 60 percent of the doll business went to three lines of dolls, Shirley Temple by Ideal, DyDee by Effanbee, and Madame Alexander's Dionnes. Of the remaining 40 percent of dolls produced at the time, most were imitations of those three.

While this was the case in the 1930s, it also held true for earlier periods. The ByeLo Baby, introduced in the early 1920s, was immediately very popular and encouraged numerous variations created by competing makers. In the late 1920s and early 1930s, it was Effanbee's Patsy that produced such a fascinating and varied group of look alike dolls. Having a basic knowledge of

such trends will definitely help collectors and researchers focus their studies.

While major companies set trends, smaller firms made their own important contributions. Their dolls should be studied with an open mind. The identification mark of a prestigious company on a head does not necessarily determine the merit of a doll.

With the passing of the year 2000, increasing numbers of American-made composition dolls will be considered antique rather than collectible or new dolls, and all collectors will want to know more about these precious playthings. Hopefully, the additional information and clear pictures provided in this book will help with this most enjoyable endeavor.

_____

American-made composition dolls with Oriental features. Manufacturer or seller unknown. Through unmarked, these three are typical examples of very collectible dolls which were made by small companies.

How to Use this Book

The Gallery of Dolls section of this book, beginning on page 9, is arranged alphabetically by manufacturer (name or subject, if a manufacturer is unknown). Subheadings list the names of dolls, designer, etc. An index which is cross-referenced will aid further with the identification of dolls.

Three Most Often Asked Questions

1. What should I put on my composition doll to preserve her?

The plain and simple answer is — nothing.

The examination of numerous dolls over many years has proven that any number of oils, creams, and other so-called preservatives only do harm. None of them are permanent in their structure. Oils become hard and change color, to name just one of the many problems. To remove a hardened and discolored film of oil from the air-brushed, painted hair (or face) of a composition doll is impossible. In other words, inappropriate preservatives have ruined many a good doll.

It has to be kept in mind that the dolls are mostly "naked" on the inside. While the outside surface has been made stable by a thin coat of oil paint, eye and mouth cuts are subject to changing temperature and humidity. While all of this may sound alarming, successful maintenance of composition dolls is relatively easy, once the requirements have been fully understood and a safe place created.

Maintaining relatively stable temperature and humidity is the only way to successfully maintain composition dolls. At a room temperature of 65 – 70 F, the humidity should be about 45 – 55%. The dolls will also have be protected from bright sunlight.

2. I have an all-original Shirley Temple doll. Her hair is still in the original set. Why do I have problems getting $500.00 for her? The book says she is worth $1,000.00.

While originality is very desirable, condition plays an equally important role. If the wig looks slightly mussed and is matted and a little dirty, the face is faded (no cheek blush left), and the clothes are also faded pale, experienced collectors might not want this doll at any price.

3. Why are composition dolls so troublesome? Whenever I buy one, she develops cracks overnight.

Drawing on almost 30 years of experience with composition dolls, not one has ever developed cracks overnight. In fact, with proper care, hardly any cracks have ever developed. As any experienced collector will confirm, when buying a doll, it is prudent to question the seller about condition, and in addition to check for cracks and other flaws, particularly in hidden areas. The doll should again be checked at home. All the clothes should now be removed and the doll looked over very carefully. If a hidden flaw is discovered, the buyer has a right to return the doll or arrange for some kind of compensation. This procedure is valid not only for composition dolls but all dolls, particularly those with breakable heads. So-called "hairlines" are sometimes difficult to see.

Once it has been determined that the doll is perfect, following the suggested guidelines for proper humidity, temperature, and light control will assure continued stability.

A Word About American-made Composition Dolls with Knee Joints

It is a commonly held misconception that if an American-made composition doll has knee joints, it must be from the World War I era (1914 – 1918).

When the import of toys from Europe was cut off during WW I, American dollmakers did try to fill the void by copying German dolly-faced dolls that featured bisque heads and ball-jointed body assemblies including jointed knees. The American copies were made of all composition. Toddlers with slanted hip joints and ball-knee joints were also offered. It is important to remember, that these dolls were copied in composition in their entirety, including, and in particular, the German bisque heads.

In 1926, both the American Character and E. I. Horsman companies introduced mama dolls with all-composition legs that featured slanted hip joints and ball joints at knee level. In all instances, these joints were actually not at knee level but somewhat higher, so that they would not be visible when the doll was dressed. As hem lines moved up, so did the knee joints. By 1926, nobody was copying German bisque heads anymore. Even if the composition doll head in question bears no identification marks, it should be recognizable as an original American design by its 1920s look. (See examples in the American Character Co. and E. I. Horsman sections.)

In 1926, Horsman stressed in their ads that they had applied for patents for this special knee joint. If they were granted a patent, it is doubtful that exclusive rights could have been enforced, as knee joints were not a new invention in 1926. When one studies the lower limb created by American Character, one sees a molded groove at knee level, which is not present on the Horsman joint, a small difference that could possibly be used as defense in an infringement court trial (or to wire on the lower leg onto a cloth upper one, in case the jointed knee turned out to be unpopular, or both could be done).

Whatever the case may be, mama dolls with knee ball joints are a rarity today. Effanbee's Patsy was introduced in 1928 and took the public by storm. One assumes that by then knee joints were passé. One also assumes that today's collectors feel otherwise and would treasure having one of these rare knee-jointed mama dolls in their collections.

Composition Doll Collecting and the Internet

The ready availability of home computers certainly has changed the landscape for people who are interested in composition dolls. Before, one would look at magazine ads placed by dealers and auction houses and fervently wish that a time would come when composition dolls would be as visible as bisques, etc. One would go to auctions and doll shows, hoping that one would see composition dolls offered. Local antique dealers and pickers would have some now and then, and one would be so overjoyed at being offered a doll that one would pay the price asked, even if the quality left some to be desired.

This all has changed with the advent of the home computer. Now composition dolls are very visible, particularly at such auction sites as eBay and those of large auction houses. On a daily basis one can compare prices and quality. This certainly has helped bring down prices for the broad range of dolls that are less than perfect. Dealers who formerly had lists for composition dolls (some of them even with illustrations), now have extensive websites with special sections for this category of doll. When formerly one illustration of an item was very much appreciated, now, with the touch of a button, several exposures and close-ups of a particular item can be examined.

Yet, when thinking about buying dolls on the Internet, one old saying comes to mind: "The more things change, the more they stay the same." When reservations are expressed about buying on the Internet, one can only say that it is not that much different from the old way of buying via mail order. Always, the prospective customer expects to be pleased with a purchase. To make this possible, two basic rules are vitally important and not new. A collector has to be knowledgeable in his field of collecting and has to be thoroughly aware of the rules the seller has established for doing business. This has mostly to do with an agreeable return policy. As with mail-order business, the dealer, regardless if dealt with directly or through an online auction site, should be willing to take the doll back if faults are discovered that were not described or if the buyer considers these faults more extensive than mentioned by the seller. Certainly, if a "no returns" policy is stated, the dealer should be avoided, regardless of how plausible the reasons he or she has for the policy.

Some things have changed with Internet buying and should be mentioned here, as collectors may not be familiar. If on receipt of a composition doll, her surface coloring seems paler, and her cheek blush less rosy, the pictures on the computer may have been enhanced. This can be done with the push of a button. If this is suspected, certainly, that would be a reason to return the doll. As with the traditional mail order business, if a doll is returned, the customer is responsible for paying the postage both ways. Though, one would wish that in cases of oversight on the part of the dealer, he or she would be willing to refund at least one way.

Besides being able to buy dolls on the Internet, this new technology also presents great opportunities for learning. Before, there was a limit as to how many doll shows one could attend. Now, only one's time available to sit at the computer sets limits. There is great opportunity for getting an idea what is available in the marketplace at any given time.

Certainly, there no longer is any validity to the statement that one cannot afford old dolls. For people on a limited budget who enjoy "rescuing" dolls, there is unending opportunity to buy, even in the under $50.00 price range.

Fear has been expressed that the Internet will put doll shows out of business. That seems unlikely for the promoter who makes a serious effort to put on a balanced show. There is no substitute for seeing and handling the real thing before buying in person at a doll show, or for that matter, going to a real live auction.

Of course, the Internet offers other activities for people interested in dolls. Online doll clubs and chat rooms can be joined for the purpose of exchanging data on doll collecting and making friends. Organizations such as UFDC (United Federation of Doll Clubs) have websites where informational materials are offered on a regular basis and research can be done. The opportunities are endless.

Harriet Flanders
Creator of Little Cherub

Harriet Flanders was a graphic artist and employee of the Averill Manufacturing Company of New York City. While working there, she designed one doll, Little Cherub.

Harriet had trained at the New York School of Design and worked as a freelance designer of greeting cards. During the Depression in the 1930s, jobs became scarce, and Harriet worked at whatever she could get in the field of illustration and the like.

One day in 1932, she studied the classified section of the newspaper and saw an ad for a doll painter. She went for an interview and was hired on the spot. Her new job was painting the features of dolls' faces at the Georgene Novelty Company.

Harriet had fond memories of her years at the Georgene Novelty Company. She and Georgene Averill became good friends. "You could get up every morning and go to work for these people and it wasn't work. It was pure joy," she commented.

The Averills were a real family business: Besides Georgene Averill and her husband Paul, there was her brother, Rudolph A. Hopf, also a partner in the company. Their daughter Maxine was working there as well. At the time they produced mostly soft dolls that were cut, sewn, stuffed, and dressed on the premises, and Harriet painted the faces. She claimed that she could paint two gross a day. Among the cloth dolls she painted were Johnny Gruelle's Raggedy Ann and Andy and the cloth Quintuplets, the latter produced by the Averills for the Alexander Company.

In 1937, Harriet wrote and illustrated a storybook entitled *Little Cherub*. The character, Little Cherub, was a very small child who, in his own words, tells of his daily exploits, both happy and scary. It is a most endearing story that any small child would love to listen to and identify with. She showed the book to Mr. Hopf, who liked it immediately and wanted to know if she could sculpt a doll like the little character in the book. Harriet set to work and came up with a successful head. The doll went into production and Harriet was paid royalties for Little Cherub for four years, which was the usual life span of a doll, according to her.

This is Harriet Flanders Rapaport when I met her in 1993.

At the time of World War II, Harriet had to leave Georgene Novelties to care for her ill mother, at the same time doing freelance work part-time. She eventually married and had a son. Harriet visited at Georgene's occasionally. Tragedy struck at the Averill's when their daughter Maxine died suddenly at a young age. According to Harriet, Georgene was never the same.

Harriet Flanders was born on May 25, 1905, and died on April 15, 1997, at age 92.

The above information is based on several personal interviews with Harriet Flanders in 1993 and 1994.

Gallery of Dolls

A.B.C. Toys

14". Marks: A.B.C. Toys
Composition flange head and lower limbs, cloth body and upper limbs,
stitched hip joints. Molded painted brown hair, blue tin sleep eyes,
closed mouth. All original. Cynthia Whittaker collection. $125.00.

17". Marks: Anette Baby // A.B.C. Toy
Composition flange head, short arms and legs to above the knee. Cloth body,
stitched hip joints. Molded, painted dark brown hair, painted blue eyes.
Closed mouth. Re-dressed. $95.00.

Acme Toy Manufacturing Co.
New York, New York
1908 – 1930s

As can be seen in the following illustrations, the Acme Toy Manufacturing Co. produced high quality dolls with well modeled faces, elaborate costumes, sleep eyes, and human hair wigs. They also offered medium priced dolls with painted eyes and hair and cloth legs. These dolls are found in simpler costumes made of cheaper fabrics.

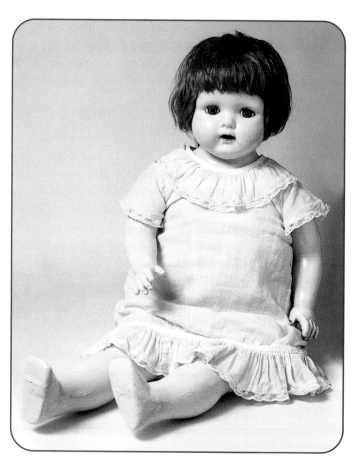

26". Marks: Acme Toy Mfg. Co. (Playthings, February 1927) Composition shoulder head, full arms, and lower legs. Cloth body and upper legs, jointed at shoulders, stitched hip joints. Brown mohair wig over molded hair, gray tin sleep eyes, open mouth. Matching underwear and dress seem original. Cynthia Whittaker collection. $275.00.

This enlarged photo of the doll seen in the previous illustration makes possible the study of a superbly and subtly molded face.

27". Marks: Acme Toy Co. — 1920s
Composition shoulder head, arms, and legs to above the knee. Cloth body and upper legs. Jointed at shoulders, stitched hip joints. Blond human hair wig, blue sleep eyes, open mouth with two teeth. All original. Cynthia Whittaker collection. $300.00.

18". Marks: Acme Toy Co.
Composition shoulder head and full arms, legs to above the knee, cloth body. Jointed at shoulders, stitched hip joints. Light brown mohair wig. Gray sleep eyes, open/closed mouth. All original. Cynthia Whittaker collection. $160.00.

20". Marks: Acme Toy Co. (ca. 1918 – 1922)
Flared composition head and short lower arms. Cloth body, upper arms, and bent legs, jointed at shoulders and hips with inside disks. Blond mohair wig over molded hair, painted blue eyes, closed mouth. Appropriate old clothes. $150.00. Cynthia Whittaker collection.

Close-up of tag as seen on 16" toddler in the previous illustration and inscribed: "ACME Means Perfection Walking • Talking • Dolls."

16" toddler. Marks: Acme Toy Co.
Composition shoulder head and arms to the elbow. Cloth body, upper arms, and legs. No shoulder joints, stitched hip joints. Molded, painted light brown hair, painted blue eyes, open/closed mouth. All original with original paper tag (see enlargement). Cynthia Whittaker collection. $150.00.

14". Marks: Acme
Composition shoulder head and short arms. Cloth body and legs. No shoulder joints, stitched hip joints. Brown mohair wig, painted blue eyes, closed mouth. All original except for shoes. Cynthia Whittaker collection. $125.00.

Albert Brueckner's Sons, Successors to Albert Brueckner 1901 – 1930 and later (Coleman II)

While this company is mostly known among collectors as a manufacturer of cloth dolls with printed faces, this ad proves that in the 1920s, they also sold mama dolls with composition heads and limbs and cloth bodies. None has ever been identified. Their heads may not have been marked.

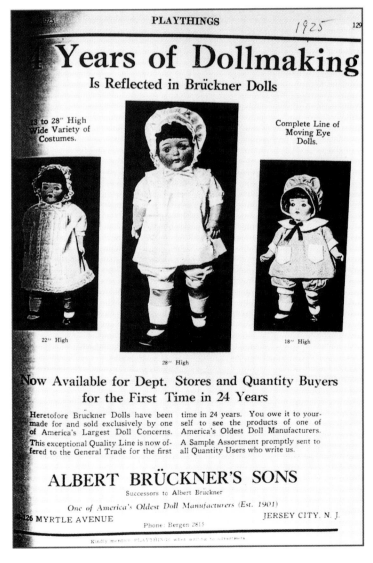

Playthings *ad, 1925.*

Alexander Doll Co.
New York City

Many dolls have been recorded in their original costumes, some of them rare, such as the 7½" Baby McGuffy or Tiny Betty in Chinese costume. Twelve of the famous but elusive Portrait Dolls from the late 1930s and early 1940s are illustrated.

Presented for the first time are 50 marionettes sold by the Alexander Company during the 1930s and designed by famous puppeteer, Tony Sarg. While some have been seen in the doll literature, few of their identities were known. Certainly, a set of Snow White and the Seven Dwarfs including Stepmother and Prince is rare. Two theaters, one of them sold by F.A.O. Schwarz in New York City, and three play books are pictured as well.

7½". Marks: Mme. Alexander
Cloth tag: Baby McGuffy
All composition, fully jointed, bent legs. Blond mohair wig over molded hair, painted blue eyes, closed mouth. All original. Note: The same head mold was used for this doll as the Dionnes. Anita Maxwell collection. $400.00.

16". Marks: Mme. Alexander (This is Pinkie.)
Composition flange head, hands, and bent legs to above the knee. Cloth body, arms, and upper legs, stitched hip joints. Molded painted brown hair, gray sleep eyes, closed mouth. All original. Cynthia Whittaker collection. $400.00.

11" Wendy Ann in pink skirt. Marks: none.
Dress tag: Wendy Ann // by Madame Alexander, N.Y. // All Rights Reserved
All composition, fully jointed. Blond mohair wig, blue sleep eyes, closed mouth. All original. Mary Lu Trowbridge collection. $375.00.

16". Marks: none. 1930s.
Label on dress: Madame Alexander // New York
Composition flange head, full arms and bent legs, jointed at shoulders and hips. Blond mohair wig, sleep eyes, open mouth with two upper teeth and molded tongue. All original. Cynthia Whittaker collection. $250.00.

7". Marks: Mme. Alexander. 1936.
Gold foil paper label: Topsy
All composition, fully jointed. Black mohair wig, painted brown eyes, closed mouth. Molded, painted black shoes. All original, including box. Anita Maxwell collection. $400.00.

7". Marks: Mme. Alexander. 1936.
Cloth tag: Madame Alexander
All composition, fully jointed. Elaborate, white mohair wig, painted blue eyes, closed mouth, colonial costume. All original. Anita Maxwell collection. $350.00.

7". Marks: Mme. Alexander. 1936.
Tag: Chinese
All composition, fully jointed. Black mohair wig. Painted blue eyes, closed mouth. All original. Note: The so-called Tiny Betty was used to create the doll seen here and the ones in the previous two illustrations. Anita Maxwell collection. $300.00.

13½" Wendy Ann, green skirt.
Marks: Wendy-Ann // Mme. Alexander // New York
Dress tag: Wendy-Ann // Madame Alexander N.Y.
All composition, fully jointed with swivel waist.
Blond mohair wig, sleep eyes, closed mouth. All
original. Mary Lu Trowbridge collection. $450.00.

11" Wendy Ann. Marks: none.
Dress tag: Wendy Ann // by Madame Alexander, N.Y. // All Rights Reserved
All composition, full jointed. Blond mohair wig, blue sleep eyes, closed mouth. All
original. Mary Lu Trowbridge collection. $375.00.

14". Marks on body: Wendy-Ann // Mme. Alexander // New York All composition, fully jointed, with additional waist joint. *Blond human hair in original set. Sleep eyes, closed mouth. All original with dress tag. Lynn Murray collection. $450.00.*

14" Wendy-Ann seen in previous illustration, modeling tagged blue wool coat with fur trim. Lynn Murray collection. $450.00.

14". Marks on body: Wendy-Ann // Mme. Alexander // New York All composition, fully jointed with additional waist joint. *Molded, painted brown hair, painted blue eyes, closed mouth. All original outfit. Lynn Murray collection. $450.00.*

13½" Wendy-Ann. Marks on back: Wendy-Ann // Mme. Alexander // New York
All composition, fully jointed with swivel waist. Blond mohair wig, sleep eyes, closed mouth. All original with blue hat. Mary Lu Trowbridge collection. $450.00.

14". Marks on body: Wendy-Ann // Mme. Alexander // New York.
All composition, fully jointed. Blond human hair wig, sleep eyes, closed mouth. Original, tagged riding outfit. Lynn Murray collection. $450.00.

19". Marks on head: Mme. Alexander // Sonja // Henie.
Dress tag: Genuine // "Sonja Henie" Doll // Madame Alexander N.Y. U.S.A. // All Rights Reserved. Paper tag: see separate illustration. All composition, fully jointed. Blond human hair wig, brown sleep eyes, open mouth with four upper teeth. All original. $2,100.00.

24". Marks: none. Dress tag: Madame // Alexander // New York Composition swivel head, shoulder plate, and limbs. Cloth body. Jointed at shoulders, stitched hip joints. Blond human hair wig, blue sleep eyes, open mouth with four upper teeth. All original. Dee Cermak collection. $400.00.

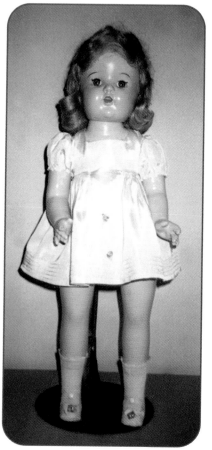

21". Marks: none on doll. Original pin: Jane Withers.
Paper tag: Authentic Jane Withers // Doll // All rights reserved // Madame Alexander // New York
All composition, fully jointed. Brown mohair wig, sleep eyes, and open mouth with four upper teeth. All original. Note: In the accompanying book, Jane Withers' name is used for the main character. The story has nothing to do with her movies. Offered as follows: "An original story featuring Jane Withers, famous motion picture star, as the heroine, by Kathrn Heisenfelt, authorized edition." Whitman Publishing Co., Racine Wisconsin. Copyr., 1944. (Compare the picture of Jane Withers, the child, on the tag and Jane Withers, a teenager, on the book jacket). On the book jacket back additional titles are listed using other famous movie star names such as Shirley Temple, Judy Garland, Ginger Rogers, etc. $1,900.00.

9". Marks: Madame Alexander // New York (McGuffy Ana). 1937.
Wrist tag: Created//by//Madame//Alexander//New York
All composition, fully jointed. Blond mohair wig, blue sleep eyes, closed mouth. All original. Anita Maxwell collection. $400.00.

9" Rumbero and Rumbera, Cuban Dancers. Marks: none. 1937.
Wrist tag front: Created // by // Madame // Alexander // New York.
Wrist tag back: An Alexander Product // Supreme // Quality and //
Design
All composition, fully jointed. Black mohair wigs, painted brown
eyes, closed mouths. All original. Anita Maxwell collection. $700.00
pair.

12½" and 15" Princess Elizabeth. 1937.
Marks, 12½": none (Tag: Princess Elizabeth). Marks, 15": Madame
Alexander (tag: Princess Elizabeth).
All composition, fully jointed. Blond human hair wigs, sleep eyes,
closed and open mouths. All original. Note: For the 12½" doll, the
more unusual Betty face mold was used. Anita Maxwell collection.
12½", $675.00. 15", $600.00.

The Portrait Dolls

Some of the most glamorous and mysterious dolls of the Madame Alexander line were the portrait dolls. First introduced in 1938, their production was interrupted at some point by the conditions created by World War II. Featured at the March 1946, Toy Fair in New York City, they were also advertised in the November 1946 issue of *Playthings*. The trade journal *Toys and Novelties* reported in their March 1947 issue that these exquisite portrait dolls had initially been intended by Madame Alexander as window display items only and were offered in a set of 12 pieces.

While most Alexander dolls carried identification marks and cloth tags attached to their dresses, giving their names, these portraits are not marked in any way. Their only identification is a cloth label attached to an inner seam of their slips, imprinted: "Madame Alexander // New York USA."

All of them are 21" tall and made of composition. An already existing mold was used for their heads, the so called Wendy-Ann face. The heads were customized by dramatizing their eye, and eyebrow treatment, which gave them an adult look.

Excellent quality mohair wigs were elaborately styled according to the character represented. As can be seen in the following illustrations, the gowns were designed and trimmed with great care.

Several of the dolls are known by various names, some documented and some, heretofore, not. Some of the costumes have been seen in different colors, such as Antoinette's. Her gown came in yellow, pink, or blue. This may account for the difference in names. The fact that the dolls were offered at two different times may explain some of the differences. The original price for these dolls was reported at about $75.00 per doll.

For more information on this subject, see "The Mystery of the Madame Alexander Portrait Dolls" by Sally Freeman, *Antique Doll Collector*, June 2002.

The next ten dolls illustrated are from the collection of Diane Hoffman, and they were photographed by Neal Eisaman.

Because of the rarity of these dolls it is difficult to report a reliable price range. Just as with other composition dolls, their condition can run from outright poor to mint in the original box. One in lesser condition might sell from $900.00 to $1,600.00. $5,000.00 per doll is the upper range.

With the help of this close-up, the excellent make-up of the Alexander portrait dolls can be studied.

This is Carmen. She has also been seen in a black dress with identical trim and decoration.

This is Orchard Princess.

This is Judy (Playthings, November 1946).

This is Antoinette, also known as Mme. Pompadour or Mme. DuBarry. In this picture she is dressed in a pink gown. But this costume has also been seen in yellow and blue. It is not known if the above names were used with a certain color costume.

This doll is identified as Renoir in an Alexander Co. archive photograph. She is also called Lady Windemere.

This doll is identified Victoria in an Alexander Co. archive photograph. She is also called Princess Flavia.

This doll is June Bride.

This doll is Melanie.

This doll is known as Degas.

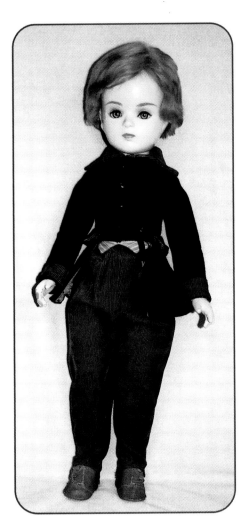

This tenth doll from the Diane Hoffman collection is commonly known as David Copperfield. No documentation for this name has been found. His height is also 21". A different head mold was used for him. It is known as the Margaret face.

The next two illustrations were graciously submitted by the Rosalie Whyel Museum of Doll Art in Bellevue, Washington. The two dolls pictured belong to the same set of Alexander portrait dolls seen in the previous ten illustrations. Therefore, the same descriptive data and value conditions apply here as well.

This beautiful example is known as Godey.

This example is known as Melanie.

14". Marks: Mme. Alexander. W.A.V.E., Soldier, Salvation Army girl, and W.A.A.C., ca. 1946. All composition, fully jointed, mohair wigs, sleep eyes, and closed mouths. All original. Anita Maxwell collection. W.A.V.E., $750.00. W.A.A.C., $750.00. Salvation Army girl, rare, $800.00. Soldier, $800.00.

11". Marks: Alexander. Tagged dress: Madame // Alexander // New York U.S.A. All composition, fully jointed. Blond human hair wig, brown sleep eyes, closed mouth. All original. Mary Lu Trowbridge collection. $450.00.

14" Jeannie Walker. Marks on back: Alexander // Pat. 2171281
Dress tag: Jeannie Walker // Madame Alexander, N.Y., U.S.A. // All rights Reserved
All composition, fully jointed, with walker mechanism. Blond mohair wig, brown sleep eyes, closed mouth. All original. Mary Lu Trowbridge collection. $850.00.

14". Marks: none. Circa 1940. Southern Girl.
Tag: Madame Alexander
All composition, fully jointed. Blond mohair wig, blue sleep
eyes, closed mouth. All original. Anita Maxwell collection.
$550.00.

14" Princess Margaret Rose, ca. 1946.
Marks: Mme. Alexander
Cloth tag: Madame Alexander
All composition, fully jointed. Blond mohair wig, blue sleep
eyes, closed mouth. All original. Anita Maxwell collection.
$850.00.

Marionettes Created by Tony Sarg for Madame Alexander

With television not yet available in the 1930s, puppet shows were a popular form of entertainment for children. Puppeteers like Virginia Austin and Tony Sarg were well known personalities. Toy companies were eager for these well known professionals to lend their name and help with the design of marionettes meant as playthings for children. The Effanbee Company hired Virginia Austin, and the Madame Alexander had Tony Sarg under contract.

The Alexander Company went all out and created several sets of marionettes, representing the characters of popular fairy tales such as Snow White and the Seven Dwarfs, Cinderella, Alice in Wonderland, as well as Walt Disney characters. As can be seen in the following illustrations, a diverse number of attractive and expressive faces were created for these puppets. Books of plays and actual theaters were also available (see the following illustrations).

Introduced in 1934, the Alexander marionettes must have been popular for quite some time as, obviously, numerous sets were offered for sale.

Construction of Marionettes

Head, body, and lower limbs are made of composition. Upper limbs are made of cloth and left empty (no stuffing). The head is attached with hook and eye. Upper arms are wired on. The cloth tube for the upper legs is fed through the hip openings and continues down to the second leg. In order to make manipulation easier for a child, attached to the wooden cross bar is a metal rod that was also hooked to the head of the puppet at its other end.

Note: Some of the marionettes do not have their original name tags but were illustrated with their names in the books of plays. Other names were passed along by previous (original) owners.

This drawing shows the construction of The Alexander/Tony Sarg marionettes. Reproduced from the book, Treasury of Madame Alexander Dolls. *Courtesy of Jan Foulke, author, and Hobby House Press, publisher, Copyright 1979.*

Front side of an original autographed hand bill, showing a portrait of Tony Sarg.

The backside of the Tony Sarg hand bill carries the following text:

"The work of Tony Sarg is so familiar to everyone that there is little that can be said, which has not already been said, about the man himself. His drawings are world famous, his designs for textiles, pottery, wall paper, rugs, furniture, and numerous other articles are fascinating to both young and old; his books have been sold throughout the world, and his marionettes have been seen and enjoyed by thousands. It is a distinct pleasure to present the creator of these marionettes to lecture audiences in programs which have been especially designed for children and adult audiences, and for banquet appearances.

Tony Sarg was born in Guatemala, in 1882. Until 1905 when he began his career as an illustrator in London, Mr. Sarg served as an officer in the German Army. In 1915, he came to the United States and in 1921 was granted citizenship. Three years later his first book, Tony Sarg's Book for Children *was published. This was followed in 1925 by* Tony Sarg's Animal Book; *in 1926,* Tony Sarg's Alphabet; *in 1927,* Tony Sarg's Wonder Zoo, Tony Sarg's New York, *and a book of marionette plays; in 1928,* Tony Sarg's Trick Book.

Mr. Sarg was the proprietor of Tony Sarg Company (marionette shows), Tony Sarg Studios, and Tony Sarg Workshops (makers of window displays).

Left to right: Three books of plays from the Dorothy W. Reiman collection.
Walt Disney Marionette Plays by Madame Alexander, *New York*
Play # 1 – Snow White and the Seven Dwarfs
    Characters: Snow White, Seven Dwarfs, Prince,
    Stepmother, Huntsman.
Play # 2 – Mickey's Mix Up
    Characters: Mickey Mouse, Donald Duck, Minnie Mouse
Play # 3 – Donald's Disaster
    Characters: Mickey Mouse, Pluto, Donald Duck

Plays for the Tony Sarg Marionette Theatre
Play # 1 – Rip Van Winkle
    Characters: Rip Van Winkle, Dame Van Winkle, Judith
Play # 2 – Alice in Wonderland
    Characters: Alice, Tweedle Dee, Tweedle Dum
Play # 3 – Hansel and Gretel
    Characters: Hansel, Gretel, Witch
Play # 4 – Lucy Lavender's Hero
    Characters: Lucy, Tippy Toes (butler), Lawrence Lightfoot
    (Lucy's hero)
Play # 5 – Tingling Circus
    Characters: Percival, Frances, Cyrus (horse)
Play # 6 – Clever Gretchen
    Characters: Master, Gretchen, Fido
Play # 7 – Red Riding Hood
    Characters: Red Riding Hood, Wolf, Grandma
Play # 8 – The Three Wishes
    Characters: Martin, Fairy, Margaret
Play # 9 – The Dixieland Minstrels
    Characters: Interlocutor, Bones, Sambo

A Marionette Play to be Used in Tony Sarg's Marionette Theatre
Production, *Adapted by Tony Sarg, Manufactured Exclusively by*
Madame Alexander, New York, U.S.A.
Play # 1 – The Three Wishes
    Characters: Martin, Margaret

Theatre sold by FAO Schwarz for Tony Sarg Marionettes in 1939. Stage front: made of wood with red cloth curtain. Side: Wood frame with yellow cloth insert. Backdrop: cloth scene hangs down from dowel. 30" high, 33" wide, 12¾" deep. Stage 31" wide, 13½" deep. Dorothy W. Reiman collection. $500.00.

Walt Disney Marionette Theatre. Marks: Walt Disney's // Silly Symphony // Marionette // Theatre // By // Tony Sarg for Madame Alexander // 1938
Made of cardboard. 38" high, 29" wide, 9" deep. Stage: 20" wide in front, 18" wide in back, 15½" deep. Dorothy W. Reiman collection. $800.00+.

Two side panels for Silly Symphony Theatre.

Front section of original marionette box. Marks: Characters PRINCESS - 73. Name of Play: Enchanted Prince. Tony Sarg Marionettes. Alexander Doll Company, N.Y. Dorothy Reiman collection.

9" Seven Dwarfs.
Tags on coats: Walt Disney's Marionette // Individual Name // by Madame Alexander, N.Y. // All Rights Reserved
From left to right: Sleepy, Grumpy, Bashful, Dopey, Happy, Sneezy, Doc. Dorothy W. Reiman collection. $525.00+ each.

12" Stepmother, Snow White, and Prince.
Marks on bodies: Tony Sarg // Alexander
Dress tag Stepmother: Walt Disney's Marionettes // Stepmother // Madame Alexander, N.Y., U.S.A.
Dress tag Snow White: Snow White // Madame Alexander, N.Y. // All Rights Reserved
Dress tag Prince: none. Dorothy W. Reiman collection. $525.00+ each.

Red Riding Hood, Grandmother, Wolf.
Marks on bodies: Tony Sarg // Alexander
11" Red Riding Hood dress tag: none.
11" Grandmother marks on head: Tony Sarg. Dress tag: Tony Sarg Marionettes // Grandmother // Madame Alexander
Wolf dress tag: none. Dorothy W. Reiman collection. Wolf, $475.00+. Other, $475.00 each.

Hansel, Gretel, and Witch.
Marked on bodies: Tony Sarg // Alexander
12" Hansel. Cloth tag on collar: Hansel // Marionette by Madame Alexander N.Y. USA // All Rights Reserved
12" Gretel. Dress tag: none.
12" Witch marks on head: Tony Sarg Dress tag: Tony Sarg // Marionettes // Witch // Madame Alexander, N.Y. Dorothy W. Reiman collection. $475.00+ each.

Alice in Wonderland.
12" Alice. Marks on body: Tony Sarg //
Alexander. Dress tag: none.
11" Tweedle Dum and Tweedle Dee. Marks on
head: Tony Sarg. Marks on body: Tony Sarg.
Dress tag: none. Dorothy W. Reiman collec-
tion. Alice, $475.00. Tweedle Dum/Tweedle
Dee, $475.00+ each.

Alice in Wonderland.
7" Humpty Dumpty. Marks: none (illustrated in book of plays).
Dorothy W. Reiman collection. $475.00+ each.

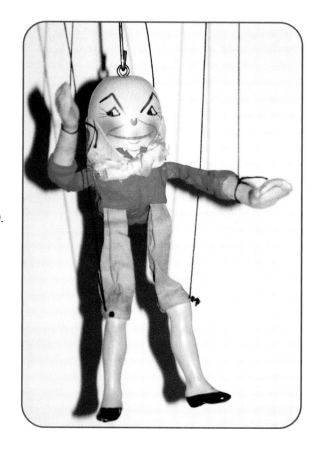

13" Pinocchio.
Marks on head: Pinocchio // Made © USA // W. Disney Ent.
Marks on body: Tony Sarg // Alexander
Dorothy W. Reiman collection. $525.00.

The Three Wishes. 12" Martin (woodcutter), 12" Margaret. Marks on their heads:
Tony Sarg. Marks on bodies: Tony Sarg // Alexander. Their clothes are not tagged.
Dorothy W. Reiman collection. $475.00 each.

Lucy Lavender's Hero. 12" Lawrence
Lightfoot (Lucy's hero), 12" Lucy
Lavender, 12" Tippy Toes (butler).
Marks on heads: Tony Sarg. Marks
on bodies: Tony Sarg // Alexander.
Their clothes are not tagged.
Dorothy W. Reiman collection.
$475.00 each.

Rip Van Winkle.
Marks on bodies: Tony Sarg // Alexander
12" Judith (daughter).
Marks on head: Tony Sarg. Dress tag: Tony Sarg Marionettes // "Judith" // Madame Alexander N.Y.
12" Rip Van Winkle.
Suit tag: Madame Alexander New York
12" Dame Van Winkle (wife).
Marks on head: Tony Sarg. Dress tag: Tony Sarg Marionettes // "Dame Van Winkle" // Madame Alexander N.Y.
Dorothy W. Reiman collection. $475.00 each.

The Enchanted Prince. Marks on bodies: Tony Sarg // Alexander.
10" Gnome Rumpel. Dress tag: Tony Sarg Marionettes // Rumpel // Madame Alexander
11" Princess. Dress tag: Madame Alexander // New York
12" Prince. Dress tag: none.
Dorothy W. Reiman collection. $475.00 each.

The Dixieland Minstrels. 12" Interlocutor and Sambo. Marks on back: Tony Sarg // Alexander. Dress tag on Sambo: Madame Alexander, New York. Dress tag on Interlocutor: none. Dorothy W. Reiman collection. Interlocutor, $475.00. Sambo, $550.00.

12" Maid and Tippy Toes (Butler)
Marks on body: Tony Sarg // Alexander
Butler also marked on head: Tony Sarg. Dorothy W. Reiman
collection. $475.00 each.

Tingling Circus. 12" Percival (riding master) and 12" Cyrus
(horse).
Marks on bodies: Tony Sarg // Alexander
Dorothy W. Reiman collection. Percival, $475.00. Horse,
$500.00+.

Tingling Circus. Fido (dog), 5" long, 4" tall. Marks: none.
11" Clown. Marks on head: Tony Sarg
Marks on body: Tony Sarg // Alexander
Fido, $475.00. Clown, $500.00+.

The following illustrations are of unknown characters. It is hoped that showing these might result in more information from collectors. If anyone owns FAO Schwarz or similar catalogs in which these marionettes are identified with individual names and titles of relevant plays, please contact the author.

Four ladies, 12". I think these are Cinderella, two Stepsisters, and Stepmother. $475.00 each.

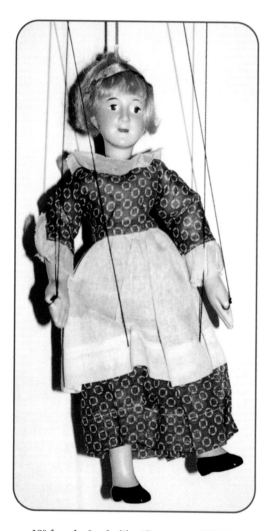

12" female. Looks like Alice to me. $475.00.

Two 12" men. $475.00 each.

12", three princes? $475.00 each.

Dog. 2½" x 2½". Composition head, brown felt body, limbs, and tail. Ribbon around neck (yellow-white). Head in poor condition. Very hard to find. 9" long, 8" high. $450.00.

Two ladies. 12" Snow White and Witch? $475.00 each.

10" Puppet. Marks: none. Cloth tag: Walt Disney's Marionettes // "Donald Duck" // By Madame Alexander N.Y. // All Rights Reserved (see illustration).
Composition head, hands, and feet, cloth upper arms, wood body and legs. All original. Gayle and Jerry Reilly collection. $350.00.

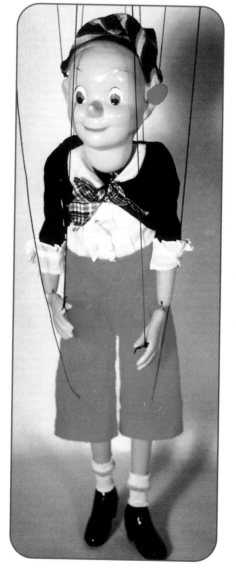

19" Pinocchio. Marks: none on puppet. Cloth tag on jacket: Madame Alexander.
Composition head, hands, and feet, wooden limbs. Molded painted brown hair and painted brown eyes, closed mouth. All original. Dorothy Reiman collection. $400.00.

Allied Grand Doll Manufacturing Co., Inc.
Brooklyn, New York

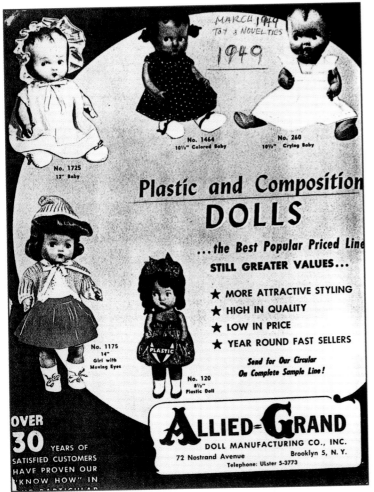

Full page ad placed in the trade magazine Toys and Novelties, *March 1949. To collectors, Allied Grand is mostly known as the manufacturer of the famous Jackie Robinson doll. This ad amply proves that other types of dolls were sold. Most of them were probably not marked. The wide-eyed baby in the upper right-hand corner (No. 260) looks rather distinctive, and the illustration should be helpful to collectors trying to identify their small unmarked all-composition baby dolls.*

12". Marks: AGD
All composition, jointed only at shoulders and hips, straight legs, spring strung. Slightly molded painted black hair, painted brown eyes, closed mouth. He is barefoot, original shirt and overalls. Margo Delaughter collection. $100.00.

Louis Amberg & Son
New York City
1878 – 1930

Many elusive and rare dolls produced by the Amberg firm have been located and researched. They are presented in the following section. Few of the early dolls, illustrated here for the first time, feature any identification marks. This may explain their invisibility. It is hoped that the illustrations will help collectors focus on these early dolls. Even if found in poor condition, they should be preserved. They are an important link in the chain of early American dollmaking. In the case of Bobby Blake and Dolly Drake, designed by Grace Drayton (never published before), they help complete the body of her known work.

Collectors of personality dolls will certainly appreciate seeing Alkali Ike from the collection of Don and Arlene Jensen, a doll so far known only from ad illustrations.

The composition doll line of the Amberg firm was sold to E. I. Horsman in 1930. Even though, in 1928, Amberg was still introducing newly created dolls, such as Amby, a character toddler with well designed, cheerful features. Since this doll's name was mentioned only on a paper hang tag, Amby may have been largely overlooked by collectors. He certainly is worthy of highlighting.

Amberg's most artistic achievement was Mibs. She was advertised in 1921 as "Mibs, A Phyllis May Dolly." It was further known that "Phyllis May was a little girl from story-book land made popular in the *New York Evening Mail* by Hazel Drukker." This information did not shed much light on the history of Mibs or Phyllis May. More information can now be presented on Mibs, Phyllis May and the story-book.

Amberg is also listed as having carried an exclusive line of mama dolls (see Coleman II, pg. 34, 1929). It must be assumed that the mama dolls were not marked, as none have ever been identified as having been made by Amberg, outside of Baby Peggy and Vanta Baby.

For more information on Louis Amberg & Son see the three-part research paper by Don Jensen in *Doll News*, summer 2003, winter and spring 2004.

11" Sunny Jim (Playthings, August 1909). Marks: none.

Flared composition head, plush body and limbs, jointed at shoulders and hips. Painted light brown hair (no hair modeling), painted blue eyes, open/closed mouth with molded tongue. Head has been restored. Note: This head was produced without a dipped top composition layer and reveals excellent, sharp modeling of the facial features. When the doll is turned upside down, it becomes more evident that when new the plush was baby blue. The original 1909 ad stated: "You'll laugh and the world'll laugh with you." It must be remembered here that Sunny Jim was sold at a time when Horsman's Billikin had met with overwhelming success and the first teddy bear craze was also in full swing. $400.00.

Bobby Blake and Dolly Drake, famous storybook characters designed by G.G. Wiederseim (G.G. Drayton).
Illustrated in Playthings, *June 1911.*

12". Marks: none. Cloth label: Original // "Bobby Blake" // Copyright by Louis Amberg & Son, 1910 Trademark Regd. // By special arrangement with the artist & originator // G.G. Wiederseim (Grace Drayton)

Flared composition head, cloth body and limbs with stump hands and sewn-in black boots. Molded, painted hair and painted blue eye, closed mouth. Original, tagged sailor suit. $360.00.

13". Marks: none on head. This is Dolly Drake, 1911.

Ink stamp on body, front: Copyright 1911//By Louis Amberg & Son NY.//Sole makers

Flared composition head, cloth body and limbs, jointed with inside disks. Striped black and white stockings and black cloth boots are part of the leg casing. Molded, painted light brown hair and painted blue eyes. Closed mouth. Re-dressed.

Note: A June 1911 Playthings *ad stated as follows: "Made by special arrangement with and after designs by the artist and originator, G.G. Wiederseim (Grace Drayton), and by contract with Fred A. Stokes Co., publishers of the books of the same name." $200.00.*

Full page ad from Playthings, *dated February 1912. Pictured are two very interesting looking character dolls, Spic and Span, that have never been seen. A Sis Hopkins doll is also illustrated.*

Pair of Tiny Tots (see separate illustration of original ads).
12" boy marks: ©///L.A. & S. 1912
12" girl marks: 504//©///L.A. & S. 1912
Flared composition heads and short lower arms. Cloth body, upper arms, and legs. No hip joints. Cardboard soles inserted into feet, making it possible for the doll to stand. Molded painted light brown hair, painted blue eyes. Open/closed mouths with white line between lips, indicating teeth.
Note: Girl's hair shows different modeling from boy's.
$150.00 each.

Undressed doll shows special construction of the Tiny Tots.

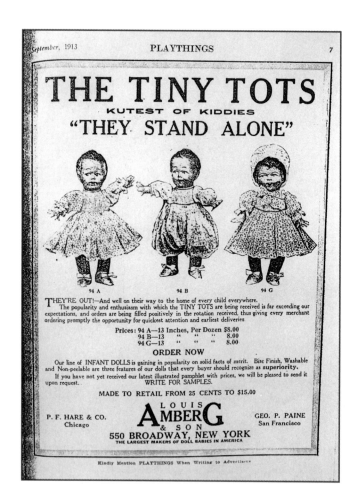

Full-page ad, Playthings, *September 1913, showing the doll with short hair dressed as a matching boy and girl pair (regular girl to the right).*

Full page ad, Playthings, *October 1913, promoting the Tiny Tots.*

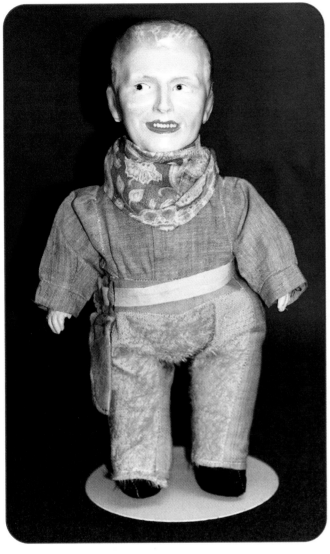

11". Marks: L.A. & S.
This is Augustus Carney in the role of Alkali Ike. Augustus Carney
appeared in many early movie shorts. The doll was sold by
Essanay Film Mfg. Co., Chicago, 1913. (Also see: article on "Early
Film Stars" by Don Jensen in the August, 2002, issue of Doll Collector.)
Composition flange head and short arms. Cloth body, upper arms,
and legs, jointed at shoulders and hips. Molded, painted hair and
painted blue eyes. Open/closed mouth with eight painted teeth. All
original. Don and Arlene Jensen collection. $600.00.

13". Marks: © 1915 // Amberg
Flared composition head and short arms. Cloth body, upper arms, and legs, jointed with inside disks. Original, blond mohair wig over molded hair. Painted blue eyes, closed mouth, three dimples. Re-dressed. $125.00.

Two Pouty Pets (See Toys & Novelties, *July, 1915).*
Left: 14". Marks: L.A. & S., © 1915.
Flared composition head and short arms. Cloth body, upper arms, and straight legs. Molded, painted light brown hair and painted blue eyes, closed mouth. Old pajamas. Right: 14".
Identical to above, except differently styled hair and bent legs. Old dress may be original.
Left: $150.00. Right, $200.00.

13". Marks: none. Cloth Tag: OO-GUG-LUG // Zulu Lucky Doll // Trade Mark // Originated - Design Patented - by J.W. Long // CopyRgt. 1915 and Mfg'd by Louis Amberg and Son, N.Y.

Flared composition head and lower arms. Cloth body, upper arms and legs made of black satin. Jointed shoulders with inside disks, jointed hips with outside disks. Head was painted a deep black, including the early molded hair. Black eyes, open/closed mouth. Face painting is all original. Holes in ear lobes and nose (earrings seem original). Other decorations are replacements but similar to ones seen on all original doll. Note: A Charlie Chaplin head was used to create this character. $800.00.

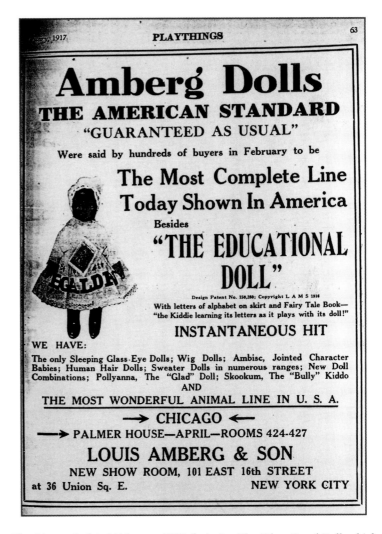

Playthings ad, dated February 1917, featuring The Educational Doll, which was offered with letters of the alphabet printed on the skirt and a fairy tale book.

Mibs and Phyllis May

A full page ad in the trade journal *Playthings*, dated August 1920, was placed by New Toy Co. Inc., announcing the arrival of "Phyllis May, a little girl from story-book land, made popular in the New York *Evening Mail* by Hazel Drukker," the very same Hazel Drukker who had been credited with the creation of Amberg's Mibs. In the meantime, a Phyllis May doll was located and is illustrated on the following pages, but it was sold by Amberg not New Toy. New information can now be presented on Hazel Drukker, both dolls and a storybook, entitled *Phyllis May and Her Dollies.*

The *Evening Mail*, one of New York City's dailies featured a daily children's corner in the section called Daily Magazine Page for Everybody. The September 24,1919, issue announced that on the following Monday "Phyllis May and Her Dollies Are Coming to Cheer The Mail Readers." An accompanying picture showed Hazel Drukker (Mrs. George Silberman) and her daughter, Phyllis May.

The picture of Mrs. Drukker and her daughter, Phyllis May, appeared in the September 24, 1919, issue of the Evening Mail, announcing the arrival of a special children's feature credited to Mrs. Drukker.

The new feature would relate day by day how Phyllis May played with her dolls, hopefully encouraging little girls to do likewise. Mrs. Drukker was quoted as saying that she regretted the little ones' lack of interest in playing with dolls, when their mothers and grandmothers had done so for many years.

Not unlike the ever-popular newspaper cartoons of the day, the layout of this new feature consisted of framed action pictures arranged horizontally, accompanied by short verses relating to the illustrations. Unlike cartoons, the pictures were created by using photographs, enhanced by some outlining. Apeda Studio and Geisler & Andrews were given credit for them. Soon a Phyllis May Letter Box was added to the new children's feature, which reproduced some of the correspondence received and Phyllis May's replies. The children were also asked to remind their parents to buy the newspaper every day. In other words, the real reason for the existence of this new feature directed at children was to enhance circulation. Before long, the feature was reduced from three pictures to one and the letter box. In a postscript it was suggested that the children cut out the pictures and paste them into a scrapbook, so that they would have a complete story. At Christmas time, three Phyllis May dolls were raffled off and sent to lucky correspondents. At one point, Phyllis May paper dolls were mentioned, and one wonders if any were ever sold.

On Saturday, December 27, 1919, the *Daily Mail* announced that Billy Bunny stories, written by David Cory, would begin on the following Monday. They were located in the spot previously occupied by Phyllis May and Her Dollies. Therefore, Hazel Drukker's special children's feature was published only for the short period of three months. It must be assumed that it did not generate the response the paper had expected.

Coming back to the New Toy Co. and their Phyllis May doll, this would explain why an example has never been located. Obviously, by the time the company was ready to market their product, the newspaper feature had already been discontinued and not many dolls may have been sold. It might also explain why, one year later, in 1921, Louis Amberg & Son could announce the arrival of Mibs and call her A Phyllis May Dolly, as Mrs. Drukker's contract with New Toy had probably expired. Though, one wonders what provided the impetus to go ahead with such a project. Maybe, Mrs. Drukker persuaded Amberg to create dolls on the basis of her book.

A book entitled *Phyllis May and Her Dollies* was published by Barse & Hopkins, New York, in 1920, citing Hazel Drukker as the author. Some of the same copy and verses

were used for the book that had appeared in the newspaper. One of the ball-jointed dolly faces seen in the book was called Phyllis May and dressed in an identical outfit as the girl seen on the cover of the book. One frequently mentioned and apparently favored playmate was named Mibs, and one is puzzled to realize that she too, according to the illustration, is a ball-jointed doll and in no way resembles the highly prized character doll which Louis Amberg & Son would offer for sale in 1921.

While Mibs was frequently promoted with illustrated ads, none were found for Amberg's Phyllis May, and we also don't know why less money was spent on producing her. While a sweet little face was created for her, the head was mounted on a standard cloth body with cloth legs and feet. Since she was dressed in an exact copy of the real Phyllis May's outfit and given her name, this was, perhaps, consid-

ered sufficient to make her appealing. The example seen illustrated in this section is the only one ever encountered, and we are indeed fortunate to be able to see her with her original clothes and original label.

While we have gained knowledge on the two Amberg dolls and the book that inspired them, various checks and research did not result in more information on Hazel Drukker. She was apparently not an author of children's books or a visual artist but a person with novel ideas and excellent promotional talents. An entry in Coleman I, page 17, states that Amberg came out with two new dolls in 1921: Mibs, created by Hazel Drukker and the other by Julio Kilenyi. The Kilenyi doll is not identified. Knowing what we do know now, the two dolls new in 1921 may have been Mibs and the Phyllis May doll, and both sculpted by Julio Kilenyi. To verify the latter will take more research.

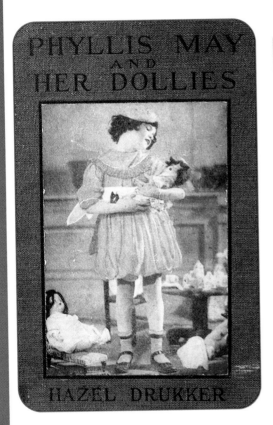

Cover of book.

Sample of double page from book Phyllis May and Her Dollies.

Example of the new feature when it consisted of three pictures and the letter box.

16". Marks: none.

This is Mibs, a Phyllis May Dolly, created by Hazel Drukker and copyrighted in 1921 (Play-things, May 1921).

Composition shoulder head with head slightly turned to the right. Composition arms to above the elbow, and specially designed composition legs which are pin jointed. Cloth body. Molded, painted light brown hair, painted blue eyes, closed mouth. Doll on left is all original. Doll on the right was re-dressed and her hair has been touched up. Shoes and socks have been repainted. She is from the Betty Houghtaling collection.

Note: Both dolls feature molded shoes. For the doll on the left, they were not painted. Though both are original, the arms are not from the same mould. $1,200.00 each.

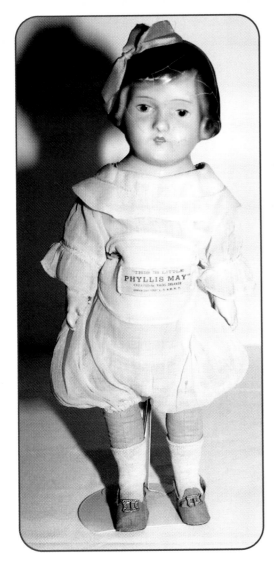

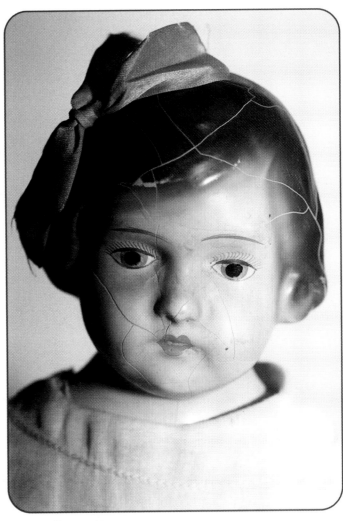

15". Marks: none.
Cloth tag on belt: "This is Little // Phyllis May" // Created by
Hazel Drucker // Copyright 1921 L.A. & S. N.Y. / (Louis
Amberg & Son, New York)
Composition shoulder head and short lower arms. Cloth body,
upper arms, and legs, jointed at shoulders and hips. Molded,
painted brown hair, painted blue eyes, open/closed mouth
with four upper painted teeth. All original. Phyllis Bechtold
collection. $400.00+.

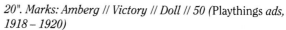

20". Marks: Amberg // Victory // Doll // 50 (Playthings ads, 1918 – 1920)
Composition socket head and ball-jointed body. Blond mohair wig, sleep eyes, open mouth with upper teeth. Redressed. Anita Maxwell collection. $375.00.

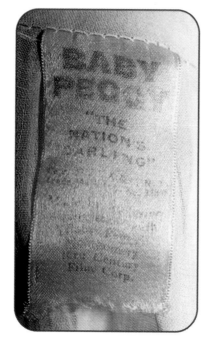

20", Baby Peggy (Montgomery) (Playthings, July 1923). Marks: none on doll. Sewn-in cloth tag: Baby // Peggy // "The // World's // Darling (rest illegible)
Composition shoulder head and lower limbs. Cloth body and upper limbs, stitched hip joints. Molded painted black hair and painted brown eyes with several painted highlights on iris, multi-stroke brows. Open/closed mouth with four painted upper teeth. All original. Don and Arlene Jensen collection. $750.00.

8" Sunny Orange Maid (Playthings, July 1924).
Marks: L.A. & S. N.Y. // D.R.G.M. // Made in Germany
German composition, jointed only at the shoulders. Molded, painted cap having the texture and color of an orange with painted green neck strap and paper blossom on each side. Molded, painted shoes and socks. Painted blue eyes, closed mouth. All original. Note: The fact that the Amberg firm had this small doll produced in Germany points out once more that relations with German toy manufacturers were close. Whoever could produce it cheapest was awarded the job. During the 1920s, it was quite common to also offer small examples of a large doll: Baby Peggy, Mibs, Little Annie Rooney, etc. However, those small dolls were made of bisque. The 8" Orange Maid illustrated here has never been seen before. $500.00.

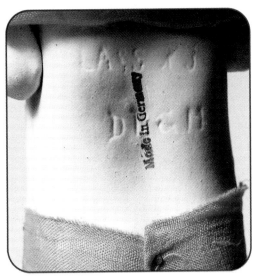

Left: 8" Sunny Orange Maid seen in previous illustration.
Right: 14" Sunny Orange Maid. Marks: L.A. & S.//1924
Composition shoulder head with molded cap having the texture and color of an orange. Short composition arms and lower legs. Cloth body and upper limbs with stitched hip joints. Painted blue eyes, closed mouth. Original dress. Replaced shoes and socks. Note: See lower legs shown in separate illustration. In the creation of this novelty doll, the lower legs of a ball-jointed body were used. They are definitely original, as has been verified by comparing with an all original model.

A short announcement in the July 1924, Playthings issue introduced Amberg's Sunny Orange Maid and mentioned that the doll "makes a noise like an orange when you squeeze it." Repeated searches have not turned up ads for this doll or the reason for her creation. This photo emphasizes the difference in height and special features of the smaller doll and her pristine originality (molded shoes and socks, dress is done differently in front). Left, $500.00. Right, $400.00.

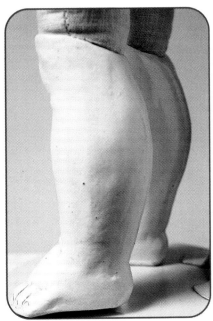

Left: 14" Horsman Peggy.
Right: 14" Amber "It" doll.
Marked on backs: Amberg // Pat. Pend. // L.A. & S. © 1928
All composition fully jointed, with additional waist joint. Molded painted blond hair and painted brown eyes, closed mouth. Peggy: Contemporary clothes. "It" doll is all original. Her dress tag reads: "An Amberg Doll With // Body Twist // all, all its own! // Pat. Pend. SFR No. 320,016.
Note: The validity of the "It" name has recently been confirmed when the doll was found in her original box marked "It" and with original "It" hang tag. (See Patsy Moyer's Modern Collectible Dolls, Vol. I, *page 22.) For information on the Peggy doll, see Horsman section. Left, $350.00. Right, $500.00.*

13½". Marks: Amberg // Pat. Pend. // L.A.S. © 1928
All composition, fully jointed, with additional swivel joint at waist level. Molded, painted reddish brown hair and painted brown eyes, closed mouth. Original dress, replaced shoes and socks.
This doll was an advertising item for Peter Pan fabrics and can be seen in various Playthings *ads offered as "Peter Pan Drest doll." Also see the next illustration of a Peter Pan-tagged dress, showing the fabric company's logo. Peggy Yale collection. $400.00+.*

Close-up of additional dress label, reading: "Made of // (not visible — inside seam) Peter Pan // Reg. U.S. Pat Off. // Fabric // Guaranteed Fast Color"
Embroidered and between the words "Peter Pan" is the figure of a Peter Pan carrying a palette and brush, the trade symbol of the fabric company.

13". Marks: Amberg // L.A. & S © Co.
This is Little Amby, Playthings, *September 1929.*
All composition, fully jointed. Molded, painted blond hair.
Painted brown eyes, open/closed mouth. All original except
dress. Pattern was taken from old, irreparable dress and the
lace and decal from it re-used. Old dress was made of light
blue organdy. $250.00.

Back row: 13". Marks: Amberg // L.A. & S. © 1928. Two compo-
sition toddlers, fully jointed, painted features and hair. Left: All
original. Right: Re-dressed.
Front row: 8" pair of Tiny Tots, also known as Teenie Weenies.
Same construction and marks as above, with additional waist
joint.
Front row, middle: Little Amby, also seen in previous illustration.
Note: The two toddlers in the back row were advertised by Amberg
with Little Amby as a group of three. See the following picture
*(*Playthings, *February 1929). All three of them are hard to find in*
today's collectors' market. The Teenie Weenies are also men-
tioned in this ad. Rear, 13", $250.00 each. Front, 8", $350.00 pair.
13" Amby, $250.00.

Playthings ad dated February 1929. In the lower right-hand corner of the ad one can see Little Amby and the other two toddlers pictured in the previous illustration.

Playthings ad, dated September 1929. In the lower right-hand corner Little Amby is illustrated and identified by a hang tag bearing his name, thus confirming his identity. To the left of him one can observe the Tiny Tots pair pictured in the previous group of five.

8". Marks: *Pat. Appl'd For // L.A.S. © 1928*
Gold color double sided tag: (See separate illustration).
All composition, jointed only at shoulders and waist. Molded, painted blond hair, painted brown eyes, closed mouth. Molded and painted socks and slippers. Re-dressed. $150.00.

American Character Doll Co.
New York City

The American Character Doll Co. was founded by Jacob Brock in 1919. Theirs was a family business. In 1923, they began using Petite as a trademark for their line of dolls. As can be seen in this section, some of their dolls were marked with such slogans as "America's Wonder Dolls" and "America's Wonder Baby Dolls." A horseshoe was also used as a symbol (a trademark) with the particular doll's name encircled by it.

The firm produced a general line of baby dolls and children, and quality was always emphasized. Some of their dolls stand out, such as Toodles, Bottletot, and Puggy, illustrated and discussed in this section.

Playthings, *May 1926.*

J. Brock and His Latest Creation, "Bottletot"

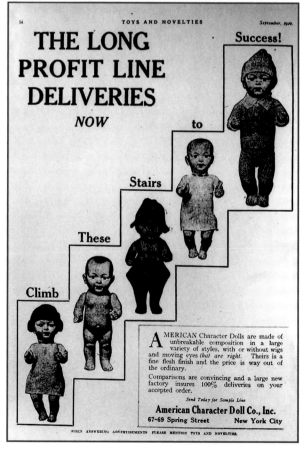

Full-page ad in Toys and Novelties, *dated September 1920, with five dolls clearly showing the German influence. They seem to have identical faces but were produced with straight legs and no hip joints and with bent legs and hip joints.*

*11". Marks: Baby // Petite (*Toys and Novelties, *Sept. 1925)*
Composition flange head and lower arms. Cloth body, upper
arms, and straight legs. Stitched shoulder and hip joints.
Faintly molded painted blond hair, blue sleep eyes, closed
mouth. Re-dressed. $150.00.

21" Bottletot. Marks: Petite // America's Wonder Baby Dolls. 1926.
Composition shoulder head to under the arms, full composition arms and
bent legs to above the knee. Right hand is molded so that it can hold a bot-
tle. Cloth body and upper legs, jointed at shoulders and hips. Molded, paint-
ed blond hair, gray tin sleep eyes, open mouth. Re-dressed.
Note: Subtle and very effective modeling of the facial features on this large
baby doll. When compared with the smaller Bottletots in the next illustra-
tion, the modeling is not as successful for these smaller versions of the same
doll. $300.00.

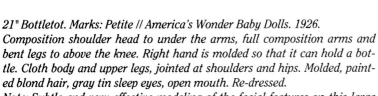

Group of three Bottletots, 13", 21", and 16" tall. 21"
doll seen in previous illustration. Both smaller dolls
are identically marked and constructed and have
original clothes, marked "Bottletot." Left to right:
$200.00, $300.00, $300.00.

19". Marks: Petite // America's Wonder Dolls
(This may be Miss Fashion, see next illustration, Playthings *ad, dated June, 1926.)*
Composition shoulder head and limbs, cloth body, jointed at shoulders and hips with additional knee joints. Dark brown wig, sleep eyes, open mouth with four upper teeth. Old clothes. Cherie Gervais collection. $350.00+.

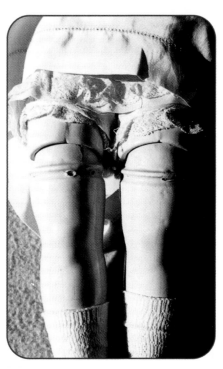

Close-up of knee joints of doll seen in previous illustration. They were actually way above the knee, probably necessitated by short skirt length. Note also the grove seen at joint level of the lower legs. The limb could have been wired onto an upper cloth leg, if the traditional leg without a knee joint was desired.

Full-page ad in Playthings, *June 1926, showing Miss Fashion. When comparing the face of the doll seen here with that of the one in the previous illustration, having the special knee joints, it seems to be identical.*
Miss Fashion was introduced and promoted with much fanfare. Elsewhere it was claimed that she was a special, new design created by an artist. Her slim, trim beauty was stressed. There was no mention of special knee joints.

15". Marks: none, see separate illustration of paper tag. Composition shoulder head and short arms. Cloth body, upper arms, and straight legs, stitched hip joints. Blond mohair wig, blue sleep eyes, open/closed mouth. All original. $200.00.

*17". Marks: Petite // Am. Character Doll Co. (*Toys and Novelties, *March, 1928)*
Cloth tag on dress: Happy Tot // A Petite Baby Composition shoulder head to below arms, composition arms and bent legs to above the knee. Cloth body and upper legs, jointed at shoulders, stitched hip joints. Molded painted blond hair, blue tin sleep eyes, open mouth with two upper teeth. All original. Cynthia Whittaker collection. $175.00.

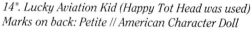

14". Lucky Aviation Kid (Happy Tot Head was used)
Marks on back: Petite // American Character Doll
Composition shoulder head to under the arms (like Bubbles), full arms and legs. Cloth body, jointed at shoulders and hips. Molded painted blond hair, blue tin sleep eyes, open mouth, all original, including red, white, and blue ribbon with small model of "Spirit of St. Louis" plane attached. Judy Johnson collection.
Note: The July 1927, Playthings *issue, announced the introduction of Lucky Aviation Kid as follows (with illustration): "The Lucky Aviation Kid was produced by the American Character Doll Co. to offer to the trade an opportunity to profit by the interest in aviation due to the Lindbergh adventure and the others who have followed it." $250.00.*

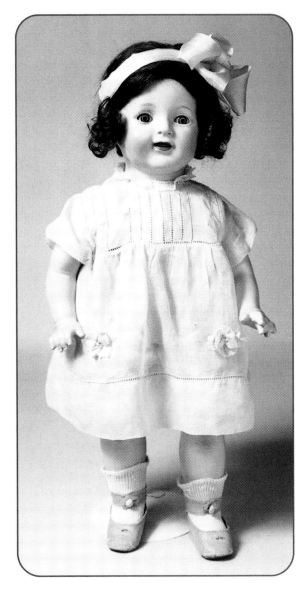

17". Marks: Petite // Amer. Char. Doll Co.
Composition head, swivel shoulder plate, arms, and legs to above the knee. Cloth body and upper legs. Jointed at shoulders, stitched hip joints. Brown mohair wig, blue sleep eyes, open mouth with four upper teeth. All original. Cynthia Whittaker collection. $250.00.

17". Marks: Petite // Amer. Char. Doll Co. 1920s.
Composition shoulder head, arms, and legs to above the knee. Cloth body, jointed at shoulders, stitched hip joints. Dark brown human hair wig over curly, molded hair. Gray tin sleep eyes, open mouth with two upper teeth. Old clothes. Replaced hair bow. $175.00.

24". Marks: Petite // Amer. Char. Doll Co.
Composition shoulder head, arms, and legs to above the knee, jointed at shoulders, stitched hip joints. Brown human hair wig, blue sleep eyes, open mouth with two upper teeth. All original. Cynthia Whittaker collection. $375.00.

12" Puggy. Marks: A// Petite Doll (Playthings, August 1929).
All composition, fully jointed. Molded, painted blond hair, painted blue eyes, closed mouth. All original. Margo Delaughter collection. $500.00+.

16". Marks: Petite // Amer. Char. Doll Co. Early 1930s.
Composition flange head and limbs. Cloth body, jointed at shoulders and hips. Blond mohair wig, sleep eyes, closed mouth. All original. Anita Maxwell collection. $350.00.

18". Marks: Petite // American Char. Doll Composition shoulder head arms, and legs, cloth body, jointed at shoulders and hips. Blond mohair wig. Gray tin sleep eyes, open mouth with four upper teeth. All original except for socks and shoelaces. $350.00.

18". Marks: Petite // American Char. Doll. Late 1920s.
Composition shoulder head, full arms, and legs, jointed at shoulders and hips. Cloth body. Blond mohair wig, blue tin sleep eyes, open mouth with four upper teeth. All original. $350.00.

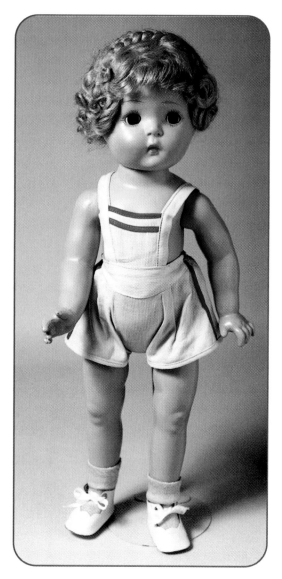

19" Carol Ann Beery (Playthings, October 1935).
Marks: Petite // Sally (on head), Petite (on body)
All composition, fully jointed. Blond mohair wig with braid across the top of head. (It is this braid that distinguishes her as a Carol Ann Beery rather than a Sally). Brown sleep eyes, closed mouth. original sun suit and socks.
Note: Carol Ann Beery was one of the film starlets of the mid-1930s. Mostly, she was the daughter of famous actor Wallace Beery. For further information on this very interesting doll, see "In the Image of Carol Ann Beery," by Nancy Carlson, Doll Reader, Sept. 1992. $250.00.

17". Marks: Petite // Amer. Char. Doll Co. 1930s.
Composition flange head, full arms, and legs to above the knee. Cloth body, jointed at shoulders, stitched hip joints. Molded, painted blond hair, painted blue eyes, closed mouth. Re-dressed in vintage, factory-made clothes. Anita Maxwell collection. $250.00.

Toodles – A Very Special Baby

Dollmakers have always tried to create dolls that are more life like in one way or another. During the early thirties, it was the feel of human flesh that manufacturers were aiming to duplicate by the use of rubber.

American Character introduced their Toodles in 1931, a truly and amazingly life-like new baby. While it still had a composition head, the limbs were made of a heavy gauge rubber. It modeled beautifully with very realistic baby features — creases and rolls of fat. But the really novel item was the body construction. A steel frame was covered with a spongy, soft rubber. When pressure is applied with a finger, it feels soft and can be slightly depressed. One of the ads stated: "An achievement in research and the development of new material, FLEX-O-FLESH looks and feels like … human flesh …?

Toodles had another special feature — unique eyes. A *Playthings* ad of August 1934, stated: "Talking about eyes, 'Toodles' is a great hit with the NEW kind of sleeping eyes. They don't merely 'plunk' shut — they go to sleep ONLY when you WANT them to."

When Toodles is put down on his back or right side, the eyes stay open. Only when the head is turned to the left, will the eyes close.

The ad further stated that Toddle-Tot, Sally, and Sally Joy had these new eyes as well. While Toddle Tot has been examined having these special eyes, Sally and Sally Joy have never been seen with them.

A *Playthings*, October 1937, ad announced the introduction of Toodles with a drink and wet feature.

*18" Toodles. Marks on head: Petite (*Playthings *and* Toys and Novelties *ads, 1931 – 1937+).*
Marked on body within the symbol of a horseshoe: "Petite."
Underneath: "Pat. Pend."
Composition head, Flex-O-Flesh body supported by a metal frame, heavy gauge rubber arms and bent legs. Molded painted blond hair, green sleep eyes with special mechanism, open mouth, tongue, no teeth. All original. $350.00.

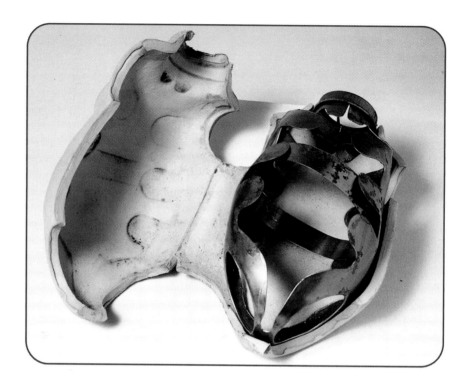

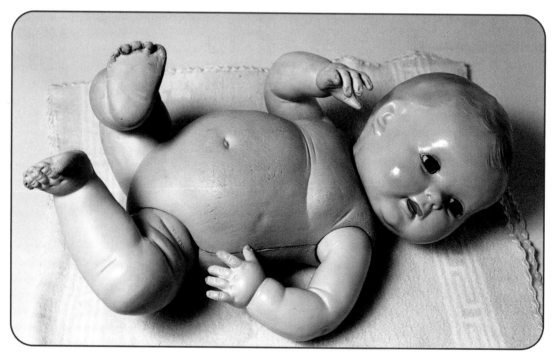

Toodles's body was supported by a special steel frame.

Sally Jane, A Paratex Unbreakable Doll

Great popularity was claimed for the Paratex dolls. In today's collector market, they are a rare find. Sally Jane is an all hard rubber doll, made from the same material as the Effanbee DyDee Baby's head. It has been proven beyond any doubt that DyDee Baby's head has survived in excellent condition. Why then is Sally Jane such a rarity?

Paratex dolls look and feel just like any composition doll. The only rather obvious difference would be her weight. If a doll seems unusually heavy for one made of composition, a closer look is warranted. At hand may be one of the rare Paratex dolls or an I-De-Lite, produced by the Ideal Novelty and Toy Company. The easiest way to do further checking would be to look at the joint areas. All hard rubber dolls did not have a dipped intermediate layer. They were painted directly onto the molded hard rubber surface. For this reason, finger and toe nails show sharper modeling detail than that of composition dolls. Their modeling was somewhat obscured and softened by the dipped intermediate layer which was applied before painting.

It is hoped that this information will help discover additional all hard rubber dolls.

17". Marks: none (Playthings, *August 1936).*
Tag front: Sally Jane // a // Paratex // unbreakable // doll
With an insurance policy guarantee
My wig can be curled because it is really human hair.
Tag back: You can // wash it
It won't crack, craze, or chip
(Inside text, see separate illustration)
All Paratex (rubber) fully jointed. Blond human hair wig, brown sleep eyes, open mouth with six upper teeth. Two dimples in cheeks. All original.
$700.00.

Once upon a time, long, long ago, little girls in Egypt played with dolls made of clay and wood. In far away Greece, they had dolls made of bone, and ivory, and clay, and wood, and even marble. The great great grandmother of your rag doll belonged to a little Roman girl. When the Pilgrims came to America, they found the little Indian girls playing with dolls made out of Cornhusks.

When Queen Victoria was a little girl, French and English and German dolls were made of wax, china, bisque, and papier mache. And then Americans learned to make dolls out of wood pulp composition which is more lifelike than any dolls ever made before.

Now, the American Character Doll Company has perfected a new kind of compound called PARATEX. That is what your SALLY JANE is made of. This wonderful new PARATEX material makes dolls look more lifelike. You can really WASH your Sally Jane—with SOAP—and she won't crack, craze or peel. And she WON'T BREAK even if she falls out of her carriage. She has a REAL INSURANCE POLICY, just like daddy's. That means that if she gets hurt, you can send her to us, and we will return her in good health.

A PRODUCT OF AMERICAN CHARACTER DOLL CO., INC. IN NEW YORK
Makers of Petite Fine Dolls.

Inside text of Sally Jane tag.

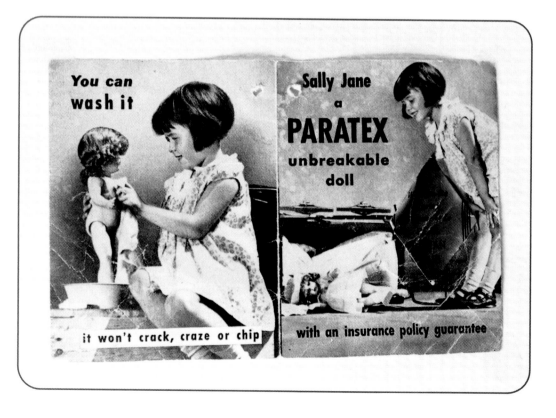

Toodles Made of Paratex

A 1937 ad proclaimed: "Toodles, She is Here! She is New! She is Different! …"

Six years had passed since the introduction of Toodles with FLEX-O-FLESH body and composition head. The ad also claimed that the firm had previously issued an all rubber Toodles. Now, they were introducing a Toodles with head and limbs made of Paratex (hard rubber), which is almost indistinguishable from composition. The really puzzling innovation for this new baby was a cotton-stuffed oilcloth body with mama voice box and drink and wet mechanism (a rubber tube attached to the inside of the mouth and leading through the stuffed body to a proper rear exit).

American Character was obviously trying to outdo the competition in more than one way. (In 1934, Effanbee's drink and wet doll Dy-Dee had been introduced with much success.) Besides having unique features, Toodles was of high quality and so was the box. Made of strong cardboard, it was covered with an elegant, expensive looking, embossed paper. Attractive illustrations covered the inside of the attached lid.

In October 1949, the firm was advertising yet another Toodles, called Toodles, the "Potty Baby," made of "fine molded rubber" and a hard plastic head (not illustrated).

Since Toodles is not marked, a close-up of the head is provided to help with the identification of collectors' unmarked dolls.

17" Toodles (Playthings, October 1937).
Marks: none on doll.
Paratex head, swivel shoulder plate, and lower limbs. Oilcloth body and upper limbs. Drink and wet feature. Molded painted brown hair, sleep eyes, open mouth, no teeth. All original including glass bottle with rubber nipple. Cynthia Whittaker collection. $500.00+.

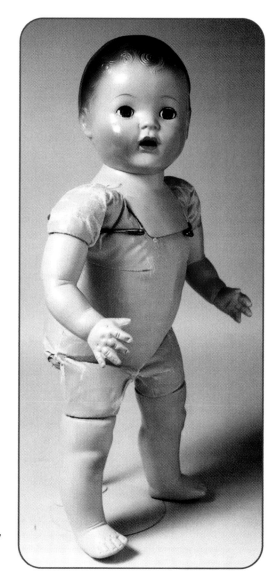

Oilcloth body stuffed with cotton, mama voice box. Drink and wet feature, with proper lower exit. $500.00+.

Toodles's original box.
Note: The identical graphics have been used as in the October 1937 Playthings *ad. Text inside box: "Toodles // The New Baby Doll That's Really Different // It Toodles, Drinks, Wets, Cries, Sleeps, and is Washable. It is Made Of The New Unbreakable, Washable, Paratex, A New Hard Rubber Material, Made With Soft, Cuddly Body . . . One Of The Fine, Long-Lasting Petite Dolls."*
Imprinted on horseshoe symbol: "A Lovable Petite Doll // Toodles."

Full-page ad, Playthings, *October 1937.*
Note: The word "Paratex" is not mentioned in this ad.
The ad states: "Toodles // She's Here! She's New! She's Different! Here's The Only Really NEW Idea In 1937 Dolls
Remember the sensational all-rubber Toodles? We predict that this NEW Toodles will be just as great a SUCCESS — the forerunner of a new vogue in dolls, just as the original Toodles was the forerunner of the all-rubber baby doll and the drinking wetting feature. If you want to be first to capitalize on Toodles in your city — see it now, or write or wire for full particulars.
It's Completely Foolproof."

This illustration was included with editorial copy in Playthings, *November 1941. The text reads as follows: "American Character Doll Company's 'Little Miss Patriot' catches the spirit of American patriotism with a modish organdy dress and bonnet, tastefully trimmed in patriotic colored stars and red, white, and blue stripes. Soft bodies, with voice, sleeping eyes, sashes, etc. $2.00 and $3.00 retail."*

Build Your Own U. S. Defense is a timely and popular number in the Standard Toykraft line. Packed in attractive boxes, the sets retail from 25¢ to $3.00. Included in the sets are figures of Soldiers, Sailors, Aviators, Boats, Tanks, etc., to be colored with either crayon or paint.

PICTORIAL
PLAYTHINGS
NOV, 1941

American Character Doll Company's "Little Miss Patriot" catches the spirit of American patriotism with a modish organdy dress and bonnet, tastefully trimmed in patriotic colored stars and red, white and blue stripes. Soft bodied, with voice, sleeping eyes, lashes, etc. $2.00 and $3.00 retail.

Illustration from Playthings, *August 1942, included with editorial copy, announcing various newly introduced toys.*

This American Character Doll Trunk Outfit, No. 913, has an 18" wood frame trunk with new and novel "pull shutter" which discreetly closes off each side of the trunk, as desired, thus contributing added play value to the item. Included with each outfit is a full composition doll, 13" tall, with sleeping eyes and lashes as well as a fine quality wig. The doll is attractively dressed in skating, skiing or party dress outfit, with added clothes consisting of blouse, shorts, skirt, jacket, hat and extra pair of shoes. This outfit retails at $1.98 and is on display with "Little Love", the new lovable infant doll, and the many other members of this well-known doll family. The complete line of this company can be viewed at their New York showrooms, 200 Fifth Avenue.

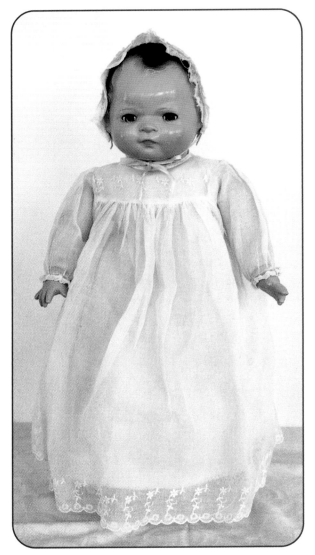

18". Marks: Am. Char. Doll. This is Little Love, 1943 – 1947. Composition flange head and hands, cloth body, arms, and straight legs, stitched hip joints. Molded painted brown hair and blue sleep eyes, closed mouth. All original. Cynthia Whittaker collection. $250.00.

15". Marks: Am. Char. Doll. 1943 – 1947.
Paper tag: Little Love // A // Petite // Baby
Composition flange head and hands, cloth body and limbs, stitched hip joints. Molded painted brown hair, blue sleep eyes, closed mouth. All original.
Note: Though definitely meant to be a baby, this doll has straight legs, with seams on both sides of the leg and a tailored heel, previously seen only on Hendren mama dolls (patented by Averill). $250.00.

American Doll Company

More information has come to light on this company. Original boxes have been found marked as follows "American Doll Co. Owned and operated by Bayless Bros. & Co., Louisville, KY." (See Patsy and Friends Newsletter, Jan/Feb., 2000, pg. 8.) Further in Coleman II, pg. 95: "Bayless Bros. & Co. 1925 – 1930 and later, Louisville, KY. Made doll's heads. 1926 – registered Honey Child as a U.S. trademark for dolls." Since it had previously been established that Honeychild was made by American Doll Co., this new information can be considered confirmed.

American Doll Co. made cheap premium dolls for at least ten years. So far, only two models had been seen: a boy with molded, short, curly hair and a girl with identical facial features but molded, marcelled hairdo. However, the girl with wig and white dress and the other in long, orange dress seen in the following illustrations, feature a new face: molded, straight hair with a part and open/closed mouth, but still with the decal eyes which many collectors identify as painted ones.

While so far it had been assumed that these dolls were used by various shoe companies only, the boy with all composition legs and molded black shoes (also illustrated here) features a cloth tag on his body marked "Manufactured for Pure Food Bakery."

(Additional shoe company mentioned in the Patsy Newsletter: "Polly Parrot Shoes.")

25". Marks: A.D. // C.
Composition shoulder head and arms, cloth body and legs, pin jointed at shoulders and hips. Molded, painted blond hair, decal eyes, open/closed mouth. Original bloomers and dress. $125.00.

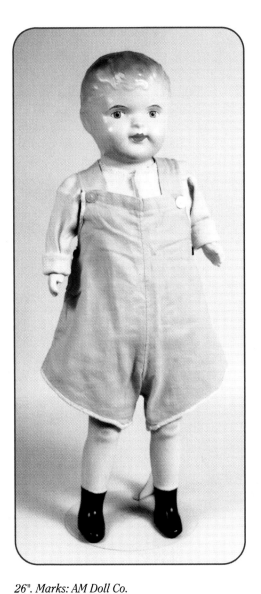

25". Marks: A.D. Co.
Dress tag: Peters // Weatherbird // Shoes
Composition shoulder head and arms. Cloth body and legs are stuffed with excelsior (wood shavings). Pin jointed at shoulders and hips. Blond mohair wig over molded hair, decal eyes, open/closed mouth. All original. Cynthia Whittaker collection. $150.00.

26". Marks: AM Doll Co.
Cloth label sewn to body: Manufactured // for // Pure Food Bakery
Composition shoulder head, all composition arms and legs with molded black boots, pin jointed at shoulders and hips. Cloth body stuffed with excelsior. Molded, painted blond hair and blue decal eyes, closed mouth. Dressed in old children's clothes. $95.00.

Close-up of label shown on dress in previous illustration.

Animal Dolls

An article in the trade magazine *Toys and Novelties* of August 1923, commented on the toys displayed in stores on the boardwalk of Atlantic City, New Jersey: "Let us take a look in one of the shops to show the vast assortment from which gifts may be chosen. Dolls — every kind in the world are here, the effective 'Flapper dolls' with their long arms and legs being used the most frequently for the window displays. Next in order of display are the animal dolls — rabbits and pussies, the old stand-by Teddies, donkeys, monkeys. Dolls are as bizarre as the age and the modern child loves the animal doll as much as her mother and grandmother loved the orthodox doll that was dressed and undressed and put to bed." (Doesn't this last sentence sound as if it had been written in 2002 and not in 1923?)

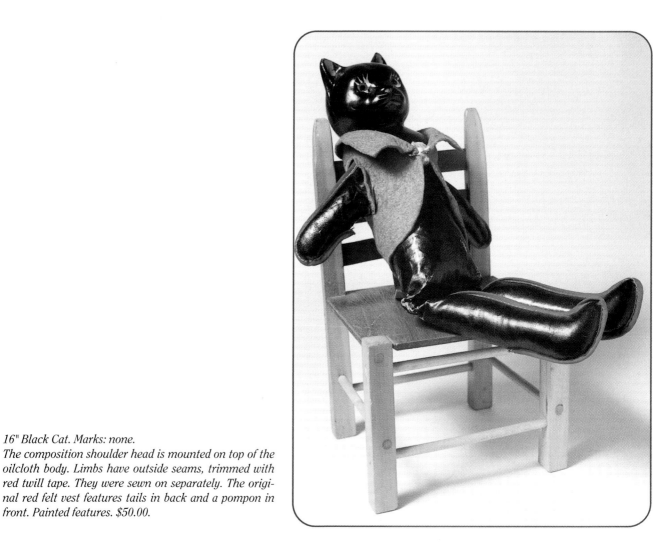

16" Black Cat. Marks: none.
The composition shoulder head is mounted on top of the oilcloth body. Limbs have outside seams, trimmed with red twill tape. They were sewn on separately. The original red felt vest features tails in back and a pompon in front. Painted features. $50.00.

16" Cat. Marks: none.
Composition flange head, cloth body and limbs. Painted, yellow eyes, open/closed mouth with molded tongue. All original, except for bow. $85.00.

15" Monkey. Marks: none.
Composition flange head, cloth body and limbs, no joints. Cardboard inserts allow the toy to stand by itself. All original. May have had a matching jacket. Facial decoration was carefully executed. Eyes were rendered more expressive by airbrushing around sockets with brown paint. $75.00.

12" Monkey. Marks: none.
Composition flange head with molded cap. Cloth body and limbs, no joints, ribbon loop on top of cap. Painted eyes and closed mouth. $50.00.

12". Marks: none.
Pair of rabbits with pink and white heads. Bodies and limbs show regular flesh color. All composition, fully jointed. Painted brown eyes. All original outfits. Sherryl Shirran collection. $150.00 each.

Arranbee Doll Company
New York City
1922 – 1958

The first doll illustrated in this section is a toddler from the mid-1920s. It features a German composition head on a cloth body with American-made composition limbs. At the time, various American companies were offering character dolls with bisque heads made in Germany and body assemblies produced domestically. Arranbee's Dream Baby was one of these. It may have been this trend that encouraged Arranbee to offer a similarly constructed doll but with a German composition head. It must not have been a great success, as this is a rarely seen item. Entirely American made composition mama dolls and babies were dominating the market during the 1920s.

After the introduction of Effanbee's Patsy in 1928, Arranbee's various Nancy dolls were very much styled in the image of this famous newcomer. This changed during the mid 1930s after the introduction of Ideal's Shirley Temple, when their Nancy was made to resemble the Shirley dolls not only in facial features but also in body shape.

The late 1930s saw the introduction of the Debu'Teen and very similar looking Nancy Lee dolls. Both featured slimmer waists and limbs. The Debu'Teen dolls seem to have been aimed at the higher end market. Molded eyelids are a special feature that distinguishes them from the Nancy Lees. Also, their eye shadow was airbrushed a pale gray, not black. The clothes are very well styled and sewn and reflected teen fashions.

An ad in the trade magazine *Playthings* of October 1946, was still offering a composition Dream Baby, Little Angel, Nancy, Nancy Lee, and Nanette. An all hard plastic Nanette was sold by Arranbee in the 1950s. An illustrated notation in *Toys and Novelties*, August 1949, was still featuring three sizes of Nancy Lee dolls on roller skates and dressed in colorful cotton dresses.

For more extensive information on Arranbee's Debu'Teens, see "Fashion Dolls of the 1930s," by Lyn Murray (*Antique Doll Collector*, November 2000).

22". Marks: on head: Simon Halbig // Arranbee // Patent No. 74720 // Germany. Mid-1920s.

German composition socket head and shoulder plate, American-made composiition lower arms and legs to above the knee. Cloth body, upper arms, and legs. Tied-on arms, stitched hip joints. Light brown mohair wig, glass sleep eyes that also move from side to side. Open mouth with two upper and two lower teeth. Old clothes. Judy Johnson collection. $350.00+.

Dolls Whose Bodies Are Marked "Kewty"

The following two dolls' bodies are embossed with "Kewty." Though they have been placed in this Arranbee section, a question remains that the "Kewty" marked bodies may have been used by other companies as well. More research is required.

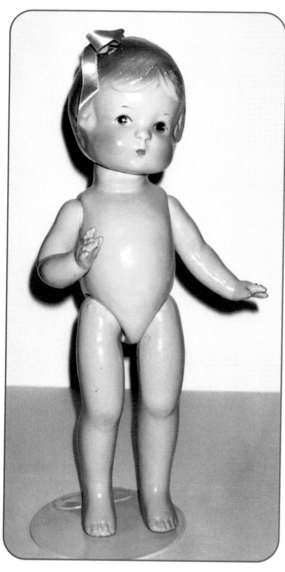

14". Marks on back: Kewty.
All composition, fully jointed. Molded, painted reddish hair, painted blue eyes. Closed mouth. Judy Johnson collection. $250.00.

14". Marks on back: KEWTY. Early 1930s.
All composition, fully jointed. Molded, painted blond hair, painted blue eyes, closed. Smiling mouth. Re-dressed. $250.00.

11". Marks on body: Arranbee.
All composition, fully jointed. Molded, painted blond hair with molded hair loop. Painted blue eyes, closed mouth. Old clothes. Joan Nickel collection. $150.00.

12". Marks on body: Arranbee // Doll Co.
All composition, fully jointed. White mohair wig over molded hair, painted blue eyes, closed mouth. All original. Note: This doll was produced on the occasion of George Washington's 200th birthday in 1932. $250.00.

1931 catalog illustration showing an Arranbee Nancy, as seen in picture above. Her paper tag reads as follows: Nancy // Arranbee // Doll. Note the short dress and large hair bow.

12". Marks on doll: none. (This is their Drink 'n Babe.)
Marks on celluloid bottle: Arranbee // Pat. Aug. 10, 26
All composition (except for right hand which is made of celluloid and glued to the arm), fully jointed. Slightly molded, painted, blond hair, gray tin sleep eyes, open mouth.
Note: The celluloid hand was used as a reservoir for the liquid in the bottle. When the right arm is raised (nipple into doll's mouth), the liquid would drain into the hand. When lowered, the fluid would return into the bottle. Was sold with suitcase and layette. $150.00. Cynthia Whittaker collection.

20". Marks: Dream Baby. 1930s.
Composition flange head, lower arms, and legs to above the knee. Cloth body, upper arms, and legs. Stitched hip joints. Molded, painted blond hair, blue sleep eyes, open mouth with two upper teeth, metal tongue. All original. $200.00. Cynthia Whittaker collection.

Note the holes in hand for draining fluid.

16". Marks: none on doll. Ca. 1940.
Box marked: Arranbee dolls (tag on clothes)
Composition flange head and limbs. Cloth body with tied on limbs, stitched hip joints (straight legs). Molded, painted blond hair and blue tin sleep eyes. Open mouth with two upper teeth. All original including basket and shipping box.
Note: Close-up of distinctive hairdo will be helpful to collectors when trying to identify their unmarked dolls. Lois Jean Adam collection. $500.00.

An Unretouched Photograph

A beautiful Dream Baby, dressed in flannel sleeping garment—a large, colorful, gorgeously trimmed basket with adjustable hood and handle—pillow and coverlet to match—and complete layette in cellophane envelope.

And All For

$4.98 Retail

Full-page ad, Playthings, *October 1940, featuring "A beautiful Dream Baby dressed in flannel sleeping garment — a large colorfully trimmed basket with adjustable hood and handle-pillow and coverlet to match — and complete layette in cellophane envelope." Further mentioned in the ad are "Featherweight Babies With Rolling Eyes." Also: Nancy Lee, Nancy, Nannette, and Newly Created Doll Wardrobes and Other Novelties."*

19". Marks on head: Nancy. Paper Tag: Nancy // R & B Quality Doll All composition, fully jointed, blond human hair wig, blue sleep eyes, open mouth with four upper teeth. All original. Lynn Murray collection. $400.00+.

90

13". Marks: none (Princess Elizabeth type face), early 1940s.
All composition, fully jointed. Blond mohair wig, blue sleep eyes, open mouth with four upper teeth. All original. Caryl Silber collection. $250.00.

15". Marks: (x)
All composition, fully jointed. Brown sleep eyes, open mouth with four upper teeth. All original, except for wig.
Note: Though this doll's head is of a different mold (a so-called Elizabeth face), she has been seen with an identical "Nancy" tag, as shown with doll in previous picture. $400.00.

19". Marks: Nancy
Paper tag: Nancy // RandB // Quality Doll
All composition, fully jointed. Blond human hair wig, sleep eyes, open mouth with two upper teeth. All original. Arlene and Don Jensen collection. $350.00.

91

17". Marks: R & B
Paper Tag: Nancy Lee//An//R & B//Quality Doll. (See separate illustration.)
All composition, fully jointed, blond human hair wig and blue sleep
eyes, closed mouth. All original, including umbrella.
Note: Dress features snap closures rather than the usual safety pins.
$400.00.

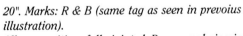

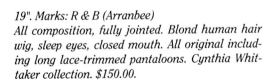

Close-up of Nancy Lee in pristine condition.

20". Marks: R & B (same tag as seen in prevoius illustration).
All composition, fully jointed. Brown mohair wig and brown sleep eyes, closed mouth. All original. $800.00.

19". Marks: R & B (Arranbee)
All composition, fully jointed. Blond human hair wig, sleep eyes, closed mouth. All original including long lace-trimmed pantaloons. Cynthia Whittaker collection. $150.00.

18". Marks: R & B (Debu 'Teen)
Paper Tag: see separate illustration.
Composition head, shoulder plate, and limbs. Cloth
body, jointed at shoulders and hips. Blond mohair
wig, sleep eyes, closed mouth. All original. $400.00.

17". Marks: none. Paper tag: "Debu 'Teen//R&B Quality Doll"
All composition, fully jointed. Reddish blond human hair wig, sleep eyes, closed mouth. All original. Lynn Murray collection. $450.00.

19". Marks on head: R&B
Paper tag: "Debu 'Teen // R&B Quality Doll"
Composition head, swivel shoulder plate and limbs. Cloth body, jointed at shoulders and hips. Blond human hair wig, sleep eyes, closed mouth. All original. Lynn Murray collection. $500.00.

21" Nannette. Early 1940s.
Marks: none on doll.
Paper tag: see separate illustration.
Composition head, swivel shoulder plate, and limbs, cloth body with mama crier. Jointed at shoulder, stitched hip joints. Blond human hair wig, blue sleep eyes, open mouth with four upper teeth. All original. Caryl Silber collection.
Note: Even though this doll is from the early 1940s and represents an older child (not a baby), she features a cloth body with inserted mama crier, and the label states that she is a "Walking and Talking Doll." This means that after more than 30 years since their introduction, mama dolls were still popular and the manufacturer considered it desirable to use the walking and talking feature to advertise this doll. Also note the Nannette in the following illustration. She has a different head, a cloth body, and bent legs, but the same label. $350.00.

Same fabric underwear as the 21" Nannette is nicely finished at neck and armholes with dark blue bias tape. Usually, raw edges are only turned under and machine stitched. This type underwear may have been intended as a playsuit.

18" Nannette. Marks on head: R & B
Paper tag: Nannette//Walking and Talking// An R & B Quality Product.
Composition head, swivel shoulder plate, and arms. Composition legs to upper mid calf. Cloth body and upper legs, jointed at shoulders, stitched hip joints. Blond human hair wig, sleep eyes, closed. Mouth. All original.
Note: Legs on this doll are slightly bent at the knee and non-supporting. Lynn Murray collection. $500.00.

8½" Jack and Jill. Marks on head: R & B
Box measurements: 10"x9"x3"
All composition, fully jointed. Molded, painted light brown hair, painted blue eyes, closed mouth. All original, including 2" high red wooden pail. $400.00.

Atlas Dolls & Toy Co., Inc.

Doll: 13". Metal frame including handle: 28"
Marks: Century // Doll Co.
(See: April 1928 ad, Atlas Doll & Toy Co., Inc., Baltimore MD)
Composition shoulder head, metal arms with attached metal "jump rope," cloth body and legs, jointed at shoulders and hips. Molded, painted blond hair and painted blue eyes, open/closed mouth with four painted teeth. All original.
Note: The ad stated: "Just What You Need For Children's Day! The Doll that Jumps Rope Just Like a Real Child!" $650.00.

The Averill Manufacturing Co.
New York City
1915 – up

Georgene Averill (nee Hopf), 1876 – 1963 (See Coleman II.)

The Women's Activities section of the *New York Times*, dated November 3, 1940, featured an illustrated two-column article, based on an interview with Georgene Averill. Some early biographical data on Georgene Averill and their doll business are excerpted here.

Apparently, the interview was conducted at the Averill's apartment in Greenwich Village, a neighborhood in New York City. It is described as being furnished with antiques and art objects including paintings done by daughter Maxine.

Around 1910, Georgene Averill was a patient at a hospital in Portland, Oregon. There she gave a cowboy doll to a little boy in the children's ward. Georgene had created the costume for this doll from felt scraps. Back home in Seattle, it was still uncertain that she would ever walk again. Encouraged by her first attempt, Georgene dressed more cowboy and Indian dolls, which her younger brother sold to novelty shops. The dolls appealed to tourists. Before long, Mrs. Averill was employing her siblings and neighborhood children, making braids and stringing beads for her creations. She did recover from her illness and moved to Los Angeles, conducting her business under the name of Mme. Georgene Hendren. When she met Paul Averill, a toy buyer from New York City, he bought her whole output. They were eventually married.

The article goes on to explain the production of a doll head from original plastic model to metal die. Mrs. Averill was quoted as saying that putting a newly designed doll into production cost $4.000.00–$5.000.00.

While Mrs. Averill designed the dolls and their clothing, her brother, Mr. Rudolph Hopf, supervised production. Stuffed animals were also mentioned. It was stated that their Broadway plant turned out 250,000 pieces a season (year). It was further reported that Mme. Georgene was planning to produce some of her creations in porcelain, to be used as bookends and decorative pieces. Because of curtailed imports of such novelties from Europe due to the war (WW II), good sales were expected. One wonders if these items went into production, as none have ever been seen.

Unusual Items

Following, many dolls in their original clothes are illustrated and have been researched. Worth mentioning are the character faces of early Indians and babies. U-Shap-Ti, the pharaoh doll, was an exciting, new discovery and the information on Mah-Jongg Kid. The three faces of the Averill's Lullaby Baby are illustrated, as well as an all original and tagged Chocolate Drop, a Grace Drayton creation so far known only in an all-cloth version. Last but not least, a Georgene Baby is pictured which has a music box inserted in her softly stuffed cloth body that plays "Lullaby Baby."

9" Dutch pair. Marks: none (St. Nicholas Magazine, 1916).
Flared composition heads and short arms. Cloth body, upper arms, and legs with light brown cloth boots, and jointed with outside disks at shoulders and hips. Molded painted brown hair (blond mohair wig with braids for girl) and black eyes, no pupils. Closed, smiling mouths. All original.
Note: The mold for these heads was obviously copied from a German source. $200.00 pair.

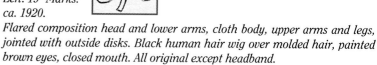

Left: 19" Marks:
ca. 1920.
Flared composition head and lower arms, cloth body, upper arms and legs, jointed with outside disks. Black human hair wig over molded hair, painted brown eyes, closed mouth. All original except headband.
Right: 20", same marks and construction as above, except jointed with inside disks. All original except headband.
Note: An identical head was used for these two Indians and for the mama doll with the same mark seen in this section. $500.00 pair.

15". Marks: none on doll. Cloth label: Madame Hendren // Character Doll // Costume Pat. May 9, 1916. Ca. 1920. Composition shoulder head and short lower arms. Cloth body, upper arms, and legs, jointed at shoulders and hips with inside disks. Black human hair wig with braids, painted brown eyes, closed mouth. All original. Cynthia Whittaker collection. $200.00.

13". Marks: Trion Toy Co. // 1915
Flared composition head and lower arms. Cloth body, upper arms and legs with brown cloth boots which are part of the leg casing. Jointed with outside disks. Molded, painted black hair and painted brown eyes, closed mouth. All original.
Note: At this early date, the Averill Company bought heads from other firms to produce their dolls, in this case from the Trion Toy Co. Further note that the heads used for the pair seen in the previous illustration were bought from yet another company (those initials as yet unidentified). $175.00.

18" Indian Chief, early 1920s.
Marked on shoulder plate: A.M. © Co. (Averill Manufacturing)
Cloth tag: Madame Hendren // Character Doll // Costume Pat.
May 9, 1915
Composition shoulder head and arms, cloth body and legs, joint-ed at shoulders, stitched hip joints. Black cotton yarn wig with braids, painted brown eyes, closed mouth. All original.
Note: Doll shows the typical mama doll construction of the early 1920s (no voice box). $250.00.

15". Marks: none on doll. Cloth label: Madame Hendren // Char-acter Doll // Costume Pat. May 9th, 1916. 1920s.
Composition shoulder head and arms, cloth body and legs, joint-ed with inside disks. Black mohair wig over faintly molded hair. Painted brown eyes and closed mouth. All original. $200.00.

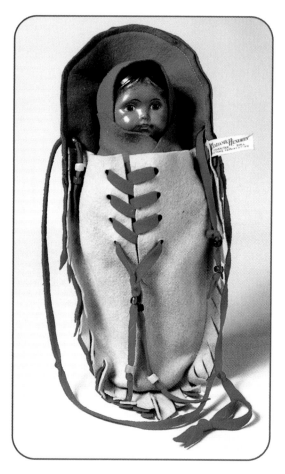

Doll 12", carrier 16" long. Can't tell if the head is marked, as the wrapping has never been removed.

Cloth tag on carrier: Madame Hendren // Character Doll // Costume Pat. May 9th, 1916.

Composition flange head and short arms. Cloth body, upper arms and legs with black cloth boots, jointed with outside disks. Molded, painted black hair and painted brown eyes, closed mouth. The doll has been wrapped in 4½" wide strip of felt, pinned in place with four stickpins. The carrying case back is constructed of two pieces of felt, sewn together. Laced in front with felt strip and decorated with glass beads. Carrying strap has been threaded through holes punched into the back piece of the carrier, also decorated with glass beads. $150.00.

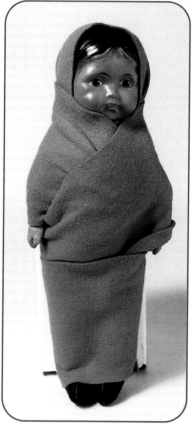
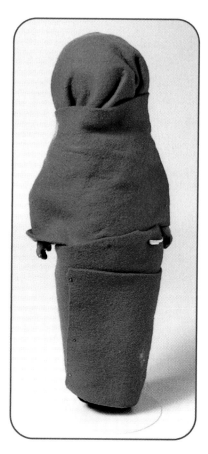

The original wrapping has never been removed, and these two pictures show how it was done. Held in place with four stickpins (three down left leg, one into rear end).

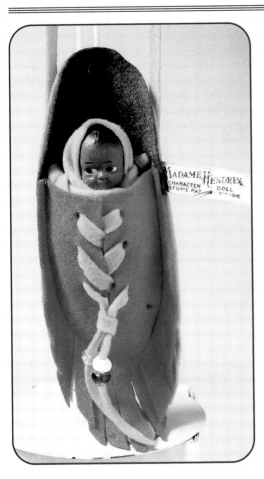

Doll: 4½". Carrier: 8" long. Marks: none.
Cloth tag: Madame Hendren // Character Doll // Costume Pat. May 9th, 1916
Painted bisque figure (no joints) is wrapped in 2" wide continuous strip of yellow felt. (For construction of papoose see caption of previous illustration).
Note: Early on, Georgine Averill used German bisque as well as celluloid dolls to create her children dressed in Indian and Dutch costumes made of felt. These are rarely seen. $45.00.

Length of papoose: 13", of doll: 9"
Marks: none on doll
Cloth tag on papoose: Madame Hendren//Character Doll//Costume Pat. May 9th, 1916
Flared composition head, cloth body and limbs with stump hands, jointed with outside disks. Body cavity is almost entirely taken up by a mama cry box. Instead of being swaddled with a strip of felt, this papoose baby is wearing a hood that extends over his shoulders. Slightly molded painted black hair and eyes, closed mouth. All original. $150.00.

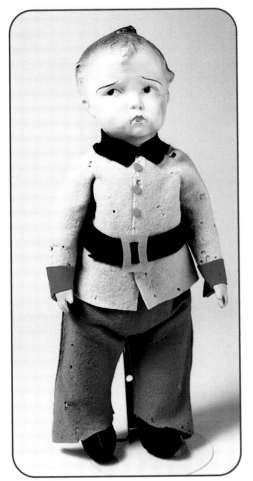

14" Grumpy. Marked: DECO
Flared composition head and short arms. Cloth body, upper arms, and straight legs with sewn-in black cloth boots, jointed with outside disks. Molded, painted light brown hair and painted blue eyes. Closed mouth.
Note: Because of his felt clothing, he is assumed to have been sold by the Averill Company. $300.00. Cynthia Whittaker collection.

16". Marks: Before 1918.

Ink stamp on body: Madame Hendren's "Life Like doll" // Patent Applied For.

Composition flange head and lower arms, cloth body and upper arms, stitched hip joints. Painted blond hair (no indication of molding), painted blue eyes, closed mouth. All original.

Note: The ink stamp on the cloth body says "Patent applied for," meaning that this doll was sold before the 1918 patent was issued. The doll in the following illustration was made with an identical head, but her stamp already gives the 1918 patent date. Further note that both heads were made without a dipped top composition layer, producing very sharp modeling of the facial features and revealing the excellent sculptural skills of the creator of this pensive looking doll baby. It also reveals why the dipping method was later used on all dolls. It ensured a very smooth surface. As can be seen in this picture, very slight depressions are evident on the forehead, which are in no way distracting by today's standards. $250.00. Cynthia Whittaker collection.

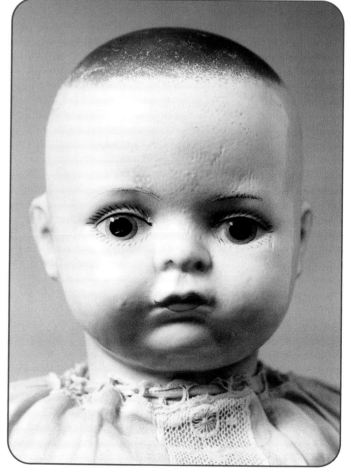

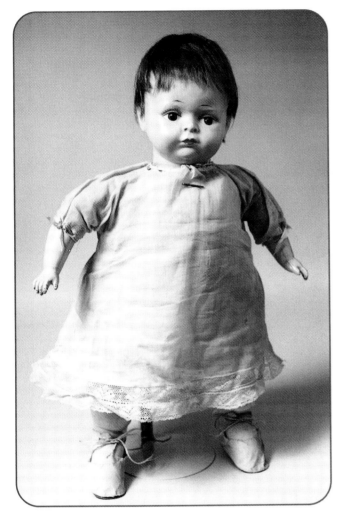

18". Marks on head:

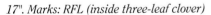

Ink stamp on body: Madame Hendren's "Life Like Doll" // patented June 11, 1918
Composition flange head and lower arms. Cloth body, upper arms and cloth legs with stitched hip joints. Brown mohair wig over molded hair, painted eyes, closed mouth. All original. Cynthia Whittaker collection. $175.00.

17". Marks: RFL (inside three-leaf clover)
Ink stamp on cloth body: Madame Hendren // Life Like Dolls // Patented June 4th, 1918
Composition flange head and lower arms, cloth body, upper arms and legs. Molded, painted light brown hair (striated), painted blue eyes with white rays on irises, closed mouth. No shoulder joints, stitched hip joints.
Note: Compare with previous two dolls. Modeling is less sharp. It is assumed that this head has a dipped composition layer. Cynthia Whittaker collection. $175.00.

Two Particularly Noteworthy Toddlers

The toddlers seen in the following two illustrations are of particular interest, as their outfits could be verified in every detail with the help of a *Playthings* ad dated January 1921.

*19" Buddy Boy (*Toys and Novelties, *January 1921)*
Marks: none on doll.
Ink stamp on body: Madame Hendren's "Life-Like Doll"//Patented June 11, 1918
Composition flange head and lower arms. Cloth body, upper arms and legs. Stitched hip joints. Molded, painted blond hair, painted eyes with rays painted onto irises, closed mouth. All original with original metal coin. Cynthia Whittaker collection.
Note: See separate illustration of the metal coin. This seems to be an earlier version not seen before. While previously examined examples showed a standing child, this one is embossed with a girl sitting, holding her doll. The back side features the usual swastika plus good luck symbols, as seen on the coin with the next doll. $400.00.

Close-up of metal coin belonging to Buddy Boy and inscribed: "Madame Hendren Dolls, Everybody Loves Them."

19". Marks: none (Toys and Novelties, January 1921).
Ink stamp on body: Genuine//"Madame Hendren"//Life-Like//Doll Patented June 11, 1918//Made in U.S.A.//20). This is the original patent date, not the date of manufacture of this doll.
Label on box: Madame Hendren//Doll//Averill Mfg. Co.
Paper tag and metal coin: See separate illustrations.
Composition flange head and lower arms. Cloth body, upper arms, and straight legs. No shoulder joints, stitched hip joints. Molded painted brown hair and blue eyes, closed mouth. Pristine condition and all original. $475.00.

Close-up of 19" Hendren Toddler. Since there are no markings on the head, being familiar with this rather unusual hairdo would help with the identification of a doll that has no body marks or tags.

Close-up of pistine face decoration.

Gold Medal — Front
Note: Also see Horsman section, 19" Gold Medal Baby, showing this coin embossed with the Hors-man name and a sitting infant. The Horsman coin was used in a joint radio advertising cam-paign with the Averill Mfg. Co.

Front and back close-ups of paper tag.

Excerpt from full-page Toys and Novelties *ad, dated January 1921, showing "Life-Like" Baby Doll and Buddy Boy.*

17". Marks: none (typical Averill leg/foot construction), early 1920s. Composition shoulder head and arms to above the elbow. Cloth body with stitched hip joints. Molded, painted light brown hair, painted blue eyes, open/closed mouth. All original, except for booties. $175.00. Cynthia Whittaker collection.

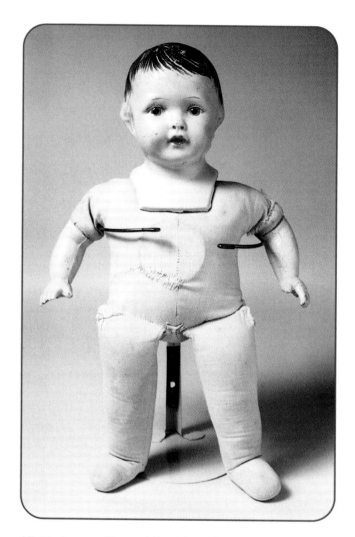

16". Marks: none (Toys and Novelties, July 1922). Composition head and arms to above the elbow. Cloth body, upper arms, and straight legs, stitched hip joints. Molded, painted medium brown hair, painted blue eyes, open/closed mouth. Note construction of legs with two side seams and tailored heel, a trademark of Averill mama dolls. The voice box imbedded in the cloth body has the depth of two regular ones. It may mean that this doll made "mama" and "papa" sounds (not in working order). $150.00.

16". Identical doll as seen in above. All original blue plaid romper. Note: excellent, sharp modeling of molded hair on forehead. Cynthia Whittaker collection. $165.00.

Tut-Ankh-Amen Dolls and Toys

When British archeologist Howard Carter and company discovered the undisturbed tomb of Tut-Ankh-Amen, an Egyptian pharaoh dead for more than three thousand years, it was a sensation. News of this exciting discovery spread worldwide and held people's attention. The Averills intended to make this fascinating event help them sell playthings.

The following quote from editorial copy in the *Playthings* issue of April 1923, gives details of the Averill's advertising campaign for these special toys: "Averill Mfg. Co. report excellent sales with their unique specialties made by special arrangement with the Tut-Ankh-Amen Products Co. Based upon the countrywide craze for everything Egyptian following the wonderful discoveries in Luxor, Egypt, 'Tut's Pup' and 'U-shab-ti' were recently offered to the toy trade and made friends everywhere immediately. 'Tut's Pup,' be it known, is a miniature of the faithful canine, which barked defiance at the enemies of the famous Pharaoh. Besides being a clever little toy or desk companion, he is a lucky dog calculated to bring success to his owners. He has a wonderful curling tail made of brightly colored beads, with a bell on the end of it. The 'U-shab-ti' dolls are offered in two distinct forms. One of the regulation unbreakable doll material of dusky hue and the other in the long leg soft body form that are so attractive with grown-ups as well as children. These latter have most interesting faces and form color spots in store window or in home. Gimbel Bros., New York, recently had a feature display and sale of these interesting Egyptian novelties."

Comment: One wonders if the second doll mentioned "the long leg soft body form" makes reference to a bed doll. Now that the "regulation unbreakable doll" can be studied in the following illustration, knowledge of the original costume of the illustrated doll should be helpful in finding the bed doll, if such an item was sold.

Full-page ad in Playthings, *dated March 1921, advertising Tut-Ankh-Amen toys.*

18". Marks: none. U-Shap-Ti (see separate illustration of tag — a copy of an original tag).

Modified composition shoulder head and short arms. Brown cloth body and limbs. Molded, painted black hair, painted brown eyes, open/closed mouth with white line to represent teeth. Stitched joints at shoulders and hips. Original skirt and headdress, replaced belt. Sandals were copied from ad illustration. Doll has been restored.

Note: The shoulder head was cut back and mounted inside the cloth body, indicating that this novelty was produced with an already existing head, to insure timely availability. The Averills wanted to make certain that the King Tut toys could be offered for sale while the excitement about the discovery of King Tut's undisturbed tomb was at its height. $350.00.

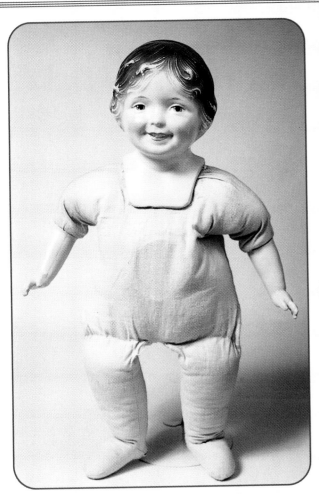

16". Marks: none. Early 1920s.
Composition shoulder head and arms, cloth body, upper arms, and legs.
No shoulder joints, stitched hip joints. Molded, painted brown hair,
painted blue eyes. Open/closed mouth with four painted teeth.
Note: Typical leg construction patented by the Averills in 1918, with
seams on both sides of the leg and tailored heel. Further note that this
head was also used in the production of U-Shap-Ti. $150.00.

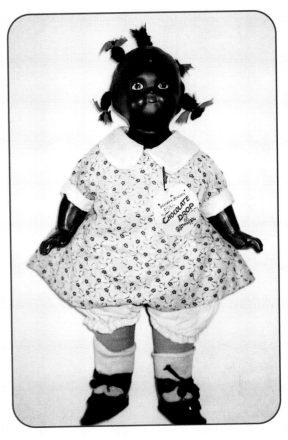

14". Marks: G.G. Drayton. 1924.
Paper tag: A // Madame // Hendren // Doll Chocolate //
Drop // G.G. Drayton
Brown composition shoulder head and lower arms.
Cloth body, upper arms, and legs, stitched hip joints.
Five black yarn pigtails have been glued into drill holes.
Painted brown eyes, closed mouth. All original.
Note: An identical head has been used for this doll and
for Sis illustrated in Collector's Encyclopedia of Ameri-
can Composition Dolls, Volume I. *Anita Maxwell collec-*
tion. $600.00.

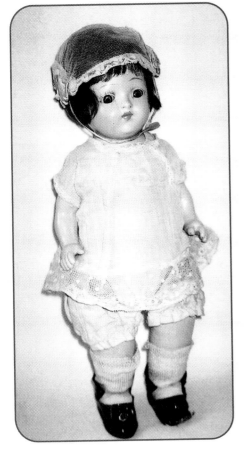

14" Rock-A-Bye Baby (Sears Roebuck catalog, 1921 – 1924).
Marks: none.
Composition shoulder head and lower arms. Cloth body, upper arms, and legs,
stitched hip joints. Brown mohair wig, blue sleep eyes, closed mouth. All origi-
nal.
Note: The doll has three mama voice boxes in her cloth body and did not close
her eyes when laid down. Only when rocked from side to side would the eyes
close eventually. Anita Maxwell collection. $350.00.

Label attached to dress of bisque baby.

Three Lullaby Babies produced by the Averill Company.
Left: 13". Marks: AM © Co. Ink stamp on body: Genuine//Madame Hendren//Doll//314//Made in USA
Far Right: 16". Marks: none. Ink stamp on body: Genuine//Madame Hendren//Doll//316//Made in USA
Both dolls have a composition flange head and hands, cloth body, arms, and straight legs, stitched shoulder and hip joints. Molded, painted light brown hair and blue tin sleep eyes, closed mouth. Both are re-dressed. (Both dolls were advertised in Playthings, *March and July 1925)*
Middle: Bisque flange head marked: AM//Germany//341//. Ink stamp on body: Genuine//Madame Hendren//Doll// (next line illegible) Made in USA. Also see separate illustration of dress tag.
Cloth body, arms, and straight legs. Celluloid hands, faintly molded blond hair and blue glass sleep eyes, closed mouth. All original. Cynthia Whittaker collection. (Re: #341, see Averill catalog in the collection of the Strong Museum, Rochester). Left to right: $150.00, $300.00, $250.00.

22". Marks: A.M. Co. (Averill Manufacturing), Playthings, *April 1924.*
Composition flange head and lower limbs, cloth body with stitched hip joints. Molded, painted blond hair and blue tin sleep eyes. Open/closed mouth with two upper painted teeth. Carole C. Chadwick collection. $400.00+.

13" Whistler. Marks: none.
Ink stamp on body: Genuine // Madame Hendren // Doll // Patented Feb. 2, 1926 // Made in USA
Composition flange head and arms, cloth body and legs, with whistling mechanism embedded in each leg. Jointed at shoulders, stitched hip joints. Molded, painted light brown hair and painted blue eyes. Drill hole in center of mouth. All original. Note: This is the "dolly face" whistler (no molded, puckered eyebrows and mouth. Unlike similar Dutch children by Madame Hendren whose outfits are made entirely of felt, this one has a cloth blouse and Dutch pants. $175.00.

Mah-Jongg Kid

A February 1924, entry in the trade magazine *Playthings* reported that the Chinese game Mah-Jongg had taken the country by storm. Now the toy men were trying to figure out how long the craze would last. Guesses ventured at the time assumed that by the second half of 1925, business would slow to steady year-round demand. The Averill Co. produced two Mah-Jongg Kids; the one illustrated here and a 10" one made of cloth, that, according to the Coleman's, was designed by Grace Drayton. They also report that the Mah-Jongg Sales Co. of San Francisco, California, was controlled by the Averill Manufacturing Co.

13". Marks: E.I.H. Co. Inc. (Playthings, August 1924).
For the production of this novelty the Averill Company used a head made by E.I. Horsman and a body assembly as used for their whistlers. When legs are pushed up, doll emits a whistling sound.
Composition shoulder head and arms. Cloth body and legs. Molded, painted black hair with drill hole in top of head to accommodate a real braid. Painted blue eyes, drill hole in mouth. Original clothes, old shoes.
Note: Though this doll is obviously meant to represent an Oriental character, the eyes are painted blue. $175.00.

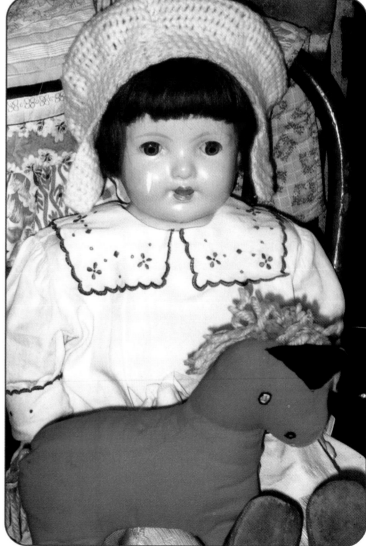

24". Marks: A.M. Co. (Toys and Novelties, March 1924).
Composition shoulder head and limbs, cloth body. Arms are tied on. Stitched hip joints. Reddish brown human hair wig. Blue tin sleep eyes, open mouth with two upper teeth. All original. $350.00.

26". Marks: A.M. Co.
Composition shoulder head, lower arms, and legs. Cloth body, upper arms, and legs with stitched hip joints. Dark brown human hair wig, sleep eyes, and open mouth with teeth and molded tongue. Re-dressed.
Note: This doll seems to be identical to the one seen in the previous illustration, the only difference being real upper eyelashes. The other doll was not produced with real eyelashes. Note the difference in expression this creates. Carole Chadwick collection. $350.00+.

19". Marks: none. 1920s.
Composition shoulder head and lower arms. Cloth body, upper arms, and legs. Legs showing the typical construction patented by Georgine Averill. Seams going down on both sides of each leg and a tailored heel. No shoulder joints, stitched hip joints. Dark brown mohair wig, painted blue eyes, closed mouth. All original, except shoes and socks. Cynthia Whittaker collection. $200.00.

18". Marked: A.M. (Averill Manufacturing), 1920s.
Composition shoulder head and lower arms. Cloth body, upper arms and legs. No shoulder joints, stitched hip joints. Dark brown mohair wig, gray tin sleep eyes, open/closed mouth. Appropriately dressed. Note: This doll was also sold with an open mouth with two upper teeth. Cynthia Whittaker collection. $150.00.

18". Marks: A.M. © Co. Early 1920s.
Round metal coin pinned to dress (see description of medal depicting standing baby described elsewhere in this section).
Composition shoulder head, arms to elbow, and legs to above the knee. Cloth body and upper limbs, stitched hip joints. Reddish brown mohair wig, blue tin sleep eyes, open mouth with two upper teeth. All original. Cynthia Whittaker collection. $175.00.

15". Ink stamp on cloth body: Genuine Madame Hendren // Doll 15 Made in USA.
Composition shoulder heads and arms to above the elbow. Cloth body, upper arms, and legs. No shoulder joints, stitched hip joints. Brown mohair wigs. Painted blue eyes, closed mouths. All original except for shoes. Cynthia Whittaker collection. $350.00 pair.

20". Marks: none on head.
Ink stamp on cloth body: Madame Hendren // Doll // Made in USA
Composition shoulder head, arms, and legs, cloth body, stitched hip joints. Brown mohair wig over molded, unpainted hair. Blue sleep eyes, open mouth with four upper teeth. All original. Hazel Coons collection. $250.00.

118

18". Marks: none. 1920s.
Composition shoulder head and lower arms. Cloth body, upper arms, and legs. Legs showing the typical construction patented by Georgine Averill: seams going down on both sides of each leg and a tailored heel. No shoulder joints, stitched hip joints. Molded, painted light brown hair and painted blue eyes. Closed mouth. Appropriate old clothes. Cynthia Whittaker collection. $125.00.

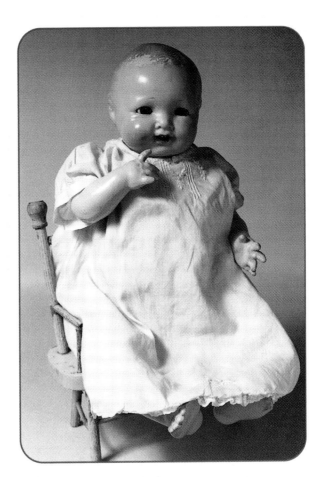

18". Baby Brite (Playthings, May 1928).
Marks: Madame Hendren
Composition flange head, arms, and bent legs, jointed at shoulders and hips. Cloth body. Molded, painted blond hair, blue sleep eyes, open mouth with two upper teeth. Re-dressed. $150.00.
Note: This is a Bubbles look alike (Effanbee). Bubbles can put his left finger into his mouth, Baby Brite the right.

18". Marks: A.M. Co. (Averill Manufacturing), 1920s.
Composition shoulder plate and short arms. Cloth body, upper arms, and legs. No shoulder joints, stitched hip joints. Molded, painted blond hair and painted blue eyes. Closed mouth. Re-dressed in contemporary clothes. Cynthia Whittaker collection. $125.00.

13" Aviator.

Marks: E.I.H. Co. Inc. (E.I. Horsman), ca. 1928. Composition shoulder head and arms, cloth body and legs, jointed only at shoulders, whistling mechanism embedded in legs. Molded, painted blond hair, painted blue eyes, closed mouth with drill hole between lips. All original, except for goggles.

Note: Dolls with the above mentioned whistler mechanism were produced by the Averill Company. It is assumed that this aviator was produced and sold by the Averills as well. A 13½" whistling aviator was offered in the 1930 Sears Roebuck catalog. One might assume that Sears placed an especially large order for these dolls with the Averill Company and they had to buy additional heads to fill this large order. Cynthia Whittaker collection $150.00.

Sunny Girl and Sunny Boy

Even though these dolls feature celluloid heads imported from Germany (not composition heads, made in the U.S.), they do belong with the American composition mama dolls of the 1920s. Little attention has been paid by collectors to these beautiful dolls. It is hoped that by including them here collectors will make a special effort to preserve the examples that did survive and treasure them in their collections.

14" Sunny Girl (also Sunny Boy), Playthings, *May 1927).*
Marked:

Body stamped: Genuine//Madame Hendren//Doll//..14//Made in USA
Ink stamp on front shoulder plate: US PAT. NO. 1.645.275
Celluloid shoulder head, composition arms and legs to above the knee. Cloth body, jointed at shoulders, stitched hip joints. Re-dressed. Was sold in sizes 14", 17", 19", 20", and 22" (Coleman II, pg. 1129). Composition limbs are of American manufacture, and the body is styled in typical mama doll fashion, with swinging legs.
Note: The head for this doll was supplied by the German firm Rheinische Gummi and Celluloid Fabrik (Turtlemark) and was adapted from a celluloid head popular in Germany since 1911. For detailed information on the history of this popular German celluloid head, see Cieslik's Puppen Magazine *2/2002, pg. 30, regular feature on celluloid dolls by Anne Stitz. $175.00.*

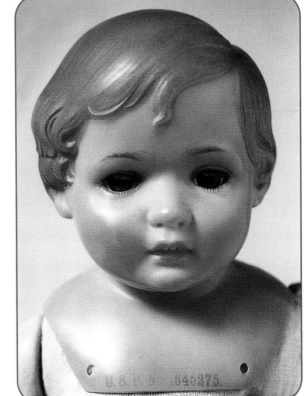

Close-up of Sunny Girl.
The glass eyes have real and painted lashes. An open mouth reveals four upper teeth. The molded hair seems to have been airbrushed but does not show the soft hairline so typical of American composition heads.
Note the beautiful, sharp modeling and luminous skin tone. Honey-colored celluloid was painted (probably sprayed) with pink, flat paint on the inside, thus creating this depth of tone. The celluloid of these heads is very fragile, and both Sunny Girl and Sunny Boy are hard to find in today's collector market.
Time and again, one can find the bodies of these dolls with only shards of celluloid remaining. Maintenance is not impossible. They should not be transported in cold weather, or be carried from a cold to a warm room. When packed, these dolls should always have their own box and never be layered in a trunk together with other dolls.

19". Marks: none.
*Tag on jacket: Madame Hendren // Dolls // "Everybody Loves Them."
Composition head on swivel shoulder plate, composition arms and legs, jointed at shoulders and hips. Cloth body. Blond human hair wig over molded hair. Gray sleep eyes, open mouth with four upper teeth. Contemporary clothes. Tagged silk jacket. Hair bow is definitely original.
Note: Original jacket was in shreds. Pattern was taken off the old item and a new one made of similar old, pink silk, using the old trim and reattaching the label. $175.00.*

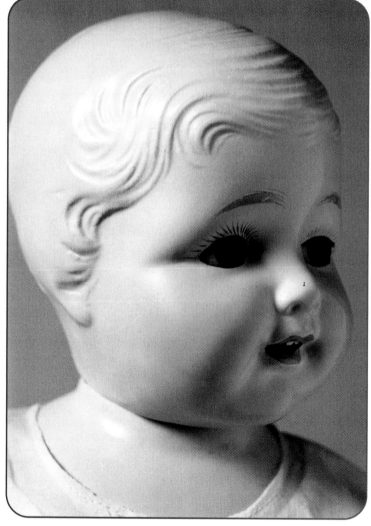

*Close-up of previous doll without wig.
This head was used frequently by the Averill firm with molded, painted hair or wig, painted eyes or sleep eyes. So far, it has never been located with identification marks. The very distinctive hair modeling seen here should be of help in identifying other unmarked Madame Hendren (Averill) dolls.*

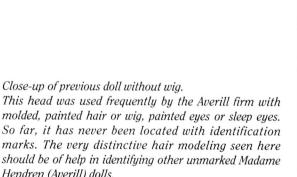

19". Marks: none.
Composition head, shoulder plate, and full limbs, jointed at neck, shoulders, and hips. Cloth body. Molded, painted blond hair, blue tin sleep eyes, open mouth with four upper teeth. Re-dressed in appropriate, contemporary clothes. New hair ribbon. $275.00.

28". Marks: none.
Composition flange head, cloth body and limbs (mitten hands). Molded, painted yellow hair with additional cotton drapery fringe glued all around the edge. The twisted fringe has been shortened in front and combed out to make bangs. Blue eyes are expertly painted with partial black outline around the iris and partial white outline around the pupil, two highlights, and grayish/brown eye shadow. Open/closed mouth. Feet are very wide and have black oilcloth soles and separate ankle straps with black shoe button closure. The body is rather short and legs extra long. Arms loosely stuffed towards top, stitched shoulder joints, not stitched at hips but loosely stuffed. Felt dress with patch pocket and "hankie." Felt cap has very long tie strings. (Face is very faded.)
Note: This popular head of a large baby resembling Effanbee's Lovums was used by various companies in the early 1930s. Also note: One definitely gets the impression that this was meant to be some kind of doll to dance with. $95.00 (very faded).

21". Marks: Baby Hendren
Dress tag: Horsman//Doll//MFD. In USA
Composition flange head, lower arms, and legs. Cloth body and upper limbs, stitched hip joints. Molded, painted blond hair and gray sleep eyes. Open mouth with two upper and two lower teeth. All original.
Note: The originality of this combination — Hendren doll//Horsman clothes — was strengthened by eBay offering No. 1276665051, dated 9/19/2001, also showing a Baby Hendren dressed in tagged Horsman clothes.
Both items may have been used in a joint radio advertising campaign by these two firms in October 1931, though the ad mentions a "Gold Medal Baby." Dolls given away during this campaign had a gold medal pinned to their chest. Also see information about Gold Medal Baby in the Horsman section. Virginia Callaham collection. $350.00.

Back view of Baby Hendren, showing markings on neck and original identification tag on dress.

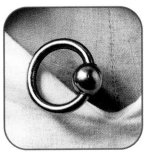

17". Marks: Georgene Baby
Composition flange head, full arms (hands with clenched fists), and bent legs to above the knee. Soft stuffed cloth body and upper legs, stitched hip joints. Molded hair with tight curls is dark brown, sleep eyes, closed mouth. Re-dressed.
Note: Inserted into the softly stuffed cloth body is a music box that plays "Lullaby Baby." It is wound by a handle protruding from the doll's back.
Further note that unlike the larger Georgene Babies illustrated in this section, this doll still has celluloid eyes, not plastic ones. $150.00.

Little Cherub Created by Harriet Flanders

These dolls were sold as a boxed set and included a picture book, written and illustrated by Harriet Flanders and published by Georgene Novelties, Inc. New York. Little Cherub was also sold wigged. Rhoda Shoemaker in *Compo Dolls Cute and Collectible, Vol. III,* reported that a nursery rhyme series was also produced, using Little Cherub. With her entry a Little Bo Peep is shown. Quote: "Her wig is quite unusual — it is made up of dozens of tiny blond silk ringlets all over her head. In one hand she carries a bouquet; a silver folder is attached to her wrist in the form of a birthday card and is marked "Georgene Dolls." (Also see biography of Harriet Flanders in front of book.)

12". Little Cherub with book and original box (box measurements: 12" x 9½" x 3½" and marked only "BLUE."
Marks: none.
All composition, fully jointed. Slightly molded, blond hair and painted blue eyes, closed mouth. All original.
Inside the box cover is a rubber band and empty packaging of a piece of clothing. Since the space under the rubber band is too narrow to hold the book, it is assumed that a piece of clothing was sold with this particular set.
Note: Most Little Cherub dolls are marked: "Harriet Flanders 1937." An identical set has been seen before. It is assumed that these sets with plain box and unmarked doll may have been sold by one of the big mail order houses. $500.00 set.

Three 20" Baby Georgene dolls, 1937 and later. Both girls are all original. The little boy with molded, painted hair has been re-dressed. For technical data, see captions of following illustrations.

This picture vividly illustrates how a product line could be created, using one and the same head. Just changing the color of the wig or using the head with painted hair created three different dolls. Back, $350.00 each. Front, $150.00.

20". Marks: Baby // Georgene
Composition flange head and limbs, loosely stuffed cloth body. Molded, tightly curled dark brown hair and blue sleep eyes, closed mouth.
Note the specially molded hands with curled-back fingers. The full composition arms with special jointing have been seen only on this doll. The upper arm features a groove and is wired on, so that the arms can be rotated. $150.00.

20". Marks: Baby // Georgene. 1937 and later.
Composition flange head, arms with curled fingers, legs to above the knee, cloth body with stitched hip joints. (These are full-length arms, wired on at shoulder level and can rotate). Blond mohair wig over molded hair (tight ringlets), blue sleep eyes, synthetic, black lashes, closed mouth. All original.
Note: It is assumed that this doll was produced during WWII or shortly after, a time of persisting shortages. Usually, these mama dolls are dressed in lace-trimmed cotton panties and matching slips. In this case, a coarse cotton diaper and a slip made of a different material showing no lace trim were used. The simple but attractively styled pink outfit is made of a strange, hard and shiny material. $350.00 (pristine condition wig in original set).

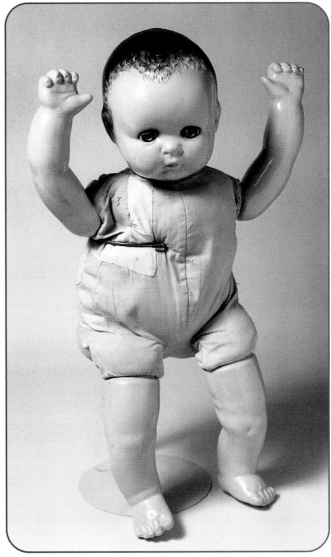

Baseball Player

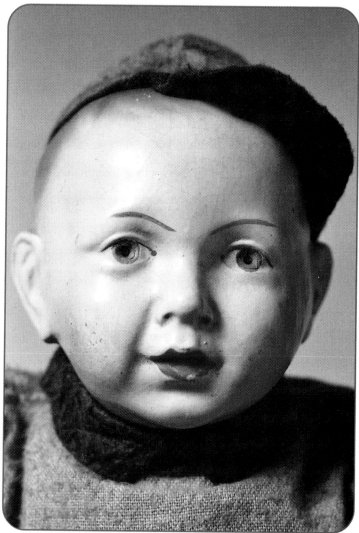

14". Marks: none. Jumper marked in front: GIANTS. Ca. 1915. Composition flange head and short lower arms. Cloth body, upper arms, and bent legs, jointed at shoulders and hips with outside metal disks. Molded, painted light brown hair, painted, blue intaglio eyes, closed mouth. All original. $300.00.

Billy and Ruth Promotions, Inc.
Box 333
Philadelphia 5 Pennsylvania

Llevelyn A. Hoeflich and William George Steltz were the owners of Suplee Biddle, a leading hardware wholesale house in Philadelphia. At Christmas time and with the help of an attractively designed toy catalog headlined "Billy & Ruth, America's Famous Toy Children," they sold toys to their hardware customers and other mom and pop toy outlets such as newspaper stores, etc. Suplee Biddle buyers assembled an attractive selection of toys, including dolls. This toy catalog had nationwide distribution. Suplee Biddle ordered in large quantities from the toy producers and could get prices that small volume buyers could not achieve. By ordering their Christmas merchandise from the Billy & Ruth catalog, the small town merchants had a chance to compete with the large department stores and mail-order houses. The catalogs were sent to participating retailers free of charge and in quantity for local distribution.

Not only did Suplee Biddle have the advantage of large volume buying but also of special and clever promotional ideas. The front cover and inside pages of the toy catalog showed pictures of two real children named Billy and Ruth. According to Charles H. Hoeflich, son of Llewellyn, these two were the children of his father's partner, William George Steltz, and their real names were used. (Both are deceased).

Inside the catalog and with the illustrations of specific items, Billy and Ruth were quoted, recommending the toys. By taking this very personal route in toy promotion, the children browsing through the catalog became quite familiar with Billy and Ruth and looked forward to getting those colorful wish books.

Apparently, this merchandising approach was very successful. The Billy & Ruth catalog was started in the late 1920s and the toy business phased out in the early 1960s. They advertised in the trade magazine *Playthings*, in the 1940s, obviously an effort to expand their toy business beyond their existing hardware store customers. By 1953, the pictures of the two children, Billy and Ruth, had changed. Additional youngsters had been introduced on the inside pages and their names used in the promotion of the toys.

While this approach to toy advertising is quite novel, it was not unique. At the time, the Effanbee Company had their Aunt Patsy and the Patsy Club. Aunt Patsy actually traveled throughout the country, demonstrating Effanbee dolls in large department stores of major cities. The Patsy Club sent out booklets to children (who had joined the club), talking about Effanbee dolls and encouraging purchases, just like the Billy & Ruth catalog did. In other words, toys were promoted directly to children, not their parents.

As can be seen on the page from the 1936 Billy and Ruth catalog, in the upper left hand corner is a picture of Ruth, and one doll has been selected to bear Ruth's name. In this case it is a mechanical walking doll that resembles Shirley Temple. Apparently there was only one mechanical walking doll resembling Shirley Temple in 1936. It was produced by the Eugene Goldberger Company (pictured in the Goldberger section).

The doll seen in the next picture whose cap is embroidered with "Ruth" resembles "Toddling Sue" illustrated in the 1939 Ideal catalog.

Discovery of the Ruth doll and the Billy and Ruth catalogs gives some idea how smaller merchants could compete with large firms like Sears and Montgomery Ward and their big Christmas catalogs.

(Ref: Phone interview with Charles H. Hoeflich)

Page from Billy and Ruth catalog.
Marge Meisinger collection.

20" Ruth.
Marks: None on doll. Cap embroidered: Ruth
All composition, fully jointed. Dark blond mohair wig, brown sleep eyes, open mouth with two upper teeth. All original with original box and studio photograph of young girl inscribed: Approved by Ruth. $800.00 mint.

Geo. Borgfeldt & Co.
New York
Established 1881

Geo. Borgfeldt & Co. were major importers and producers of dolls and toys. For more extensive information on this company, see two articles by Jennylou Hamilton Schoelwer, UFDC (United Federation of Doll Clubs) *Doll News*, Summer 2000 and Summer 2001.

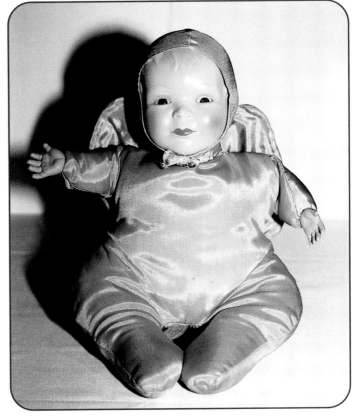

13". Marks: Fly Lo // Copyright // G. S. Putnam
Compostion flange head, celluloid hands and soft sutffed cloth body with attached, wired wings. Blue cap is removable. Molded, painted blond hair, glass sleep eyes and closed mouth. All original. Sandra Strater collection. $900.00+.

11" Happifat. Marks: none.
Cloth tag: Happifat // U.S. Pat. Office (designed by Kate Jordan)
Composition flange head and short arms. Cloth body, upper arms, and legs. Faintly molded whisp of brown hair, painted in back in the shape of a swallow's tail, painted brown eyes, closed mouth. All original. $350.00.
5½" Plaster figurine of Happifat inscribed on all four sides of pedestal: Be A Happifat; Take Life Easy; Turn Your Back on Care; Kick Out The Grouch. $60.00.
Note: George Borgfeldt & Co. as well as Louis Amberg & Son advertised Happifat dolls (1917 – 1920)
Feb. 1917, Borgfeldt: Happifat girl and boy
1920, Amberg: Happifat girl in bonnet and apron.
Jan. 1921, Amberg: Freshi, A Happifat Youngster (boy)

13". Marks: K And K // Made In Germany
Dress label: see separate illustration.
Box label: K And K Doll // Made under sanitary conditions
Bisque shoulder head, American-made composition lower arms, cloth body with inserted cry box, slightly bent cloth legs, stitched hip joints. Brown mohair wig, brown real glass sleep eyes, open mouth with two upper teeth. All original.
Note: It is a little known fact that in the 1920s Borgfeldt and the Horsman Company (there may have been others) produced some mama dolls with German-made bisque heads. They always used American-made composition limbs for these and construction was identical to the composition mama dolls. $375.00.

18". Marks: K & K X
Cloth tag sewn in front of dress: KandK // The Doll of Quality// Reg. U.S. Pat. Off. (see separate illustration). Composition shoulder head and lower limbs, cloth body and upper limbs, stitched hip joints. Blond mohair wig over molded hair, gray tin sleep eyes, open mouth with four upper teeth. All original including box. $250.00.

Label on front of box: KandK Doll, Made Under Sanitary Conditions. The latter phase was frequently used by Borgfeldt in their advertising.

20". Marks: KandK Toy Co.
Composition shoulder head, full arms, and legs, cloth body, jointed at shoulders and hips. Blond mohair wig, blue sleep eyes, open mouth with two upper teeth. All original. Cynthia Whittaker collection. $250.00.

Bride

18" Bride. Marks: none.

All composition, jointed only at the shoulders with steel spring. Original mohair wig. Painted black eyes and closed mouth (molded shoes and socks are not painted). All original.

NOTE: This was obviously done for a wedding, possibly by a dressmaker, as all is expertly done. Sewn on silk panties and slip, crepe silk dress with rhinestone braid trim at neck and arm holes, dropped waist and hem. Both veil pieces are gathered to a rosette and attached to the head band on each side. The bridal bouquet with streamers is sewn to the dress. A piece of silk ribbon is tied around her left wrist. $125.00.

Butler Bros.
New York City (and Sonneberg, Germany)
Established 1877

Butler Bros. was a large mail-order house similar to Sears Roebuck or Montgomery Ward.

13½". Marks on back: TOOTSE
Sold by Butler Bros. (See their 1928 catalog.)
All composition, fully jointed. Molded, painted brown hair, painted brown eyes, closed mouth. Contemporary clothes. Peggy Viskocil collection. $150.00.

Bye-Lo Look-Alikes

The Bye-Lo Baby, created by Grace Storey Putnam and introduced by the Borgfeldt Company in 1922, was immensely popular. This caused various firms to offer dolls that looked very similar.

13" Twins in original pillow.
Marks: none.
Composition shoulder head and full arms, jointed with long pin that turns around on itself on one arm. Cloth body and legs with stitched hip joints. Molded, painted blond hair and painted blue eyes, closed mouth. All original. Set $150.00.
Note: All is very cheaply made, but still has a lot of eye appeal.

12½" brown Bye-Lo type twins.
Marks: none.
Composition flange heads and short arms. Cloth body with crier and legs. Very short upper cloth arms. No joints at shoulders, stitched hip joints. Original slip, white infant dress and blanket bunting. Heads and hands repainted. Sweaters and caps added. Each $150.00.

Cameo Doll Co.
New York City and Port Allegany, Pennsylvania

20" Baby Blossom, ca. 1927.
Marks: Des. & Copyright // By J. L. Kallus // Made in U.S.A.
Composition shoulder head to under the arms (like Effanbee's Bubbles). Composition arms and legs to above the knee. Jointed at shoulders, slanted hip joints. Molded, painted blond hair and gray tin sleep eyes, closed mouth. Old clothes. Cloth body. Cynthia Whittaker collection. $450.00+.

16". Marks on hat and chest band: RCA Radiotrons Label on foot: Art-Quality // MFRS. // Cameo Doll Co. // N.Y.C. // Pat. appld // for (1930)
Composition head and torso molded as one piece. Wood segmented hat and limbs, jointed with steel springs. Molded, painted blond hair and painted blue eyes, closed mouth. All original. Susan Ackerman collection. $800.00+.

Little Annie Rooney

Pictured in the following illustrations are two versions of the comic character, Little Annie Rooney, one with black hair and a "hard" hairline, as would be proper for a figure from a cartoon. In the second picture, Little Annie Rooney is seen with a hairdo that shows a "soft" hairline. Apparently, both versions were sold.

Front and back of original tag, Little Annie Rooney.

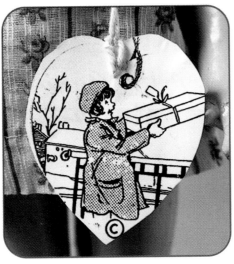

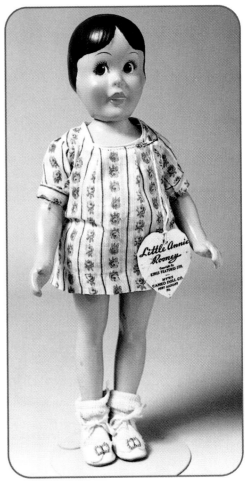

13". Marks: none. 1938.
Paper tag: Little Annie // Rooney // Copyright By // King Features Syn. // MFR'S // Cameo Doll Co. // Port Allegany // PA.
All composition, fully jointed. Molded painted, black hair, painted blue eyes, open/closed mouth with white line between lips to indicate teeth. Contemporary clothes. Susan Ackerman collection.
Note: This Little Annie Rooney is the main character of King Features' comic strip by the same name. Scripted by Brandon Walch and drawn by Darrel McClure. (Ran: 1927– 1966). $475.00 +.

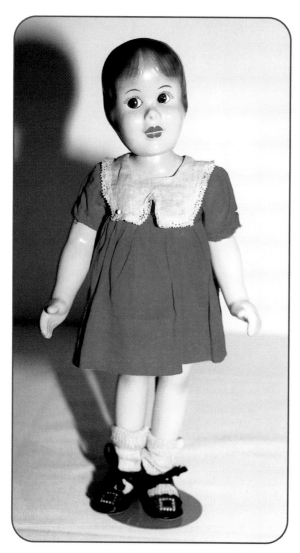

13". Marks: none (Playthings, May 1938).
Dress tag: Annie Rooney // King Features, Syn.
All composition, fully jointed. Molded, painted brown hair, painted blue eyes, open/closed mouth with white line between lips. All original. Collection of Gayle and Jerry Reilly.
Note: Main character from popular newspaper cartoon by Jack Collins. Doll designed by Josef L. Kallus. $475.00+.

13". Marks: Pete // Des. & Copyright by J.L. Kallus. Ca. 1942. Composition head and wood segmented body and limbs. Black painted eyes, closed mouth.
Note: This Pete has thick wooden shoes and an inset string tail. All original. Susan Ackerman collection. $450.00.

9". Marks: Cameo Dumbo © WDP. 1942.
Tag: "Dumbo" // The Flying Elephant // c Walt Disney Productions. Composition head, body, and trunk, light blue, pressed felt ears, inset celluloid eyes with floating pupils, jointed trunk and neck. Original ruff with tag. Betsy and Ray Baker collection. $500.00+.

Ca. 9½" long, 8" tall.
Collar marked: Streak - Des. & Copyr. by Jos. L. Kallus
Body marked: Charmo Toys // Reg. U.S. Pat. Off.
Composition head, wood segmented body, limbs, and tail. Painted brown eyes. All original. Susan Ackerman collection. $800.00.

12". Marks: none. Late 1940s.
Paper tag: "Giggles" // Designed and Copyright // Rose O'Neill // A // Cameo Doll
All composition, fully jointed. Molded, painted light brown hair with drill hole at lower back of head for insertion of ribbon. Painted blue eyes, closed mouth. All original.
Note: Kewpie box was used with Giggles label glued to front and back. $850.00.

13". Marks: Howdy Dowdy // Bob Smith. Late 1940s.
Label on foot: Illegible (Cameo)
Composition head, wood segmented body and limbs. Molded, painted reddish-brown hair and painted blue eyes, closed, smiling mouth. Freckles on cheeks. All original. Susan Ackerman collection. $450.00.

12" Kewpie. Marks: none. Late 1940s.
All composition, fully jointed. Three molded tufts painted blond. Painted black eyes, closed mouth. All original.
Box: Kewpie Doll // Design and Copyright // by Rose O'Neill // A Cameo Doll // Made in USA // Printed in USA // No. 9713.
Sticker on box: FRAGILE // Do not Drop or Throw // Sears Roebuck and Co., 4640 Roosevelt Blvd. Phila. 32, PA ... Rev. 7-21-48. $500.00.

Carneval Doll

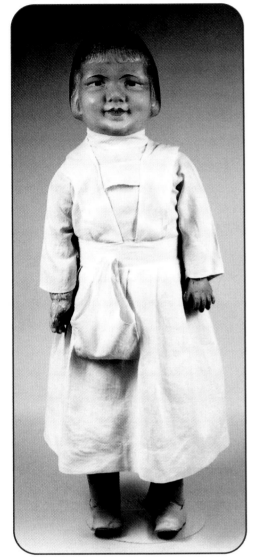

30" Nurse. Marks: None. WWI era.
Composition shoulder head and short arms. Cloth body, upper arms, and legs, jointed at shoulders and hips with outside disks. Molded, painted brown hair and painted eyes. Closed mouth. All original, including cloth slippers. Cynthia Whittaker collection. $150.00.

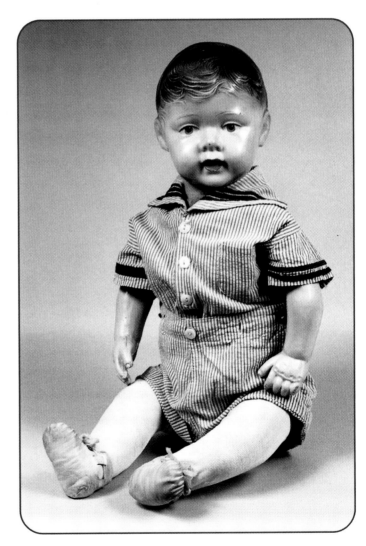

28". Marks: none.
Composition flange head and full arms. Cloth body and bent legs, jointed at shoulders and hips with outside cardboard disks. Molded painted blond hair, painted blue eyes, open/closed mouth. Re-dressed in old childrens's clothes. Cynthia Whittaker collection.
Note: Sharp, clear modeling of hair and face. $150.00.

Century Doll Co.
New York, New York
1909 – 1930 +

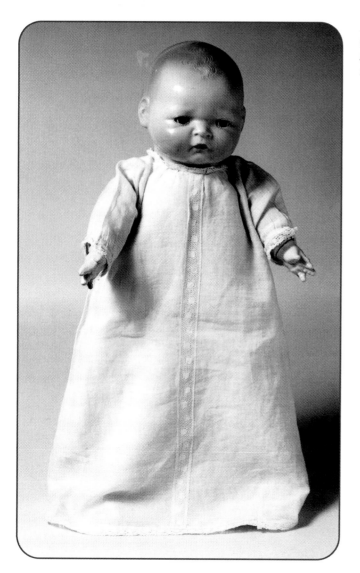

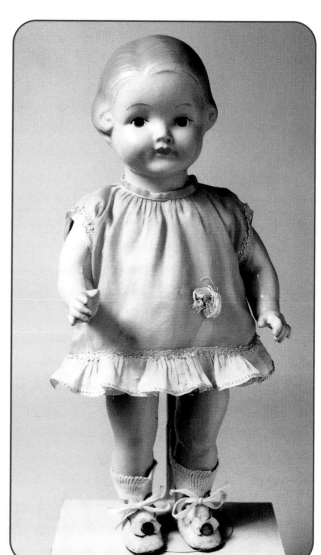

15". Marks: Century // Doll Co. 1920s.
Composition flange head and hands, cloth body, arms, and straight cloth legs. Stitched hip joints. Molded painted blond hair, blue eyes, closed mouth. All original. $175.00.

13". Marks: Century // Doll Co.
Composition shoulder head, limbs, and cloth body, jointed at shoulders and hips. Molded, painted blond hair, painted blue eyes, closed mouth. All original. $200.00.

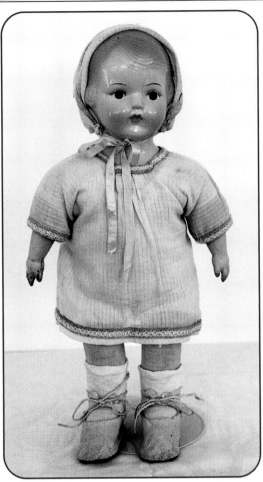

14". Marks: Century // Doll
Composition shoulder head and lower arms. Cloth body, upper arms, and legs, stitched hip joints. Molded, painted blond hair and painted blue eyes, closed mouth. All original. Cynthia Whittaker collection. $150.00.

14". Marks: Chuckles // A Century Doll
Composition shoulder head, arms, and legs, jointed at shoulders and hips. Cloth body. Molded, painted blond hair, painted blue eyes, open/closed mouth. Old clothes. Cynthia Whittaker collection. $125.00.

15". Marks: Century // Doll Co.
Composition shoulder head and short arms. Cloth body, upper arms, and bent legs, jointed with inside disks. Molded hair is not painted. May have had a wig. Painted blue eyes, closed mouth, dimple in chin. Old dress.
Note: This shoulder head has drill holes at the four corners of the shoulder plate. $85.00.

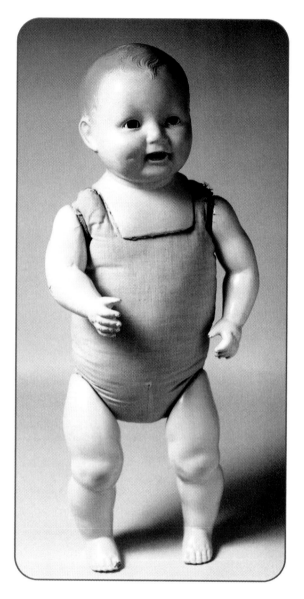

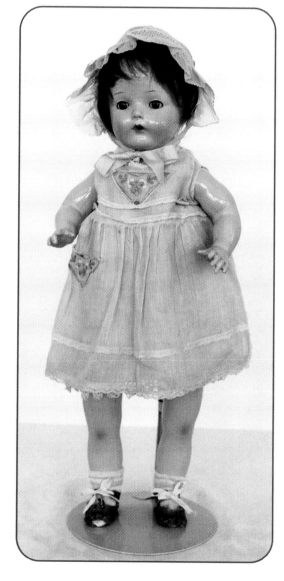

*22". Marks: Chuckles // A Century Doll. Late 1920s.
Composition shoulder head and limbs, cloth body, jointed
at shoulders and hips. Molded, painted blond hair, blue
sleep eyes, open mouth with two upper teeth. $150.00.*

*19". Marks: Century // Doll Co.
Composition shoulder head, arms, and legs to above the knee.
Cloth body and upper legs, jointed at shoulders, stitched hip
joints. Brown mohair wig over molded hair, blue tin sleep eyes,
open mouth with two teeth. Nice old dress. Cynthia Whittaker
collection. $125.00.*

Coleman Walking Doll

28". Marks: none. 1917.

Composition shoulder head and lower arms, wooden body frame covered with wire mesh and felt like padding. Wooden upper arms, legs, and feet, jointed at elbows and knees with metal hinges. Knee hinges are loaded with springs, so that knee joint will shut automatically when there is no pressure on the leg. Dark brown, long-curl, human hair wig, sleep eyes, multi-stroke eyebrows, open mouth with four upper teeth. Appropriate clothes. Mary Soleberg collection.

Note: The doll illustrated here with long curl human hair wig, sleep eyes, and open mouth has not been seen before and would have been the more expensive version of this novelty doll. $400.00.

Colonial Doll Mfg. Inc.

14". Marks on front shoulder plate: Trade (next illegible) Mark
Back shoulder plate: Colonial Doll Mfg. Inc. // Pat.Appl.For//NY
Full composition shoulder plate (similar to Effanbee's Bubbles) and all composition arms. Cloth body and legs jointed with inside disks. Arms are jointed with elastic. Light brown mohair wig. Painted blue eyes, closed mouth. All original. Crocheted hat came with doll. $150.00.

Colonial Toy Manufacturing Co.
New York City
1915 – 1920

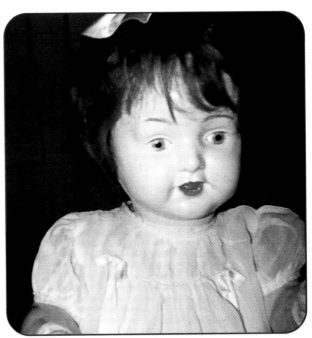

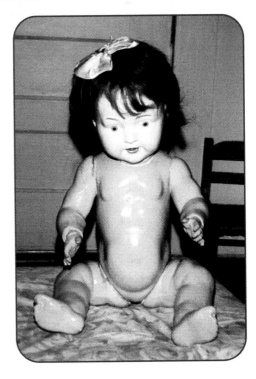

14". Marks: Zaiden//Doll//Colonial Toy MFG. Co. Ca. 1918.
All composition, fully jointed with stell springs. Molded, painted light brown
hair and painted blue eyes. Open/closed mouth. Old clothes. $125.00.

24". Marks: Colonial Toy MFG.Co.
All-composition, fully jointed, including wrists. Brown human hair wig, painted blue eyes, open/closed mouth with molded tongue.
Redressed. Mary Henshaw collection. $250.00.

Columbia MFG. Co.

12". Marks: None on doll. Box front: Baby Patty // She drinks // She wets // Washable //
Durable // All composition. On side panel: A beautiful lovable baby. Looks and acts like a
real baby. She has a soft smooth appearance. She's adorable. Give her the bottle and she
wets her diaper. // Care-Mar Doll - By Berk-Winn Products, Inc. New York, NY USA // 1947
by Columbia Mfg.Co.
All composition, fully jointed. Molded painted blond hair, painted blue eyes, open mouth.
All original, with glass nursing bottle tied to her arm. Cynthia Whittaker collection.
$125.00.

Comic Dolls
(Manufacturer Unknown)

14" Little Lulu
Title character of comic strip and books created by Marjorie "Marge" Henderson Buell, 1935 – 1984.
Marks: A Pullan Doll
All composition, fully jointed. Molded painted black hair and painted solid black eyes, closed mouth. Old clothes, replaced shoes. Gayle and Jerry Reilly collection. $500.00+.

13". Marks: none. This is Kayo from Moon Mullin comic strip by Frank Willard, 1923 – 1991.
All composition, with molded black hat, molded dark brown hair and painted brown eyes. Jointed jaw and neck. Gayle and Jerry Reilly collection.
Note: Kayo was the main character's, Moon Mullin's bratty little brother. $400.00.

19". Marks: none.
Composition flange head and molded "gloved" hands. Cloth body, arms, and legs, stitched joints at shoulders and hips. Molded, painted brown hair and painted brown eyes. Open/closed mouth with four painted teeth. Original pants and vest. $150.00.

Crown Toy

10". Marks: Pinocchio // Made © USA // W.D. Prod. // C.T. (Crown Toy)
Left: Jointed at shoulders only, molded clothes and hat, painted features.
Right: Jointed at shoulders and hips, painted features, felt hat, cotton blouse and pants, bow
tie. Molded gloves and shoes. All original. John axe collection.
Note: Produced under license from Walt Disney Productions. $350.00 each.

Dancing Couples

13". Dancing Couple.
Marks: none.
Composition shoulder heads, cloth bodies and limbs. Stitched joints at shoulders and hips. Buttoned together at head, hands, and shoulders. Molded, painted blond hair and painted brown eyes, closed mouth. Cord attached at head joint. When cord is held and rapid up and down movements made, the couple dances. $150.00 set.

12". Marks: none.
Composition flange heads, cloth bodies and limbs, stitched joints. Both feature black cloth boots which are part of the leg casing. Slightly molded dark brown hair for the boy, lady's hair style for the girl. Both have painted blue eyes and a closed mouth. Both are held in place by a double loop attached to an elastic cord. When this elastic cord is bobbed up and down the dolls dance. All original. $75.00 both.

Otto Ernst Denivelle
Established 1910

Otto Ernst Denivelle produced a glue base type of composition from which he made doll heads. Both Louis Amberg & Son and Effanbee bought doll heads from Denivelle. Most often, they were marked DECO. Some heads made for Effanbee can be seen illustrated in their 1915 catalog, and corresponding dolls could, therefore, be assigned to Effanbee. The identity of addional dolls by either company has in the past been verified through illustrated magazine ads. Following, two dolls are shown which could not be identified as having been made for a specific company. Rather than arbitrarily assigning them to one or the other firm, it was decided to list DECO marked dolls under Denivelle. Hopefully, additional information as to identity of sellers will become available in the future.

For additional, extensive information on "Devnivelle and His DECO Dolls," see Don Jensen's article in the spring 1991 issue of UFDC's *Doll News*.

16". Marks: DECO. Ca. 1918.
Flared composition head and short arms. Cloth body, upper arms, and bent legs, jointed at shoulders and hips with inside disks. Molded, painted brown hair and painted brown eyes. Open/closed mouth with two painted upper teeth. Re-dressed. $75.00.

13". Marks: DECO. (Copy of German bisque head produced by Gebr. Heubach (7977 series), ca. 1915.
Flared composition head with molded cap, short composition arms. Contempory cloth body, arms, and bent legs, jointed with inside disks. Painted blue eyes, closed mouth, re-dressed. $250.00.

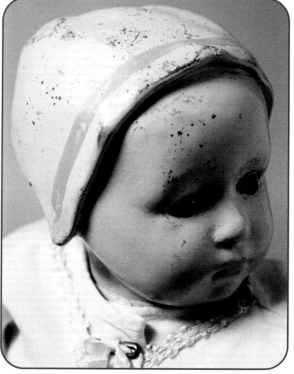

Doll Craft Novelty Co.
New York

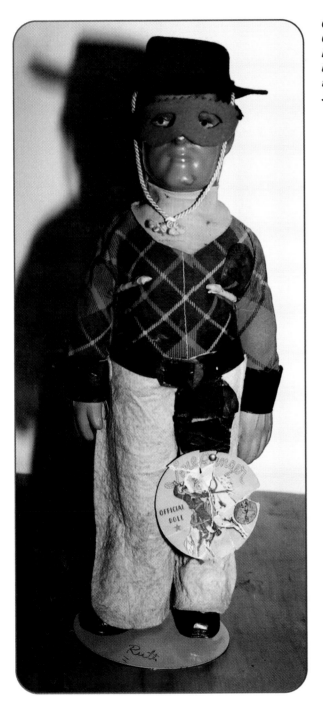

Ca. 16" Lone Ranger. Marks: none (Playthings, *1937).*
Composition flange head, hands, and molded boots. Cloth body and limbs, stitched shoulder and hip joints. Molded painted black hair, brown skin and painted brown eyes, closed mouth. All original including belt, holster, gun, hat, and label. Susan Ackerman collection.
$500.00+.

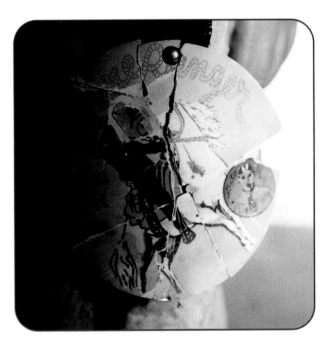

Label front: Lone Ranger // Official Doll // © 1938 // TJR Inc.
Label back: Dollcraft Novelty // Licensed by // Lone Ranger Inc. // Reg. U.S. Pat. Off.

Dollspart Supply Co.
New York, New York

The catalog and two dolls illustrated here were acquired from the estate of Mrs. Esther Sahr of Schenectady, New York, who in the 1950s bought dolls from Dollspart. They were dressed by her and then sold to the Karl Department Store in Schenectady, New York. This is further proof that Princess Elizabeth look-alikes and those resembling certain Arranbee dolls and Mary Hoyer dolls, were used by various companies in the 1940s and into the 1950s.

The catalog is not dated but seems to be from around 1950, judging by its contents. The dolls pictured on the next page are not in the Dollspart catalog. The catalog lists similar ones made of hard plastic.

The human- and mohair wigs offered bear names reminiscent of popular composition dolls, such as Nancy and Princess. Sparkle Plenty wigs were also listed as well as Tousle Fur Wigs.

A distinction was made between teen-age dolls with slim waists and girl dolls (the latter not pictured).

Composition Bye-Lo Baby heads were offered with circumferences of 12", 13" and 15" and replacement composition hands. Additional baby heads were available in composition and hard plastic.

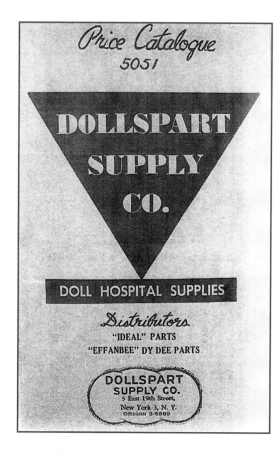

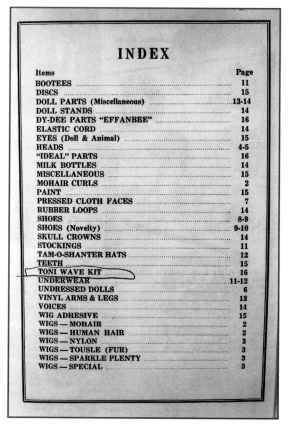

Dollspart Supply Co., Doll Hospital Supplies catalog from about 1950. Melody R. Howarth collection.

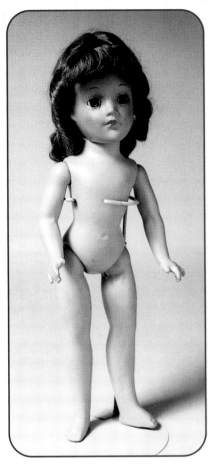

14". Marks: none (Arranbee type). All composition, fully jointed. Blond mohair wig, brown sleep eyes, closed mouth. Melody R. Howarth collection. $150.00.

15". Marks: none (Princess Elizabeth type).
All composition, fully jointed. Blond mohair wig, brown sleep eyes, open mouth with two upper teeth. Melody R. Howarth collection. $150.00.

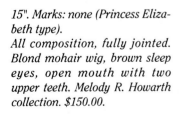

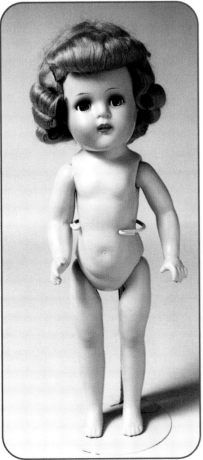

Domec Toy Co.,
New York City
1918 – 1930+

In 1928, Domec merged with the Century Doll Co. to form the Doll Corporation of America. The factory was located in Lancaster, Pennsylvania. After the merger the name Domec was kept as a trade name (Coleman II).

22". Marks on doll: Fiberoid. Late 20s – early 30s.
Paper hang tag: Babs // A Domec Product
All composition, fully jointed. Blond human hair wig, gray tin sleep eyes, open mouth with two upper teeth, all original. Patricia N. Schoonmaker collection.
Note: Some Madame Alexander dolls have also been seen with the "Fiberoid" mark. $350.00+.

Hair is very lightly molded and hardly stands out, even at sides. Since she is not marked, this should help identify her, if she is found minus the original case.

12". Marks: none. 1930s.

Box label: Polly Prim // The Little Aristocrat // A Dress For Every Occasion // A Domec Product No. (box measurements: 13" x 13" x 4½")

Doll is all composition and fully jointed. Molded, painted brown hair, painted brown eyes, closed mouth. All original. Additional clothes: Navy blue coat, shorts, and tam, two dresses and sun suit. $375.00.

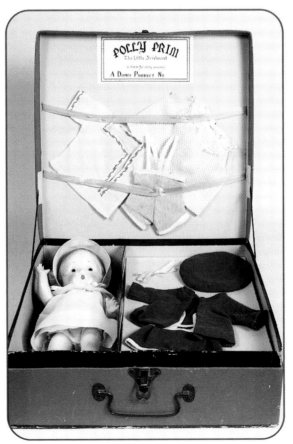

Eagle Doll

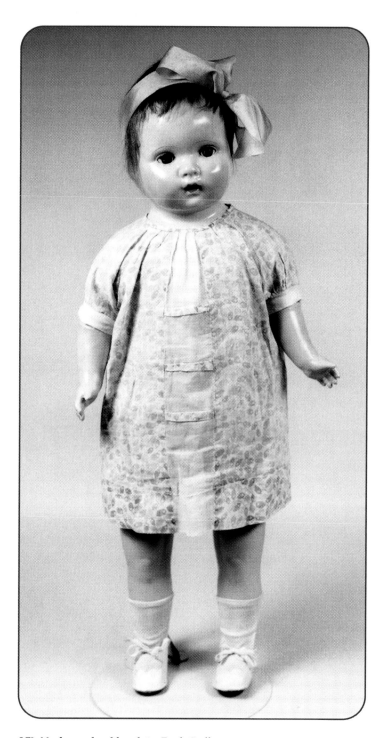

25". Marks on shoulder plate: Eagle Doll
Composition shoulder head, lower arms, and legs. Cloth body, upper arms, and legs. Stitched hip joints. Medium blond mohair wig over molded hair, tin sleep eyes, open mouth with two upper teeth and molded tongue. All original except for hair bow. $125.00.

Effanbee

Fleischaker & Baum
Manufacturers of Effanbee Dolls
1910 – Present

Newly discovered were the Anne Shirley dolls designated as America's Children, not to be confused with Dewees Cochran's American Children.

A special find was a 12" Portrait Doll in her original, unique box. It was to be hung on the wall just like a picture frame.

Effanbee produced several sets of marionettes during the 1930s and 1940s. They are also illustrated and discussed in the following section.

The re-issue Patsy dolls from the late 1940s are a rare find. Three all original Patsy Joans are shown.

Description for this 17" doll, see next page.

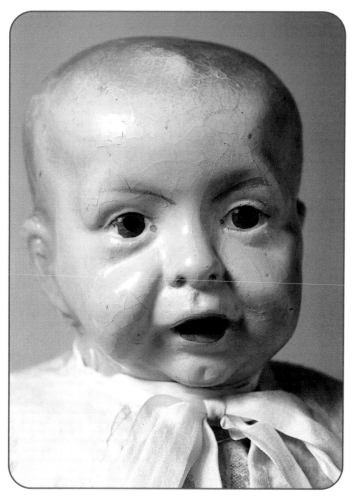

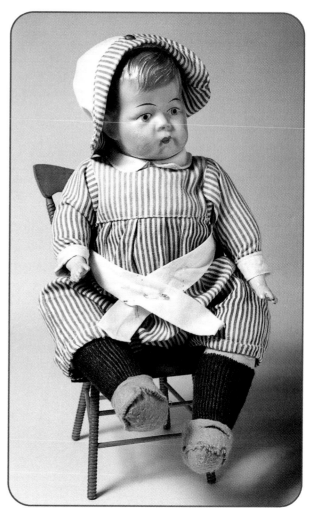

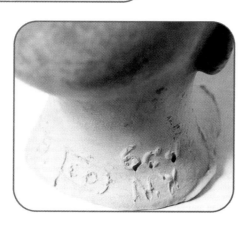

Ca. 18". Marks: none (copy of Fiamingo head). Ca. 1915. Composition flange head and short arms. Cloth body, upper arms, and bent legs, jointed with inside disks. Molded, painted brown hair and painted blue eyes, closed mouth. Original suit and hat. $350.00.

17". Marks: F+B CO 6cj // NY. Ca. 1912. Copy of German bisque head #100 by Kaemmer & Reinhardt. Flared composition head, cloth body and limbs, jointed with outside disks, bent legs. Lightly Molded, painted brown hair and painted blue eyes. Open/closed mouth. Re-dressed. $150.00.

Three Early Babies

The babies seen in the following three illustrations seem from the same mold and were produced over a period of at least five years. The first two were made of glue base composition, seen with molded hair and wig (1915 Effanbee catalog). The third one was made of wood pulp composition (ca. 1919). This unusually large doll (25") features most unusual cloth legs. They were constructed with several pattern pieces and stitched toe indications, which have never been seen before on an Effanbee baby.

16". Marks: DECO // 56 (1915 Effanbee catalog).
Flared composition head and short arms, cloth body, upper arms, and bent legs, jointed with inside disks at shoulders and hips. Brown mohair wig glued directly to head (no wig cap). Painted blue eyes, open mouth with two molded, painted upper teeth, two dimples. Re-dressed. $125.00.

18". Marks: DECO // 58 (1915 Effanbee catalog)
Flared composition head and short arms. Cloth body, upper arms, and bent legs, jointed with inside disks. Slightly molded light brown hair and painted blue eyes. Open mouth with two upper molded, painted teeth. Pacifier came with doll. Re-dressed. $125.00.

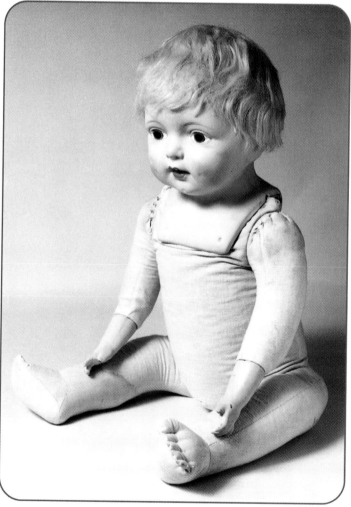

25". Marks: none. Ca. 1919.
Dress tag: Effanbee // Trade Mark
Composition shoulder head and lower arms. Cloth body, jointed at shoulders and hips. Blond mohair wig over molded hair, open mouth with two upper molded, painted teeth. All original including pacifier (rubber section missing).
NOTE: This unusually large baby has several unusual features. Painted eyelashes all around the eye opening are expertly done as are the multi-stroke brows. The bent cloth legs are well shaped and have stitched toe separations. The foot was also carefully formed, showing a well defined heel. Cynthia Whittaker collection. $350.00.

25" baby seen in previous illustration, showing the specially designed legs. A very realistic looking foot was created by using two pattern pieces for the foot and stitched toe separations.

17". Oriental Baby. Marks: none on doll. Copy of Kestner #243.
Cloth tag on kimono: Effanbee // Trade Mark
Flared composition head and short arms. Cloth body, upper arms, and bent legs, jointed with inside disks. Black human hair wig glued onto scalp (no wig cap). Painted brown eyes, deep, open/closed mouth with two upper molded, painted teeth. Original kimono and pants.
Note: Head is very faded. $350.00.

14". Marks: none.
Whistler: Modified version of a Grumpy head.
Flared composition head and short lower arms. Cloth body, upper arms, and legs, black cloth boots, jointed at shoulders and hips with inside disks. Molded, painted light brown hair and painted blue eyes. Open mouth shaped in whistling position (no whistling mechanism). All original. $850.00.

Ever Popular Mama Dolls of the 1920s and 1930s

The following mama dolls from the 1920s and 1930s document their popularity in all their variety. Some examples are seen with molded hair and painted eyes in simple cotton frocks, while the more expensive types were available with sleep eyes and good quality wigs, dressed in outfits of organdy, batiste, and even silk.

Left: 20" Betty Lee. Marks: Effanbee. Dress tag: Effanbee // Dolls // Finest And Best
Metal button shows a blue bird and inscription.
Right: 23" Alice Lee. Marks on shoulder plate and upper arms: Effanbee
Necklace with heart pendant inscribed Effanbee (Playthings, August 1924).
Composition shoulder heads, full arms, and legs to above the knee. Cloth bodies and upper legs, jointed at shoulders, stitched hip joints. Blond mohair wigs, blue tin sleep eyes, open mouths with two upper teeth. Both are all original, wearing identical outfits.
Note: In the above ad it is pointed out that Alice Lee is the big sister of Betty Lee. Cynthia Whittaker collection. 20", $350.00. 23", $400.00.

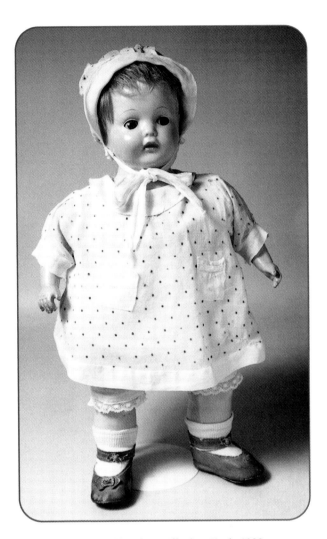

19". Marks on shoulder plate: Effanbee
Composition shoulder head and lower limbs. Cloth body, upper arms, and legs. No shoulder joints, stitched hip joints. Brown mohair wig over molded hair, blue sleep eyes, open mouth with four upper teeth. All original. Cynthia Whittaker collection. $250.00.

18". Marks on shoulder plate: Effanbee. Early 1920s.
Composition shoulder head and lower limbs. Cloth body and upper limbs. No shoulder joints, stitched hip joints. Dark blond mohair wig over molded hair, blue sleep eyes, open/closed mouth. All original. Cynthia Whittaker collection. $150.00.

24". Marks: Effanbee (on shoulder plate and upper arms)
Composition shoulder head, arms, and legs above the knee. Cloth body and upper legs. Jointed at shoulders, stitched hip-joints. Light brown mohair wig over molded hair, blue sleep eyes, open/closed mouth. Re-dressed. Cynthia Whittaker collection. $200.00.

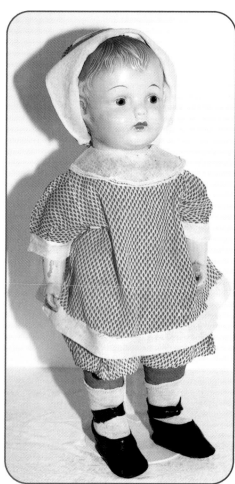

16". Marks: Effanbee
Cloth tag on romper: Effanbee // Trademark
Composition shoulder head and short arms, cloth body, upper arms, and legs. No shoulder joints, stitched hip joints. Molded, painted light brown hair and painted blue eyes, closed mouth. All original. Cynthia Whittaker collection. $100.00.

23". Marks: Effanbee (in script)
Composition shoulder head, lower arms, and legs. Very wide cloth body, upper arms, and legs. No shoulder joints, stitched hip joints. Molded painted, light brown hair, painted blue eyes, closed mouth. All original. Cynthia Whittaker collection. $150.00.

26". Marks: Effanbee (in script)
Composition shoulder head and short arms. Cloth body, upper arms, and legs. No shoulder joints, stitched hip joints. Lightly molded painted blond hair and painted blue eyes, closed mouth. All original (tagged romper). Cynthia Whittaker collection. $175.00.

18".
Dress tag: Effanbee // Dolls // Finest and Best // Made in U.S.A.
Composition shoulder head, lower arms, and legs to above the knee, cloth body, upper arms and legs. Stitched hip joints. Brown mohair wig, blue sleep eyes, closed mouth. All original. Cynthia Whittaker collection. $300.00.

27½". Marks: Effanbee
Composition shoulder head, full arms, and legs to above the knee. Cloth body and upper legs. Jointed at shoulders, stitched hip joints. Blond mohair wig, blue sleep eyes, open mouth with four upper teeth. All original. Cynthia Whittaker collection. $250.00.

18". Marks: Effanbee Dolls Walk Talk Sleep
Composition shoulder head, arms, and legs to above the knee, cloth body. Jointed at shoulders, stitched hip joints. Blond mohair wig over molded hair. Blue sleep eyes, open mouth with two upper teeth. Metal necklace with heart pendant inscribed "Effanbee." All original except for shoes and socks. Cynthia Whittaker collection. $200.00.

10". Marks on shoulder plate: Effanbee (in script)
Tag on dress: EFFanBee // Doll // Finest & Best // Made in U.S.A.
Composition shoulder plate to under the arms (like Bubbles). Composition arms. Cloth body and bent legs, jointed with outside disks. Molded painted blond hair and painted blue eyes, closed mouth. All original. $175.00.

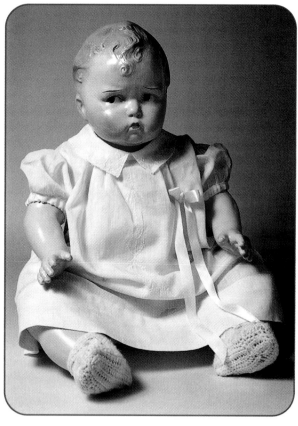

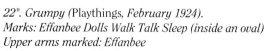

22". Grumpy (Playthings, February 1924).
Marks: Effanbee Dolls Walk Talk Sleep (inside an oval)
Upper arms marked: Effanbee
Composition shoulder head, all composition arms and bent legs to above the knee. Cloth body and upper legs, jointed at shoulders and hips (diagonal hip joints). Molded, painted blond hair, painted blue eyes, (pupil, retina, concave). Closed mouth. Re-dressed. $350.00.

20" Black Bubbles.
Marks: 19 © 24 // Effanbee // Dolls // Walk Talk Sleep // Made in USA
Composition shoulder head to under the arms, full composition arms and legs to above the knee. Cloth body and upper legs. Jointed at shoulders with steel springs, stitched hip joints. Molded, painted, black hair, brown sleep eyes. Open mouth with two upper teeth. All original, including necklace with heart pendant, inscribed "Effanbee." $400.00.

This picture of Bubbles originally accompanied the dolls. Measurements: 3" x 4½".
An entry in the 1926 Montgomery Ward catalog stated: "With each Bubbles Baby, we send six of her photographs. Grandma and Aunty will certainly want one."

13". Marks: Effanbee (Baby Effanbee)
Tag on dress: Effanbee // Dolls // Finest and Best
Composition flange head and arms to above the wrist. Cloth body, upper arms, and legs. Slightly molded, painted blond hair, blue sleep eyes, closed mouth. All original. Cynthia Whittaker collection. $250.00.

Two 14". Pat-O-Pats.
Marks: Effanbee // Made in USA
Composition flange heads and hands, cloth body, and limbs, bent legs. Molded, painted blond hair. Blue eyes and closed mouth have been repainted. Stitched hip and shoulder joints. Metal mechanism inserted in chest. The mechanism is depressed in front, hands clap together. Re-dressed. $150.00 each.

Side view of clapping mechanism imbedded in chest.

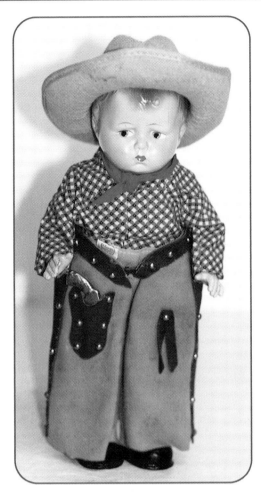

11". Marks: *Effanbee // Dolls // Walk Talk Sleep* (Grumpy)
Composition shoulder head to under the arms, full arms, and legs with molded boots, cloth body. Molded, painted blond hair, painted blue eyes, closed mouth. All original tagged cowboy outfit. Don and Arlene Jensen collection. $400.00.

14" Harmonica Joe.
Marked: Effanbee (in script)
Shirt tag: Effanbee // Trademark (Playthings, *June 1924)*
Paper tag glued to pants: see illustration picturing tag
Metal pin on cap: Bluebird pictured. Effanbee Dolls // Finest and Best.
Composition shoulder head and arms. Cloth body and legs. Jointed at shoulders, stitched hip joints. Rubber ball inside abdomen. Molded, painted blond hair, painted blue eyes. Open mouth with rubber mouth piece and metal harmonica.
Harmonica marked: F. A. Rauner // Made in Germany
Reverse side: My little Chamer // D. R. W. Z. No. 92551
All original, including shoes and socks.
Note: Rubber ball is still very flexible, but mouth piece has hardened and lets air escape. Harmonica works. $425.00.

14½" brown version of Harmonica Joe.
See description with previous illustration. Arlene and Don Jensen collection. $450.00.

173

18". Marked within oval: *Effanbee // Rosemary // Walks. Talks. Sleeps.* Early 1930s. Sewn in cloth tag in back: *Effanbee // Durable // Dolls // Made in USA.* Metal pin marked: *Effanbee // Durable // Dolls*

Composition shoulder head, full arms, and legs, jointed at shoulders and hips. Cloth body with voice box. Red human hair wig, brown celluloid sleep eyes, open mouth with four upper teeth. All original, including shoes, socks, and hair bow.

Note: Label on original box states the hair color as being "Auburn" and the dress color as "Maize." $400.00.

Original box for Rosemary in yellow dress and hair bow.

20". Marks on head: © // *Mary Ann*
On shoulder plate: *Effanbee // Lovums // © Pat. No. 128558*
Paper label: "*I'm the new // Bloomingdale // Red Head // Everybody's // talking // about // me!*"
Composition shoulder head and limbs, jointed at shoulders and hips. Cloth body. Red mohair wig, brown sleep eyes, open mouth with four upper teeth. All original.
Note: This was a store special for Bloomingdale's, well-known New York City department store, which is still in existence today. Arlene and Don Jensen collection. $1,500.00.

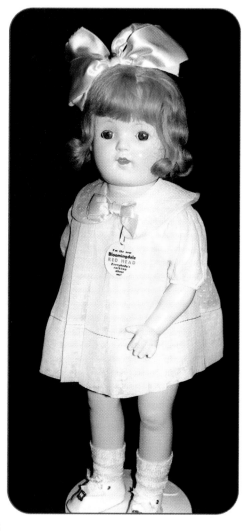

174

The Anne Shirley/Little Lady Dolls

Sold under both names, these dolls were very popular from the late 1930s throughout the 1940s. Initially made with celluloid sleep eyes, the later ones already featured new eyes with plastic irises. Due to material shortages during WWII, the dolls were produced with yarn wigs for a period of time.

21". Marks on head: Effanbee // USA
Marks on body: Effanbee // Anne Shirley
All composition, fully jointed. Brown human hair wig, brown sleep eyes, closed mouth. All original. Special, original box with provision for owner's and doll's name (next illustration). Caryl Silber collection. $400.00.

Original box of 21" Anne Shirley seen in previous illustration, inscribed: "I Belong To ...//My name is..."

15". Marks on back: Effanbee // Anne Shirley
All composition, fully jointed. Original, blond mohair wig in original set. Brown sleep eyes, closed motuh. All original. $175.00.

18". Marks: Effanbee // USA. 1945.
Lining of cape embroidered: Little Lady
All composition, fully jointed. Light brown yarn wig, blue sleep eyes, closed mouth. All original with maribou cape and hat. Anita Maxwell collection. $450.00.

14½". Marks on head: Effanbee // Anne Shirley
Paper tag: Effanbee // Magic Hand // Doll
All composition, fully jointed. Blond human hair wig, sleep eyes, closed mouth. All original including metal heart bracelet. Original box is also marked: Magic Hands.
Note: Magnets are imbedded in the doll's hands. Accessories such as flowers (shown on doll), a flag, parasol, and hankie also have a magnet attached, making it possible for the doll to hold these items. Mary Lu Trowbridge collection. $350.00.

15". Marks on back: Effanbee // Anne Shirley
Paper tag: I am // Little Lady // An // Effanbee // Durable // Doll
All composition, fully jointed. Blond human hair wig, blue sleep eyes, closed mouth. All original including metal heart bracelet and original box. Mary Lu Trowbridge collection. $350.00.

18". Marks on back and head: Effanbee // U.S.A.
Heart shaped paper tag: I am // Little Lady // an // Effanbee // Durable // Doll
All composition, fully jointed. Brown human hair wig, blue sleep eyes, closed mouth. All original, including metal heart bracelet and original box. Mary Lu Trowbridge collection. $400.00.

15". Marks on back: Effanbee // Anne Shirley
All composition, fully jointed. Sleep eyes, closed mouth. Blond human hair wig with curls and braids tied up. All original, except bunch of flowers.
Note special features: Magic Hands. Magnets have been imbedded in the palms of the hands so that the doll can hold items that have small metal pieces or wire attached. $350.00.

14" Majorette, 1940s.
Marks: Effanbee // Anne Shirley
Heart-shaped hang tag front: I Am an // Effanbee // Durable Doll // The Doll // with // Satin Smooth // Skin
Back: A new // Effanbee // Playmate // For ... // From ... // May you and Dolly// have many happy // times together // Trade Mark Reg. // Made in USA
All composition, fully jointed. Blond mohair wig, blue sleep eyes, closed mouth. All original. $350.00.

19". Marks: Effanbee // Sugar Baby
Composition flange head, arms, and legs to above the knee. Cloth body. Jointed at shoulders, stitched hip joints. Molded, painted blond hair and painted blue eyes, closed mouth. All original. Cynthia Whittaker collection. $250.00.

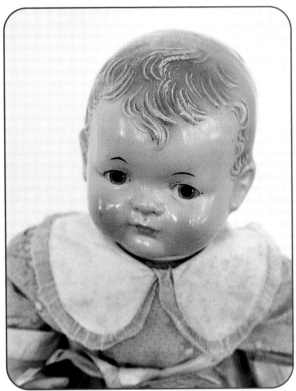

Close-up of Sugar Baby's head shows distinctive modeling of hair.

8". Marks: Effanbee (on back). This is Betty Butin-Nose.
All composition, fully jointed. Molded, painted brown hair, painted blue eyes, closed mouth. All original, except for shoes and socks.
Note: This doll's arms are made of composition. Some Butin-Nose dolls were sold with hard rubber arms. Not all Butin-Nose dolls were identified with that name. $225.00.

8". *Marks on back: Effanbee*
All composition, fully jointed. Molded, painted brown hair and painted brown eyes, closed mouth. All original.
Note: There is no mention of Butin-Nose on either doll, tag or original box. Judy Johnson collection. $350.00.

8". *Marks on back: Effanbee*
All composition, fully jointed. Molded, painted black hair and painted brown eyes, closed mouth. All original Spanish costume. Judy Johnson collection. $350.00.

The Patsy Family

Effanbee's Patsy, created by famous designer, Bernard Lipfert, was introduced in 1928. Patsy became very popular and a trendsetter. Soon, Effanbee introduced Patsy dolls in various sizes and gave them such names as Patsy Joan, and Patsy Ann. Anyone interested in the in-depth study of Patsy should consult Patricia N. Schoonmakers *Patsy Doll Encyclopedia, Vol. I* and *II*.

Full page Playthings *ad, dated April, 1928.*

14". Marks: *Effanbee // Patsy // Pat. Pend. // Doll*
Cloth tag: *Effanbee // Dolls // Finest and Best // Made in USA*
All composition, fully jointed. Molded, painted brown hair and painted brown eyes, closed mouth. Origianl dress and matching teddy. Replaced shoes and socks. $275.00.

16". Marks: *Effanbee // Patsy Joan (on back)*
Dress tag: *Effanbee // Durable // Dolls // Made in U.S.A.*
See Playthings, *May 1933. Doll was advertised as Patsy in Wonderland, obviously trying to take advantage of the Paramount film* Alice in Wonderland *introduced in 1933. All composition, fully jointed. Blond mohair wig over molded hair with two pigtails. Sleep eyes, closed mouth. All original, except for apron, which is a copy of an origi-nal apron. $400.00.*

16". Marks: *Effanbee // Patsy Joan*
All composition, fully jointed. Molded, painted reddish brown hair and green sleep eyes, closed mouth. All original, except for hair bow. Original, matching felt cap missing. $400.00.

Two 19" Patsy-Anns. Marks: Effanbee // "Patsy - Ann" // PAT. # 1.283.558
All composition, fully jointed. Molded, painted auburn hair, blue sleep eyes, closed mouth. Both are all original. Boy features original Effanbee pin, but has his fabric beret missing. $500.00+ each.

11½". Marks on head: Effanbee, on body: Effanbee // Patsy Jr. // Doll
Paper tag: I am // Anne Shirley // Inspired by Ann Shirley in RKO Radio's // Anne of // Green Gables // An Effanbee Durable Doll
Tag on dress: My wig can be combed and curled because it is real human hair.
All composition, fully jointed. Blond human hair wig, brown sleep eyes, closed mouth. All original. Arlene and Don Jensen collection. $1,000.00.

19" Patsy Ann.
Marks: Effanbee // Patsy Ann // © // Pat. No. 1283558
All composition, fully jointed. Molded, painted brown hair, blue tin sleep eyes, closed mouth. All original, including heart-shaped paper tag. Arlene and Don Jensen collection. $850.00.

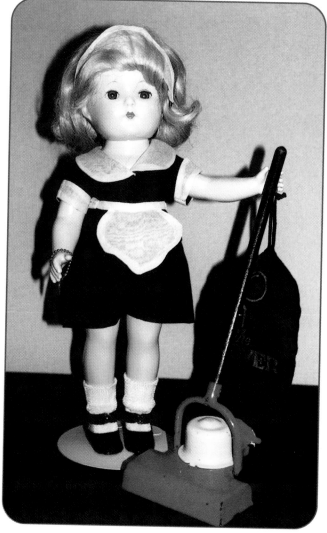

11½" Paticia-Kin.
Marks on head: Effanbee, on body: Effanbee // Patsy Jr. // Doll
For inscription of heart-shaped paper label, see above.
All composition, fully jointed. Blond human hair wig, blue tin
sleep eyes, closed mouth. All original. Arlene and Don Jensen
collection. $800.00.

14½". Marks on back: Effanbee // Patricia
All composition, fully jointed. Blond human hair wig, brown
sleep eyes, closed mouth. All original. Arlene and Don Jensen
collection. $900.00.

26". Marks on head: Effanbee // Patsy Ruth
Marks on shoulder plate: Effanbee // Lovums // © // Patent No. (illegible)
Dress tagged with NRA label.
Brown composition head, shoulder plate and limbs. Brown cloth body, jointed at neck, shoulders, and hips, stitched hip joints. Black human hair wig, brown sleep eyes, closed mouth. All original. Don and Arlene Jensen collection. $2,500.00.

29". Marks on head: Effanbee // Patsy Mae
Marks on shoulder plate: Effanbee // Lovums // © Pat. No. 1, 283,558
Composition head, swivel shoulder plate, full arms, and legs to above the knees. Cloth body and upper legs. Jointed at shoulders, stitched hip joints. Blond human hair wig, brown sleep eyes, closed mouth. All original including necklace with heart pendant. Arlene and Don Jensen collection. $2,000.00+.

9". Marks on back: Effanbee // Patsy Babyette
All composition, fully jointed, bent legs. Molded, painted blond hair and blue tin sleep eyes, closed mouth. All original. $325.00.

9½". Marks on back: Effanbee // Patsyette // Doll
All composition, fully jointed. Red mohair wig over molded hair, painted brown eyes, closed mouth. All original with original metal bracelet and heart-shaped pendant. Arlene and Don Jensen collection. $500.00.

9½". Marks on body: Effanbee // Patsyette // Doll
All composition, fully jointed. White mohair wig over molded hair. Painted blue eyes, closed mouth. All original with original box. Round metal pins show portait of George Washington and are inscribed: George Washington 1732 – 1932. $1,500.00.

8" Tinyettes dressed as Texas Rangers.
Marks on head: Effanbee
Body: Effanbee // Baby Tinyette
Tag left (double sided): I am // an // Effanbee // durable // doll trademark in U.S.A.
Tag right (doubled sided): This is Patsy Tinyette trademark pat. Pend. // The Loveable Imp // with tiltable head // and moveable limb // An Effanbee Durable Doll
All composition, fully jointed. Molded painted brown hair, painted blue eyes, closed mouth. All original including paper hang tags. $800.00 pair.

11". Marks: Effanbee//Patsy Jr.// Doll. 1930.
All composition, fully jointed. Molded, painted brown hair and painted light brown eyes, closed mouth. All original, including extra bonnet with rabbit ears. $500.00.
Tag right: (double sided) This is Patsy Tinyette trademark Pat. Pend. The loveable imp with tiltable head and moveable limb an Effanbee durable doll

Anne Shirley Dolls Designated as "America's Children"

Pictured in the following two illustrations are Anne Shirley dolls carrying paper tags designating them as "America's Children."

While both dolls are of excellent quality and all original, they do not reach the level of exellence in facial modeling or design and quality of clothes evidenced by the Amerian Children created by famous artist, Dewees Cochran. It is easy to confuse the two, as both types of dolls feature identical bodies and limbs (hands with separated fingers, so gloves can fit).

For indepth information on this matter see "American Doll Showcase," *Doll Reader*, August 2001.

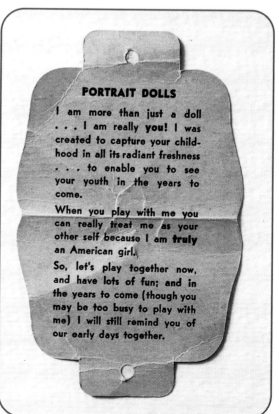

17". Marks: Effanbee Dolls // USA (head and body)
Paper "pocketbook" marked: "I am Betty Jane, // An Effanbee Durable Doll // One of America's Children
Metal heart braclet: Effanbee Durable Doll
All composition, fully jointed. Blond human hair wig, gray sleep eyes, closed mouth. All original, including real leather gloves tucked inside the pocketbook-shaped paper hang tag. $475.00.

Close-up of tag.

14½". Marks: Effanbee // Anne Shirley
See separate illustration of heart-shaped hang tag, designating her as one of America's Children.
Dress is tagged in back: Effanbee // Durable // Dolls // Made in U.S.A. (also see label of original box).
All composition, fully jointed. Blond human hair wig, brown sleep eyes, closed mouth. All original.
Note: This doll was outfitted with arms other than those designed by Dewees Cochran. Mary Lu Trowbridge collection. $1,000.00.

Original hang tag of 14½" Anne Shirley.

Original box of 14½" Anne Shirley.

The American Children Dolls Designed by Dewees Cochran

Famous designer and sculptor, Dewees Cochran, had created and executed portrait dolls of individual children, ordered by well-to-do parents. Most of these dolls were made of latex composition (not illustrated).

Based on this experience, Ms. Cochran was commissioned by Effanbee to design four basic types, representative of American children. These American Children dolls were introduced in 1937 and in 1939, *Life* magazine carried a well illustrated report on the subject. The article claimed that while the individually crafted dolls had been sold for $85.00, the Effanbee composition American Children dolls had been introduced at Saks Fifth Avenue in New York, and were selling at $25.

The bodies and limbs which Ms. Cochran had created for the American Children were of excellent design. The hands had individually sculpted fingers so that gloves could be fitted. These bodies and limbs were used for other dolls as well such as the Historical Series and the Anne Shirley dolls.

As can be seen in this section, Effanbee labeled some Anne Shirley dolls America's Children. While of excellent quality, they should not be confused with Dewees Cochrans' American Children.

20". Marks: Effanbee // American // Children. Late 1930s.
Designed by Dewees Cochran.
All composition, fully jointed. Blond human hair wig. Painted blue eyes, closed mouth.
Re-dressed in Arranbee outfit, homemade shoes.
$800.00.

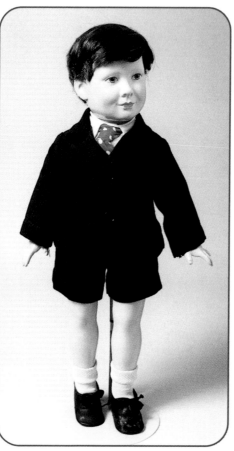

17". No marks on head. Marks on back: Effanbee // USA
Designed by Dewees Cochran.
All composition, fully jointed. Brown human hair wig, painted blue eyes, closed mouth. All original.
Note: The same Anne Shirley/Little Lady body assembly designed by Dewees Cochran was used for this boy. $1,200.00.

Marionettes Produced by the Effanbee Company

Clippo the Clown was created by well-known puppeteer, Virginia Austin, and introduced in 1937. Other marionettes joined the Clippo family: A white girl, a black boy and girl, and a Scottie dog named Pet-Pup Poochie (the latter not illustrated), were introduced in 1939 (*Toys and Novelties*, May 1939). Clippo was well publicized and promoted. A new innovation at Marshall Field's, the large department store in Chicago, was a Clippo Club. Saturday classes gave instructions in "fancy steps" and an average attendance of 75 youngsters was claimed.

Clippo was sold by Effanbee over a long period of time. Eventually, Virginia Austin-Curtis sold Clippo herself. A Clippo coloring book autographed by Virginia Austin-Curtis and with a copyright date of 1975 stated: "Clippo is still being made for a few special stores." "Clippo's Puppet Book," authored by Virginia A. Curtis and copyrighted in 1968, gave instructions on how to make puppets. The cover showed pictures of Clippo, Emily Ann, and the Scottie dog.

Virginia Austin also created the Workshop Puppets for Effanbee. These sets allowed children to assemble their own puppets (see illustration).

Effanbee offered yet another set of marionettes for sale in the 1940s. They were called Talentoon Talentoys. Talentoon probably because with each marionette came a record. These imaginatively designed playthings had wooden heads and legs and metal hands. An illustration of the group of five is included in this section.

(Also see "Those Enchanting Effanbee Puppets" by Rosemarie H. Trinko, *Doll Reader*, May 1986.)

Meet—
Miss Virginia Austin

Creator of Clippo, Charlie McCarthy, W. C. Fields and finally irresistible little "E Pluribus"—ventriloquist dolls and marionettes—made and marketed by Fleischaker & Baum

Puppeteer and creater of puppets, Miss Virginia Austin, seen holding Clippo, the clown. Toys and Bicycles, *April 1938.*

14". Marks © // Effanbee // V. Austin
Paper heart (both sides): "Clippo" // Reg. U.S. Pat. Off. //
© 1936 Virginia Austin // Exclusive Manufacturers //
Fleischaker & Baum // New York City
Composition head, lower arms, and shoes. Wooden upper
and lower body and legs. Body parts connected by cloth
tapes. At ankles, a wire is threaded through shoe and
wooden ankle and fastened, creating a joint. All original.
Note: Included with Clippo were all kinds of paper items,
such as posters, admission tickets, directional signs, etc.
$200.00 (mint in box with paper items).

14". Later Clippo. Marks: © // Clippo // V. A. Curtis
Sole of shoe marked: Curtis Crafts // Made in U.S.A.
Note: This particular example of Clippo is a late model. He came with an
instruction booklet copyrighted (1938/1961 Virginia A. Curtis). His head,
hands, and shoes are made of some type of hard plastic rather than wood
pulp composition as the earlier examples. His construction is identical to
the older types: separate, hinged wood pieces for the body and legs. Mold-
ed, painted black hair and eyes, closed mouth. All original suit and plastic
cap. $150.00.

13". Marks: Emily Ann // V. Austin // Effanbee. Late 1930s.
All original with box. $300.00 (mint in box).

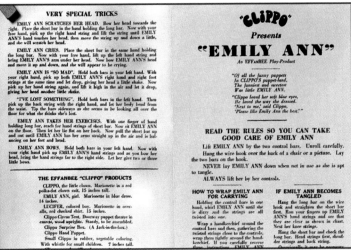

Instruction booklet of Emily Ann.

Instruction booklet for Emily Ann.

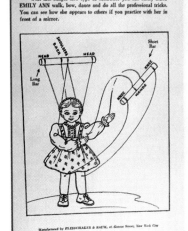

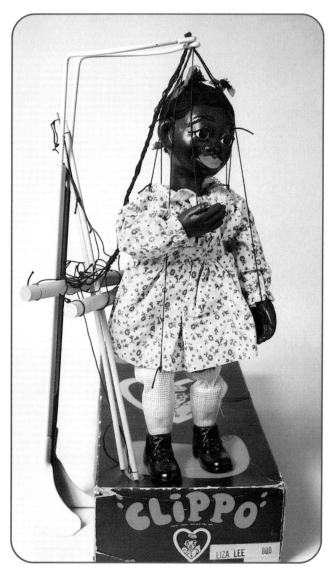

14" Liza Lee. Marks: Lucifer // V. Austin // Effanbee
Was sold in Clippo box, ink stamped "Liza Lee."
Note: Four cotton pigtails with red ribbons. $350.00 mint in box.

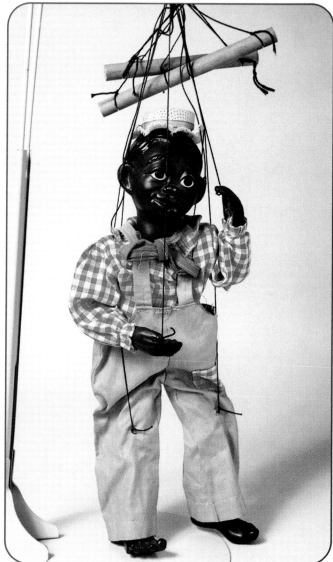

14". Marks: Lucifer // V. Autin // Effanbee
In an article in Toys and Novelties *of April 1938, pg. 124, this marionette was called "E Pluribus" (Bus for short).*
Note: While the other members of this group feature molded shoes, his marionette has beautifully molded bare feet. $250.00 (no box).

10" Workshop Puppet, late 1930s.
In original box, designed by Virginia Austin.
Composition head and arms. Plastic shoes. Marionette has been partially assembled. Materials for making wigs still in box. See pictures of different wigs shown in instruction booklet. $175.00.

Family of Workshop Puppets
10 – 13" tall (copyright 1939 Viriginia Austin).
Marked on heads: F & B // U.S.A.
Composition heads, hands, and molded shoes, wood bodies and leg sections, jointed with strips of cloth tape. Painted features, yarn hair, all original except for man's hat.
Four different heads were available: Man, woman, boy, and girl.
Note: See previous illustration showing a partially accembled puppet in the original box. Each family member came unassembled in a similar box. Assembly instructions also explained and illustrated how to string the puppets and how to work them. Clothes were sold separately by Effanbee. $75.00 ea.

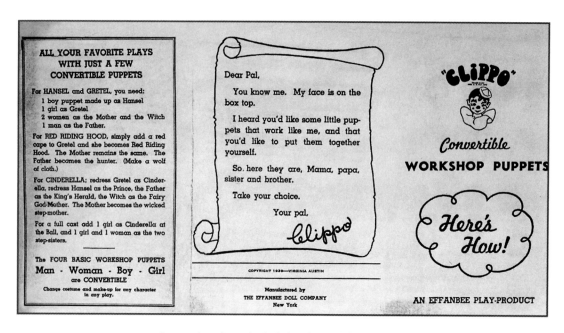

ALL YOUR FAVORITE PLAYS WITH JUST A FEW CONVERTIBLE PUPPETS

For HANSEL and GRETEL, you need:
1 boy puppet made up as Hansel
1 girl as Gretel
2 women as the Mother and the Witch
1 man as the Father.

For RED RIDING HOOD, simply add a red cape to Gretel and she becomes Red Riding Hood. The Mother remains the same. The Father becomes the hunter. (Make a wolf of cloth.)

For CINDERELLA; redress Gretel as Cinderella, redress Hansel as the Prince, the Father as the King's Herald, the Witch as the Fairy God-Mother. The Mother becomes the wicked step-mother.

For a full cast add 1 girl as Cinderella at the Ball, and 1 girl and 1 woman as the two step-sisters.

The FOUR BASIC WORKSHOP PUPPETS
Man - Woman - Boy - Girl
are CONVERTIBLE
Change costume and make-up for any character in any play.

Dear Pal,

You know me. My face is on the box top.

I heard you'd like some little puppets that work like me, and that you'd like to put them together yourself.

So, here they are, Mama, papa, sister and brother.

Take your choice.

Your pal,

Clippo

COPYRIGHT 1939—VIRGINIA AUSTIN

Manufactured by
THE EFFANBEE DOLL COMPANY
New York

"CLiPPO"

Convertible

WORKSHOP PUPPETS

Here's How!

AN EFFANBEE PLAY-PRODUCT

Instruction sheets included with Workshop Puppet.

First — ASSEMBLING THE PUPPET BODY

1. Remove all the parts from the chart and use the drawing as a guide for assembly. SPACING OF ALL PARTS MUST BE EXACTLY AS INDICATED ON THE CHART.

2. Lay CHEST and HIP blocks on the chart to match drawing. (Hip block has holes in sides.) Cut four pieces TAPE two inches long and tack CHEST and HIP together, both front and back.

3. UPPER LEGS. Cut two pieces TAPE four inches long. Push TAPE through holes in HIP block and tack to UPPER LEGS. Notice back of knee is cut away.

4. LOWER LEGS. First tie SHOES on LOWER LEGS with strong white THREAD. Three knots, please. (Thread will loosen enough for ankle action.) Cut four pieces TAPE 1¼ inches long and tack UPPER and LOWER LEGS together.

5. ARMS. Cut two pieces TAPE each six inches long. Push through holes in elbows and tack to CHEST block.

6. HEAD. Cut piece TAPE three inches long and run through loop in neck. Tack to front and back of CHEST block.

CHECK your work:

Third — WIG AND MAKE-UP CHANGES

Look in your picture-books for suitable hair-styles and costumes for the characters you want to make.

Lay the TWINTAK TAPE all over the head according to the natural hairline. Choose color yarn suited to the character.

EYEBROWS, MUSTACHES, BEARDS: Cut narrow pieces of "sticky" tape and lay on face where desired. Press strands of WOOL on tape. Trim.

WRINKLES: Pencil lines drawn on the face and rubbed with fingers. Red pencil rubbed all over the face makes an Indian; Brown, a Negro; Yellow, an Oriental. Wash off with soap and water. (DO NOT use oils or lacquers, as they will spoil the finish of the face.)

WINGS for fairy God-Mothers are shaped of wire and covered with thin material. SILVER SLIPPERS: Cover shoes with tinfoil held on with rubber paper cement. BOOTS: Black oilcloth. LEGGINS: Strips of cloth wrapt around.

These are a few of the many make-up changes possible. Your picture-books will suggest more.

MODERN HAIR STYLES

Making the WIG

Fourth — STRINGING THE PUPPET

THE PUPPET MUST BE DRESSED BEFORE HE IS STRUNG

HOW TO ASSEMBLE YOUR WORKSHOP PUPPE

Set of five Talentoon Talentoy marionettes, 12" tall, called Kilroy the Cop, Jambo the Jiver, Pim-bo the Clown, Mac Awful the Scot, and Toonga from the Congo. Copyright 1948. A folder with play suggestions and a record with music was included with each item. The marionettes were made of wood with metal hands. They are included here for completeness sake.

For more detailed information, see two articles in Doll Reader, *November 1995 and August 1996.*

$150.00 each (mint in box w/record and instructions).

All Talentoy marionettes were contained in such a box, properly marked and accompanied by a record and instruction sheet.

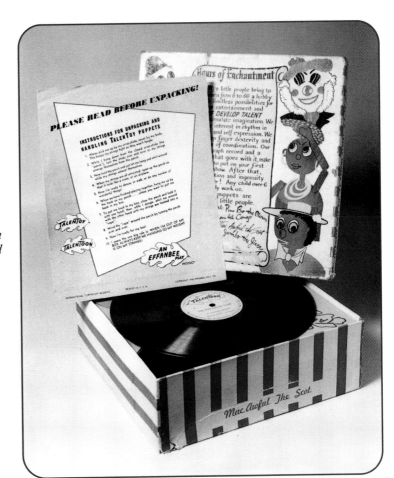

Pim-bo the Clown is the most skillful of the group. He can balance his bar and balls on hand, foot, and nose.

The 12" Portrait Dolls

Pictured in the following two illustrations are three examples of the 12" Portrait Dolls offered by Effanbee in 1940. As can be seen from the first picture, they were called Portrait Dolls because they were sold in a cardboard box with clear top that was supposed to be hung on the wall with the doll in it, "just like a portrait."

In Kelly Ellenberg's book *Effanbee, The Dolls with the Golden Hearts*, an original Effanbee catalog illustration features five sets, two of them showing pairs and three containing single dolls. No names were given. Shown were what seems to be a ballerina in very short skirt, Bo Peep, A Gibson Girl with umbrella and fashionable hat, a bridal pair, and what looks like a Spanish pair. There may have been additional sets.

In the first illustration following, we obviously have Bo Peep. In the second illustration, we see the ballerina on the left and on the right the Spanish lady. In the catalog illustration, her partner wears the typical bull fighter outfit of black pants, bolero, and wide brimmed hat.

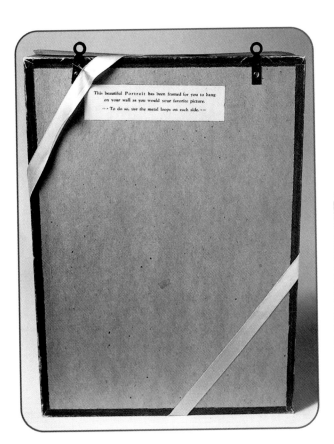

12". Marks: none.
Heart-shaped label on front of picture frame box: Another in the // Portrait Series // of // Effanbee // Durable // Dolls
Back of box: This beautiful Portrait has been framed for you to hang on your wall as you would your favorite picture. To do so, use the metal loops on each side.
All composition, fully jointed. Blond mohair wig, blue sleep eyes, closed mouth. All original. Long wooden dowel tied to her right hand with a bow. $800.00.

12". Marks: none, from Portrait Dolls series. ca 1942.
All composition, fully jointed. Blond and brown mohair wigs,
blue sleep eyes, closed mouths. Both dolls are all original. Anita
Maxwell collection. $350.00 each.

13½" Nurse.
Marks on back: Suzanne // Effanbee // Made in
U.S.A.
Marks on head : Effanbee
Paper tag: I Am An // Effanbee // Durable Doll //
The Doll // With // Satin Smooth // Skin
All composition, fully jointed. Blond human
hair wig, blue sleep eyes, closed mouth. All orig-
inal. Mary Lu Trowbridge collection. $400.00.

12" Suzette. Marks: none, Effanbee Heart Bracelet
14" Suzanne. Marks: Suzanne (tagged dress)
All composition, fully jointed. Brown human hair wigs
(Suzanne with braid on top of her head), brown
sleep eyes, closed mouth. All original. Anita Maxwell collection. Suzette, $350.00. Suzanne, $400.00.

13". Marks: FanB // Made in USA
Paper tag: Mickey and Katie. (See close-up of tag.)
Composition flange heads, hands, and bent legs to above the knee for Katie. Mickey has straight all-cloth legs (same shoes as Katie but brown). Cloth bodies, stitched shoulder and hip joints. Blond human hair wigs over molded hair, blue sleep eyes that also move from side to side, closed mouths. All original. Cynthia Whittaker collection. $400.00 pair.

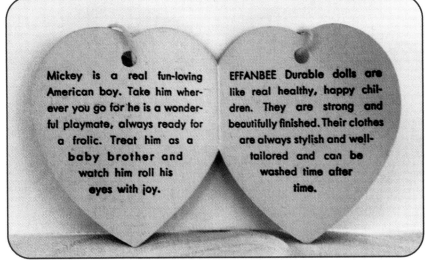

Mickey is a real fun-loving American boy. Take him wherever you go for he is a wonderful playmate, always ready for a frolic. Treat him as a baby brother and watch him roll his eyes with joy.

EFFANBEE Durable dolls are like real healthy, happy children. They are strong and beautifully finished. Their clothes are always stylish and well-tailored and can be washed time after time.

A NEW EFFANBEE PLAYMATE

FOR.............................

FROM.............................
May you and Mickey have many happy times together.
Trade Mark Reg.
MADE IN U.S.A.

I AM Mickey WITH MOVING EYES An EFFANBEE DURABLE DOLL

19". Marks: Effanbee // ©. This is Sweetie Pie.
Composition flange head, arms, and bent legs to above the knee.
Cloth body and upper legs. Jointed at shoulders, stitched hip joints.
Light brown skin wig, blue sleep eyes that also move from side to
side, closed mouth. All original fleece snow suit. Cynthia Whittaker
collection. $300.00.

Right: 19". Marks: Effanbee // Made in USA
Composition flange head, full arms and bent legs to
above the knee. Cloth body, jointed at shoulders,
stitched hip joints. Human hair wig over molded hair,
blue sleep eyes that also move from side to side, closed
mouth. All original.
Left: 24". Marks: Effanbee // Made in USA
Composition flange head and hands. Cloth body, arms,
and straight legs. Cloth arms sewn onto shoulders,
stitched hip joints. Mohair wig over molded hair. All
original except beanie.
Note: Different construction for these dolls with identi-
cal heads. $350.00 each.

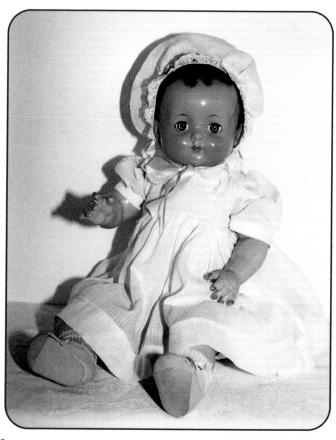

20". Marks: Effanbee. 1940s.
Composition flange head, full arms, and bent legs to above the
knee. Cloth body, jointed at shoulders, stitched hip joints. Molded,
painted dark brown hair, blue sleep eyes, closed mouth. All origi-
nal. Note original, painted fingernails. Outfit has faded. Originally
it was light blue. Cynthia Whittaker collection. $250.00.

Half page ad placed by Fleischaker & Baum (Effanbee) in Toys and Novelties, *April 1941, listing quite a number of dolls from their 1941 line.*

*18". Marks: none (*Toys and Novelties, *April 1941 Effanbee ad mentions "New Pat-O-Pat Dolls").*
Cloth mask face, cloth body, and limbs with stitched shoulder and hip joints. Wig was made from yellow yarn braid. Painted blue eyes, closed mouth. All original except for socks and shoes.
Note: Though not made of composition, this doll is included for completeness sake. $50.00 (in fair condition).

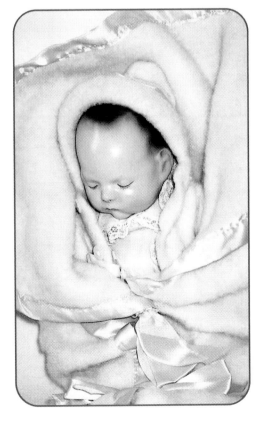

12". Marks: Babyette. 1945.
Composition flange head and hands, cloth body and limbs. Molded, painted brown hair, closed eyes and mouth. All original, with christening gown and bunting. Anita Maxwell collection. $400.00.

21" Honey. Marks: Effanbee (on head and body) For inscription of heart-shaped hang tag see separate illustration.

All composition, fully jointed. Blond human hair wig, blue sleep eyes that also move from side to side, closed mouth. All original.

Note: Effanbee's Honey was made of composition for a short time only. Honey dolls made of hard plastic can be found more readily. Arlene and Don Jensen collection. $500.00.

17" Patsy Joan, 1946.
Marks: EFFANBEE on back. No mark on head.
All composition, fully jointed. Molded, painted light brown hair, blue sleep eyes, closed mouth. All original. Arlene and Don Jensen collection. $500.00.

17" Patsy Joan, 1946.
Marks: EFFANBEE on back. No mark on head.
All composition, fully jointed. Molded, painted black hair, sleep eyes, closed mouth. All original. Arlene and Don Jensen collection. $800.00.

14" Candy Kid Boy and Girl, Toys and Novelties, *September 1947.*
Marks: none.
All composition, fully jointed. Molded, painted brown hair, blue sleep eyes, closed mouth. Original outfits, replaced shoes and socks. $500.00 pair.

17" Patsy Joan, 1946.
Marks: EFFANBEE on back. No mark on head.
Heart-shaped paper tag: This // Patsy Joan // The Loveable Imp // with tiltable head // and movable limb // An //. Effanbee // Durable // Doll
All composition, fully jointed. Molded, painted light brown hair, blue sleep eyes, closed mouth. All original. Arlene and Don Jensen collection. $500.00.

19" Howdy Doody.
Marks: None.
Paper tag front: I am an // Effanbee // Durable Doll // The Doll/with // SatinSmooth // Skin
Paper tag back: A new // Effanbee // Playmate // May you and your Dolly // Have many Happy Times Togther // Trade Mark Reg. // Made in USA
Tag inscribed by hand: For Lorraine and Elaine // May 11, Wed., 1949
Composition flange head and arms to below the elbow. Cloth body, upper arms, and legs. Molded, painted reddish brown hair, brown sleep eyes, open/closed mouth with four painted teeth. All original.
Note: Howdy Dowdy does not have a jointed jaw, only on outline where normally such a jointed jaw would be cut out. Arlene and Don Jensen collection. $600.00.

Elektra Toy & Novelty Co.
New York City

10". Marks: E.T. & N. Co. N.Y. // Copyright
Composition flange head, cloth body and limbs (stump hands), jointed at shoulders and hips with outside disks. Molded, painted light brown hair with molded hair ribbon in front that has been painted the same color. Painted blue eyes, open/closed mouth. All original. $50.00.

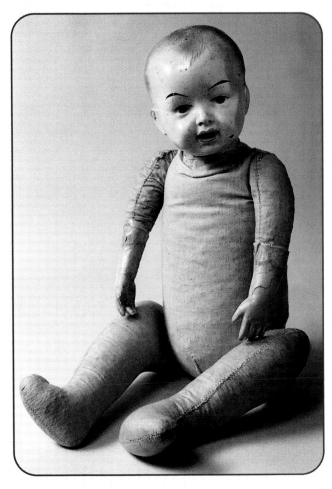

22". Marks: Elektra T. NC. NY // Copyright
Flared composition head, upper cloth arms glued into composition lower arms. Jointed at shoulders with inside disks. Jointed at hips with outside disks (bent legs). Lightly molded light brown hair and painted blue eyes. Open/closed mouth.
Note: Pink sateen was used for the limb casing and white cloth for the body. Doll is extremely faded. $85.00.

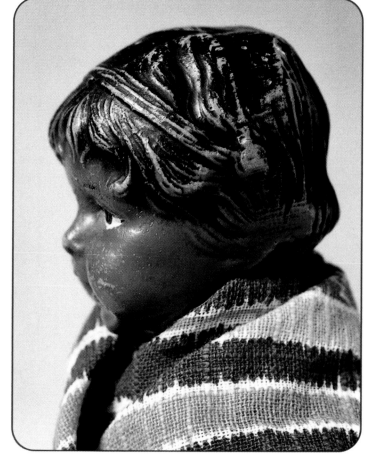

13". Marks: E.T. & N. Co. // Copyright. Ca. 1915.
Composition flange head and hands, cloth body and limbs, joint-
ed with outside disks. Molded, painted black hair with molded
headband in front and molded rosettes on each side. Painted
brown eyes, open/closed mouth. The original long-sleeved dress
is decorated at the hem with a leather fringe (fringes have fallen
off in front). Scarf seems original. Composition hands are appro-
priate replacements. Leather moccasins have been added.
Note: An identical head was used as for the little white girl in the
previous illustration. $50.00.

Eugenia Doll Co.
New York, New York

6". *Marks: none on doll.*

Box marked: Eugenia Doll // Tuesday // Eugenia Stays Home // A Touch of Paris // Copyright 1948, same text on front of package insert. For back side, see next illustration.

All composition, jointed only at shoulders and hips. Blond mohair wig, blue painted eyes, closed mouth. All original. $35.00.

6". *Marks: none on doll.*

Box marked: Eugenia Doll // Sunday // Eugenia Goes To Church // A Touch of Paris // Copyright 1948, same text on front of package insert. Backside is pictured with doll.

All composition, jointed only at shoulders and hips. Dark brown mohair wig, painted blue eyes, closed mouth. All original. $35.00.

7". Marks on head and shoulders: Eugenia // Doll. (See ad illustration where this doll is named "Beloved" 1948.)
All composition, jointed only at neck and shoulders. Molded painted blond wisps of hair on top, sides, and back. Painted blue eyes, closed mouth. Molded union suit and molded shoes painted blue. All original. $150.00.

Front and back view of previous doll, showing the molded union suit and molded painted shoes, which are almost identical in style to those of the Horsman HeBee SheBees. At this point, there is no explanation for this.

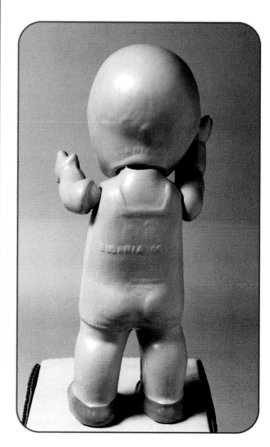

Eugenia's New Baby Beloved, advertised in Playthings, *July 1948.*
Note: Obviously, this ad does not explain why the baby has molded shoes and underwear.

16". Marks: none. This is one of a set of five Personality Pla Mate dolls produced by Eugenia Doll Co., for Montgomery Ward in 1948. Her name is Kathryn (Kathie).
All composition, fully jointed. Original blond mohair wig, blue sleep eyes, closed mouth. Re-dressed. $125.00.
16" composition – Kathie and Sandy
17" composition – Bobbie
18" hard plastic – Carol
20" hard plastic – Babs

18". Marks: none. 1940s.
Sewn-in dress tag: Made in U.S.A. // Eugenia Doll Co., N.Y.
3, N.Y. // America's Finest Dolls (see separate illustration
of tag).
All composition, fully, jointed. Blond mohair wig, blue
sleep eyes, closed mouth. All original. $250.00.

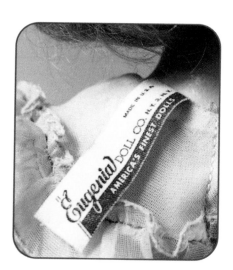

Exposition Doll & Toy Manufacture Co.
New York City
1921 – 1930+

14" Scrappy. Marks: none.
Composition flange head and hands with four fingers, molded shoes. Molded, painted black hair and eyes, open/closed mouth with faintly molded tongue. All original. Striped red stockings are his leg casing.
Note: Scrappy was the star character in a cartoon created by Charles Mintz in 1931, entitled Help Wanted. Screen Gems, a division of Columbia Pictures, filmed this cartoon in 1935. For further information, see Doll Reader, Nov. 1994, pg. 104, article by Susan Girandot. Susan Ackerman collection. $400.00+.

*Front and back of Scrappy's original tag. Last two lines on back:
© C-P-C 1935 Made in USA*

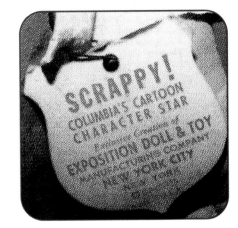

Half page ad placed by the Exposition Doll & Toy Manufacturing Co., Inc. in the August 1937 issue of Playthings, advertising The Scrappy Doll. This is obviously a so-called movie tie-in.

Famous Doll Studio

Left: Marks: none.
Composition shoulder head and lower arms. Cloth body, upper arms, and straight legs,
jointed with inside disks. Molded, painted brown hair and painted blue eyes. Open/closed
mouth with white line between light to simulate teeth. Old clothes.
Right: Marks: none. Sani Doll (Playthings, *March 1917).*
Same construction as above, except for bent legs. Old clothes.
Note: Since the modeling of these two faces seems to be identical, it is assumed that the
doll on the left was also sold by the Famous Doll Studio. $150.00 each.

Madeline Frazier

20". Marks: none. 1940s.
Tag in dress seam: La Madelon Dolls // by // Madeline Frazier
All composition, fully jointed. Blond mohair wig, blue sleep eyes, closed mouth. All original.
Note: No information was found on Madeline Frazier, obviously a small outfitter who bought blank dolls and dressed them. $250.00.

Ralph A. Freundlich, Inc.
New York City and Clinton, Massachusetts
1929 – ca. 1945

In 1934, the Freundlich Company employed 500 people and claimed to manufacture 25,000 dolls daily. They produced a varied line of medium priced dolls, their main stay being mama dolls, all-composition children and babies. While some of the specialties such as Baby Sandy and their World War II military dolls are well known, it is almost impossible to find children and babies that can be attributed to Freundlich. Few of their dolls seem to have been marked.

Photographer Richard Merrill visited the Freundlich factory in Clinton in 1938 and took many pictures of their doll-making process, starting with a vat of wood pulp and ending with finished dolls of all kinds. (See *Doll Collectors of America, Inc. Manual*, 1967, pg. 101 – 115.)

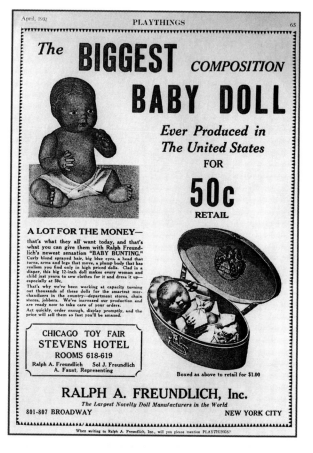

The three ads from 1932 and 1934 placed in Playthings *by the Ralph A. Freundlich Company give some idea of their ingenuity in designing attractive new products. Since neither the trunk with the cut-off corners or the oval one were probably marked, the illustrations will help collectors identify their finds. The same goes for the scale with baby. This item has never been seen.*

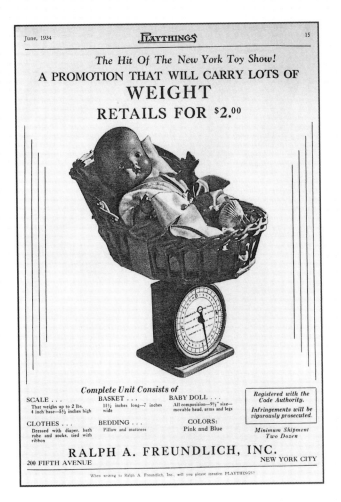

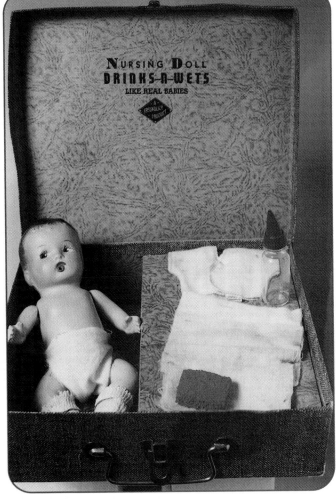

8". Marks: none on doll.
Suitcase marked: Nursing Doll // Drinks-N-Wets // Like Real Babies // A. Freundlich Products.
All composition, jointed only at shoulders and hips. Molded, painted brown hair and painted blue eyes. Open mouth with round insert (another insert at the bottom). All original with extra accessories consisting of a shirt, three diapers, a sponge, and nursing bottle.
Note: Insert at mouth and bottom of doll are connected by a rubber tube. This constituted the Drink and Wet mechanism. $95.00.

20". Marks: none. This is Dummy Dan.
Composition flange head and arms to under the elbow. Cloth body, upper arms, and legs, stitched joints at shoulders, hips, and above the knees with empty space in knee area. Black stockings to above knee are also the leg casing. Molded, painted black hair and painted brown eyes. Jointed jaw. All original, replaced shoes. $100.00.

17" Cowboy marionette. Marks: none.
Composition head with molded-on hat and jointed jaw, composition hands and shoes. Legs are wooden dowels attached to the shoes. Wood body. Upper bar which controls the marionette is also made of composition. All original. Painted features.
Note: For this marionette the head of Freundlich's Dummy Dan has been used. $75.00.

17" Clown marionette. Marks: none.
Composition head with molded-on hat and jointed jaw. Composition hands and shoes. Legs consist of only a dowel attached to the shoes. Wood body. All original. Top control bar is missing. See cowboy marionette also pictured and described in this section, which has the control bar. Painted features.
Note: For this clown marionette, the head of Freundlich's Dummy Dan was used. $75.00.

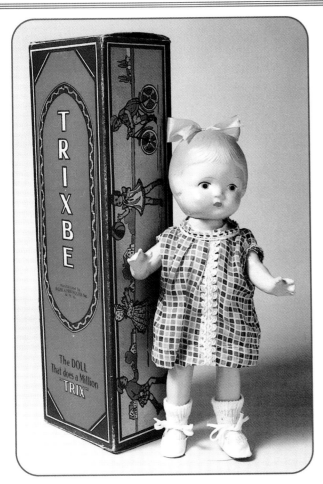

11". Marks: none.
Original box: Trixbe // Manufactured by // Ralph A. Freundlich, Inc. // N.Y.C. The Doll // That does a Million "Trix"
All composition, fully jointed. Molded painted, blond hair with pin hole into head and stick pin that holds hair bow. Painted blue eyes, closed mouth. All original. Box measurements: 14½" x 3¼" x 4⅖".
Note: The box is three inches taller than the doll and one wonders if roller or ice skates (or both) were provided with the doll. This would somehow validate the claims made on the box. $150.00.

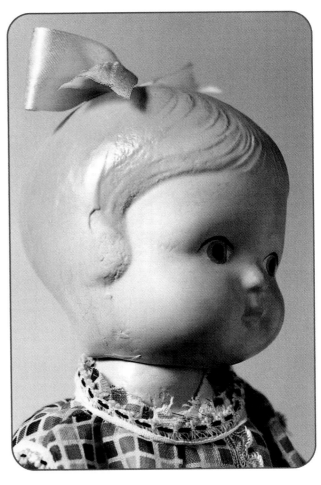

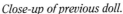

Close-up of previous doll.
This doll was also used for play sets consisting of the doll, a trunk, and additional outfits, also extra shoes and roller skates. The dolls are always unmarked. This illustration, showing clearly the non-specific modeling of the hair at the lower end, should be helpful with identification.

12" Charlie McCarthy look-alike figure. Marks: none.
All composition, jointed at neck, movable jaw. Molded hat, clothes, and shoes. Painted black eyes. $90.00.

8" and 12" all original Baby Sandy shown with book entitled Baby Sandy, The Life Story of the New Universal Pictures Wonder Baby Who has appeared in *East Side of Heaven* with Bing Crosby, *Unexpected Father* with Mischa Auer, *Little Accident* with Hugh Herbert. Baby Sandy's Own Story as Told by Her to Jane Danton. *Rand McNally & Company, Chicago.* Copyright 1939 by United Pictures co., Inc. The book is autographed as having been given "Christmas 1940." 8" closed mouth, painted eyes, $150.00. 12" open mouth with two upper teeth, painted eyes, $250.00. Book, $45.00.

12". Marks on head: Baby Sandy (Playthings, September 1939). Original photo pin: Universal Star // Genuine Baby Sandy Doll All composition, fully jointed. Molded, painted light brown hair, blue tin sleep eyes, open mouth with four teeth. All original and pictured with Baby Sandy fork and spoon set. Also see "Baby Sandy Dolls" by Edward R. Pardella, Doll Reader, June/July 1992. Judy Johnson collection. $400.00.

16" Pinocchio. Marks: none on doll. Paper tag: Original // Pinoccio // As Portrayed by // C. Collodi // Manufactured by // Ralph A. Freundlich, Inc. // 200 Fifth Ave. // New York City
Composition head and body, wooden limbs, fully jointed. Molded, painted red hair, painted blue eyes, closed mouth, all original. John Axe collection. $500.00.

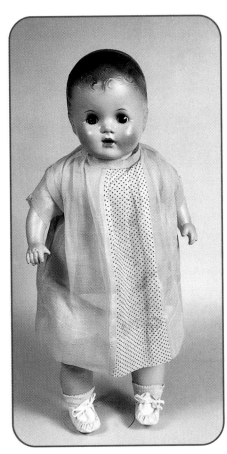

22". Marks: none (may have been sold by Freundlich).
Composition flange head and lower limbs. Cloth body and upper limbs with stitched hip joints. No shoulder joints. Molded, painted dark brown hair, celluloid sleep eyes, open mouth with two upper teeth and felt tongue. All original, except for the ostrich feather trim, which has been replaced. Only remnants of the orginal trim and rubber pants remained.
Note: This was a popular priced doll. The doll is of fairly good quality. Dress and slip are made of a very cheap, open weave material, heavily sized. Likewise, the trim and lining of the bonnet is of mediocre quality. The feather trim on the bonnet and muff gives the impression of a much higher priced doll. $190.00.

221

GEM Toy Company
New York
1913 – 1930+

In their early years, the Gem Toy Company produced dolls whose molds were obviously developed from German examples. GEM continued this copying process. In 1926, they were advertising their new GEM Baby Doll, which was a copy of Horsman's Tynie Baby. Horsman took them to court and lost, as their dolls were marked with initials only rather than their full name. Besides mama dolls, they later had a baby doll that looked very similar to Horsman's Dimples and the Effanbee's Lovums. In 1931, they were advertising a Patsy look-alike (Effanbee). They produced the Five-in-One Doll in about 1924 (see *Doll Reader*, September 1993 — "The Five-In-One Doll" by Susan Girardot), obviously a take-off on Berwick's Famlee Doll.

11". Marks: GEM. ca. 1915
Composition flange head, cloth body and limbs with stump hands. Jointed at shoulders and hips with outside disks. Molded, painted light brown hair, painted blue eyes, closed mouth. Re-dressed.
Note: Probably copied from German doll. $75.00.

13". Marks: none (see label on original box). ca. 1925.
Compostion flange head, hands, and interchangeable legs to above the knee. Cloth body, upper arms, and upper legs. Jointed at shoulders, stitched hip joints. Molded, painted blond hair, painted blue eyes, closed mouth. All original including box.
Note: This is the copy of Horseman's Tynie Baby. Cynthia Whittaker collection. $125.00.

12". Marks: none (see 1929 Sears catalog, page 633).
Cloth tag sewn to jacket: GEM Trade Mark Registered, Made in USA // Billy Boy
All composition, jointed only at shoulders and hips. Molded, painted blond hair and painted blue eyes. Closed mouth. All original. Cynthia Whitaker collection. $125.00.

George Washington

16". Marks: none. George Washington with original cardboard hatchet, probably produced on the occasion of George Washington's 200th birthday in 1932.

All composition, fully jointed. White mohair wig with ponytail over molded hair (no wig cap). Painted brown eyes, closed mouth. All original.

Note: A Patsy look-alike type was used to produce this doll. $250.00.

Gerling Toy Co.
New York

19". Marks: none. Winsome Baby Doll (see separate illustration of paper tag). Mid 1930s.

All composition, fully jointed. Molded, painted dark brown hair. Brown tin sleep eyes, open mouth with two upper teeth. All original.

Note the dark brown hair and brown eyes. It is assumed that this doll was sold to compete with the very popular Dionne Quintuplets, offered by Madame Alexander under excluisve license. $225.00.

Close-up of 19" Winsome Baby Doll seen in previous illustration.

The very distinctive hair modeling should be helpful to collectors when trying to identify their unmarked all composition toddler.

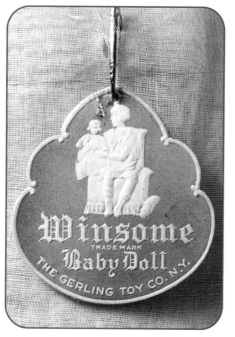

Original tag belonging with 19" toddler.

Eugene Goldberger
Brooklyn, New York

Eugene Goldberger produced a general line of dolls. From 1923 on, they used the trademark EEGEE. Apparently, they did not mark many of their dolls, as few have survived that can be attributed to this company.

The following two dolls illustrated, Baby Charming and Miss Charming, were offered at the peak of popularity of Madame Alexander's Dionne Quintuplets and Ideal's Shirley Temple, famous movie starlet of the 1930s. Both companies held exclusive licenses for these dolls and Goldberger, for example, could not produce Quints or a Shirley Temple. Nevertheless, other companies did offer similar looking dolls but gave them different names. Baby Charming, certainly, reminds one of the Quints (brown eyes, dark, curly hair) and Miss Charming, with her blond curls, comes very close to looking like Shirley Temple.

The second Miss Charming pictured here, which is also not marked, brings to our attention that companies often used the same name for different dolls and thus these dolls can be identified as to name only when they have their original tag.

18" Baby Charming. Marks: none. Original metal button: Baby Charming. I walk and turn my head. On rim of pin: A Goldberger Product Pat. Pend.
All composition, fully jointed, with walker mechanism. Brown mohair wig over molded hair. Brown sleep eyes, open mouth with two upper teeth. All original except for socks. $250.00.

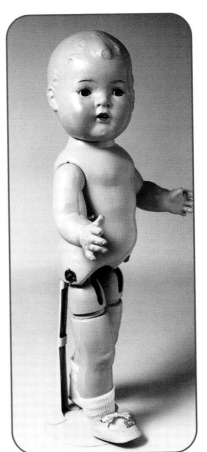

While an unmarked Baby Charming doll found without original clothes and pin would be recognizable by her walker mechanism, the distinctive modeling of the hair in front will also be helpful in the identification process (face of doll has been repaired).
Please also note: A 15" Baby Charming with bent legs and molded hair was also available. The metal pin for this doll reads: "Everybody Loves Baby Charming."
(See Doll Reader, May 1994, Compo Corner, Patricia N. Schoonmaker.)

17" and 20". Marks on dolls: none.
Original oval metal pin on left doll: Miss Charming // I Walk and Turn My Head.
All composition, fully jointed. (Same walker mechanism as show for Baby Charming.) Blond mohair wigs in Shirley Temple style, green sleep eyes, open mouth with six upper teeth. All original.
Note: Little Miss Charming was available in sizes from 12" to 27".
17", $250.00. 20", $375.00.

Full page Playthings *ad placed by the Goldberger firm, July 1936, showing both Miss Charming and Baby Charming.*
Note: In the lower left-hand corner of the ad the oval pin is pictured with a different inscription than the actual one on the dolls: Miss Charming // Everybody Loves Me.

Game card, measuring 7" x 7".
On the back, boy's and girl's names are listed in alphabetical order. Round circles in front had to be pushed out. The winner was promised a Little Miss Charming doll. $15.00.

15". Marks: none on doll.
Paper tag: See illustration on right.
All composition, fully jointed glossy, blond mohair wig, brown sleep eyes, open mouth with six upper teeth. All original.
Note: While this doll is also called Miss Charming and was produced by Goldberger (An EE-Gee product, Brooklyn, NY). She is of lesser quality in terms of construction and clothes than the dolls previously pictured. She does not have a walker mechanism. For stringing only simple hooks were imbedded in the ends of the limbs and mold seams were poorly finished. As we can see in the illustration above, right showing a game board, a Miss Charming was promised as a prize there. The doll discussed here may have been used for this purpose. $175.00.

19". Marks: none. This is Chiki.
All composition, fully jointed. Molded, painted brown hair and blue sleep eyes, open mouth with four upper teeth. Clothes are contemporary.

Note: See Composition and Wood Dolls *by M. Karl. On page 214 this doll is shown in all original condition with paper tag inscribed "Chiki, Another EE-Gee Doll."* $125.00.

13½". Marks: Gold Doll Co.
Composition shoulder head with molded hair loop, full composition arms. Cloth body and legs with sewn in black boots. Pin jointed at shoulders, stitched hip joints. Molded, painted blond hair, painted blue eyes, closed mouth. Contemporary dress. $50.00.

Goodyear Toy Co.
New York City
1923 – 1930+

Manufactured mama and infant dolls. Heads and costumes designed by Madame Blanche. Factory agent was S.O. Ludwig (Coleman II).

As the company apparently marked very few of their dolls, not many can be found that are attributable to this firm.

Full-page ad, Playthings, January 1925.
17" cloth bodied composition mama dolls are shown dressed as Peter Pan and Wendy. They represent economy priced models. The ad copy reads as follows: "First the Book — then the Play — then the Picture — and now Peter Pan and Wendy Dolls." This is a typical example of how doll manufacturers tried to take advantage of current events. Obviously the Peter Pan movie was shown in 1925 and must have been popular.

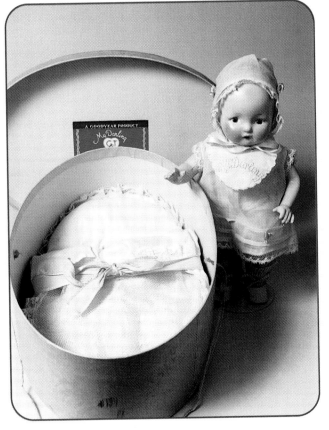

10½". Marks on doll: none.
Box lid marked: A Goodyear Product // My Darling // GT Co.
Composition flange head, full arms, and lower legs. Cloth body and upper legs, stitched hip joints. Hidden joints at shoulders. No crier. Faintly painted blond hair (not molded), painted blue eyes, closed mouth.
Oval box is equipped with cotton stuffed mattress, lace-trimmed pillow and lace-trimmed cover with ribbon ties. Box is 12" long and 4" high. All original. Bib is embroidered "My Darling." $175.00.

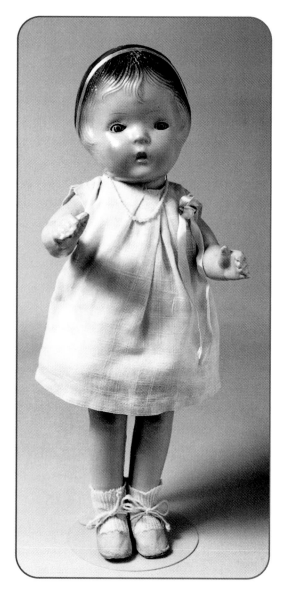

16". Marks: Goodyear // Toy Co.
All composition, fully jointed. Molded, painted brown hair, blue sleep eyes, closed mouth. Contemporary, old clothes.
Note: The arms and legs of this Patsy-type doll are stung with hooks that wre inserted directly into the upper ends (no movable S-hooks) indicating cheaper construction. $75.00.

This close-up of the previous doll shows more clearly the three molded wisps of hair on her forehead.

Halco

*18". Marks: none on doll. Paper tag: Halco Quality Doll //
Made in U.S.A. 1930s.*
*Composition shoulder plate, full arms, and legs to above the
knees. Cloth body and upper legs, jointed at shoulders,
stitched hip joints. Blond mohair wig, brown tin sleep eyes,
open mouth with two upper teeth. All original. Joann Ide
collection. $200.00.*

Hedwig Dolls
created from the characters of the books
by Marguerite de Angeli.

In all, seven dolls were created, dressed in costumes copied from the book illustrations and designed by Hedwig Ryglewicz, Mrs. de Angeli's friend.

1. Elin in Swedish costume from *Elin's America*.
2. Lydia in Amish costume from *Henner's Lydia*.
3. Suzanne in French Canadian costume from *Petite Suzanne*.
4. Hannah (not illustrated) from *Thee, Hannah*.
5. Aniela (not illustrated) in Polish costume, from *Up the Hill*.
6. Cecilia (not illustrated) in Polish costume, from *Up the Hill*.
7. April (not illustrated and a plastic doll) a black girl, from *Bright April*.

The dolls were initially made by Ideal Novelty & Toy Co. Some of the later dolls were bought from other companies. Sleep and painted eyes were used.

References:
1. "Hedwig Dolls," by Z. Frances Walker, *Doll Reader*, Aug./Sept. 1983.
2. "Marguerite de Angeli and the Hedwig Dolls," Ann Bahar, *Doll Reader*, May 1988.

15". Marks: none.
Paper tag: Elin (see separate illustration of tag)
Pin: Sweden
All composition, fully jointed. Blond mohair wig with braids, blue tin sleep eyes, closed mouth. All original. Susan Ackerman collection. $500.00+.

Front and back sides of label that originally was attached to all Marguerite de Angeli dolls.

15". Marks: none.
Paper tag: Lydia (Amish)
All composition, fully jointed. Brown mohair wig, painted blue eyes, closed mouth. All original including slate. Susan Ackerman collection. $500.00+.

15". Marks: none.
Paper tag: Suzanne (French Canadian)
All composition, fully jointed. Blond mohair wig, painted blue eyes, closed mouth. All original. Susan Ackerman collection. $500.00+.

Highgrade Toy Manufacturing Co.
New York City
1916 – 1921

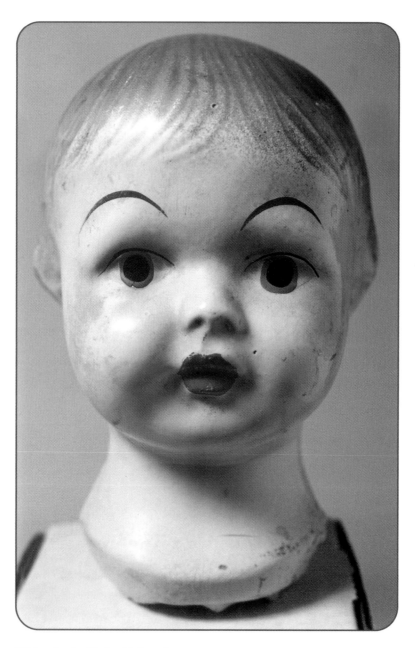

5½" head only. Marks: Highgrade
Flared composition head. Molded, painted blond hair, painted brown eyes,
closed mouth. $40.00.

Hoo Choy

14" Hoo Choy. Marks: none.
Copy of original paper tag reads: "Hoo Chou, the Little Godess of Good Luck". The backside rim of an original tag was encircled with what seemed to be Oriental characters.
All composition, jointed only at the shoulders with a steel spring. Molded, painted black hair and painted brown eyes, closed motuh. Molded, painted black shoes. All original.
$150.00.

E. I. Horsman & Company
New York City

Many Horsman dolls have been discovered and recorded, particularly from the period of 1910 – 1920. It is hoped that this new visual material will enhance collectors' awareness and appreciation of this early, extraordinarily vital period of the Horsman firm. In this connection, Don Jensen's *Collector's Guide to Horsman Dolls, 1865 – 1950* should also be consulted. In his chapter "Dolls Face a New Look, he presents his extensive research on Helen Fox Trowbridge, Horsman's chief designer of dolls during the early years. Getting detailed information on this talented artist will definitely deepen the appreciation of anyone interested in Horsman's early character dolls, such as Baby Suck-A-Thumb, illustrated in this section.

Many babies and mama dolls from the 1920s in original clothes can be studied, including Peterkin, introduced in 1928, the latter so often mistaken for a Campbell Kid. The line-up of Horsman's four Patsy look-alike dolls should help with the familiarization of their names. They now have all been positively identified as Horsman dolls through original, tagged clothing.

The Horsman/Hendren radio campaign highlighted in this section introduces us to new advertising techniques used by the doll industry in the 1930s.

Two all original Bright Star dolls illustrated in the following pages confirm the fact that Horsman used different head molds for this creation. Bright Star was produced when Ideal's Shirley Temple was all the rage.

For most companies, the 1940s were not a creative period. This was largely due to World War II with its material shortages. By the mid-forties, firms were experimenting with plastic materials. Routine composition dolls were offered for sale throughout the decade, many of them unmarked and the blanks used by several companies simultaneously.

For more extensive information on the development of this firm, see Don Jensen's new book *Collector's Guide to Horsman Dolls, 1865 – 1950*.

13" Indian. Marks: unknown (covered by nailed on clothing).
Flared composition head and short lower arms. Cloth body, upper arms, and legs, jointed with inside disks. Molded, painted black hair and black eyes, closed mouth. All original, including the typical Horsman shoes made of felt. Dickie under blouse is nailed to neck in back. Head band is also nailed on with three small nails.
Note: One of the famous Horsman Campbell kids from 1910 has been transformed into an American Indian doll. $250.00.

Chantecler.
Height: 10" (with felt comb), Playthings, April 1910.
Marks: none.
Celluloid mask face with molded, painted hair, painted blue eyes and closed mouth. Body is made of plush, legs of velour, comb, wings, and tail of felt. Jointed at neck and hips.
Note: Chantecler was the main character in a play by French playwright Edmond Rostand (1868–1918). It was based on an ancient French tale of Reynard the Fox and Chantecler the Cockerel, where the actors were dressed in animal costumes. The play opened in the spring of 1910 in Paris and was a great success. Introduced in the fall of 1910 in New York, it was not well received and closed soon. $750.00.

14" Campbells Kid. Marks: E.I.H. © 1913
Tag sewed to sleeve: The // Campbell Kid // Trade mark // LIC'D. By E. I. Horsman //
Name gesetzlich geschuetzt in Deutschland (translation: Name patented in Germany)
(See 1915 Horsman catalog. Identical outfit is pictured.)
Composition shoulder head and lower arms. Cloth body, upper arms and legs, jointed at shoulders and hips with inside disks. Molded, painted light brown hair, painted blue eyes, open/closed mouth. All original. $350.00.

Puppy and Pussy Pippin.
10" Long (head to tail), 7½" high Puppy Pippin. Marks on head: E.I.H. © 1911
Cloth label: Puppy Pippin // Cpyright 1911 // by E.I. Horsman // Trademark
Composition head sewn to body. Velour body and legs, jointed at shoulders and hips. Painted black eyes, closed mouth.
11" long, 8" high Pussy Pippin. Marks: none.
Cloth label: Same as Puppy Pippin.
Identical construction as Puppy Pippin. $400.00. each.

13" Sun Bonnet Sal. Marks: E.J.H. © 1911 (Playthings, July 1912). Composition flange head and short arms. Cloth body and limbs, jointed at shoulders and hips with inside disks. Molded, painted light brown hair and painted blue eyes. Open/closed mouth with white line to represent upper teeth. All original. Light blue, plaid dress and white lace-trimmed apron. White bonnet with sun visor in back. Cynthia Whittaker collection. $250.00.

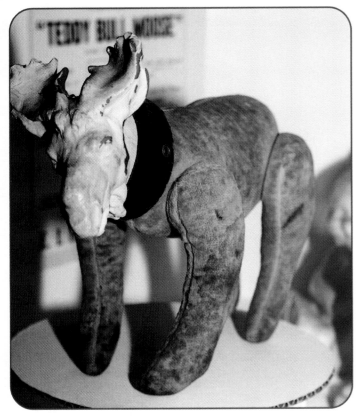

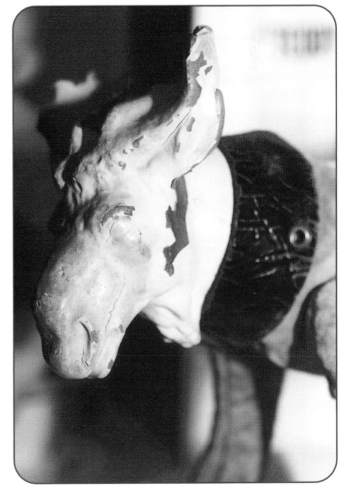

*11" long, Bull Moose (*Playthings, *September 1912)*
Composition head, velour body and limbs, jointed at shoulders and hips. Original leather collar. Top layer and paint have peeled almost completely, but the head reveals very competent modeling. (same construction as Horsman's Puppy Pippin).
Note: Though the above Playthings *ad does not make reference to Teddy Roosevelt, a connection exists. President Roosevelt left office in 1908 and was succeeded by fellow politician and friend, William Howard Taft. During the Taft years, things did not go as Roosevelt had expected, and he decided to run for president one more time. He joined the newly formed Progressive party, also known as the Bull Moose party. President Roosevelt's campaign was called the Bull Moose campaign. Obviously, he still held people's attention, and the Horsman Company must have thought that a toy moose would sell well. It is a rare collector's item today. Ruth and Bob Zimmerman collection. $1,000.00+.*

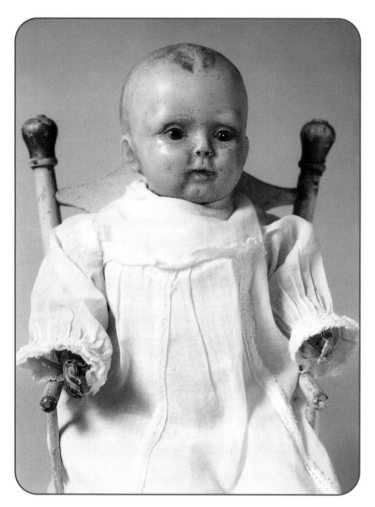

12". Marks: E.J.H. © 1910
Flared composition head and short lower arms. Cloth body, upper arms, and bent legs, jointed with inside disks. Molded, painted blond hair and painted blue eyes. Closed mouth. All original. Cynthia Whittaker collection. $150.00.

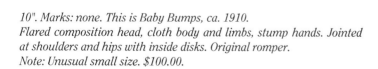

10". Marks: none. This is Baby Bumps, ca. 1910.
Flared composition head, cloth body and limbs, stump hands. Jointed at shoulders and hips with inside disks. Original romper.
Note: Unusual small size. $100.00.

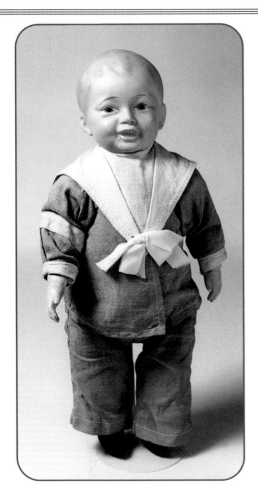

12". Marks: none. This Jack Tar (*Playthings*, May 1911).
(Head is a copy of SFBJ #227.)
Flared composition head and short arms. Cloth body, upper arms, and legs with black cloth boots (head stitched to body). Jointed at shoulders and hips with inside disks. Molded, painted blond hair and painted blue eyes. Open/closed mouth with four upper, molded teeth. All original sailor suit pinned to body with stick pins. $150.00.

Three dolls with identical head mold, 10", 12", and 14" tall. For description see caption of previous illustration for 12" doll. All three all original. (Black doll pants marked: Cotton Joe.)
Note: Varying sizes and outfits create very different looking dolls, though their heads are identical. Also note the variation in sharpness of molding, most noticeable at the hair line. Black, $250.00. 12", $150.00. 10", $100.00.

Girl: 15", boy: 14". Marks: none. (Illustrated in 1911 *Playthings* ad and called Dutch Gretchen and Hans.)
Flared composition heads stitched to body. Composition hands to above the wrist. Cloth bodies, upper arms, and legs, jointed with inside disks. Horizontally striped leg casing constitutes stockings for Gretchen, solid red casing for Hans. Mohair wigs. All original except for buttons on Hans's top.
Note: Identical head mold for both dolls was taken from German bisque model. See close-up on page 246. Top of head on both dolls shows identical construction.

14". Marks: E.J.H. © 1911
Sleeve label: The Jap Rose Kid // Trade Mark/ Process Pat. Nov. 1911 // LIC'D by Jas. S. Kirk & Company by E.I. Horsman Co.
Flared composition head sewn to body and short arms. Cloth body, upper arms, and legs, jointed with inside disks. Molded, painted black hair and painted brown eyes. Open/closed mouth, original clothes.
Note: The Jap Rose Kids were advertising symbols for the Jas. S. Kirk Company, large manufacturers of soap, talcum powder, etc. Don and Arlene Jensen collection. $350.00.

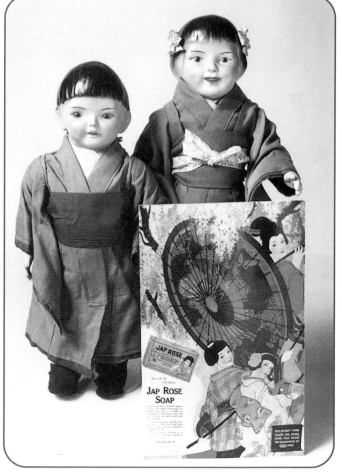

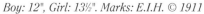

Boy: 12", Girl: 13½". Marks: E.I.H. © 1911
Boy's sleeve label: The Jap Rose Kid // Trade Mark // Process Pat. Nov. 1911 // LIC'D by Jas. S. Kirk & Company //Copyright by E.I. Horman Co.
Flared composition heads sewn to cloth body, short composition arms. Cloth body, upper arms, and legs. Black foot casing simulating boots. Molded, painted black hair, painted brown eyes, open/closed, mouths with painted upper teeth. Boy all original, Girl has been re-dressed. Original ad for Jap Rose Soap from Ladies' Home Journal, *April 1919, placed by the James S. Kirk & Company, Chicago, makers of Jap Rose Talcum Powder. Collection of Mary Stuecker. $350.00 each.*

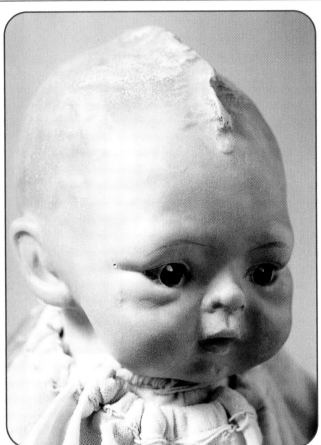

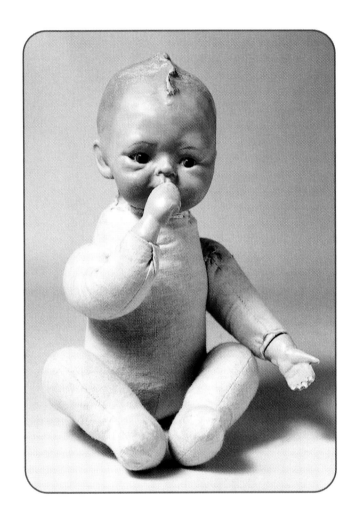

11" Suck-A-Thumb. Marks: EIH © 1911 (designed by Helen Trowbridge) (Playthings, Sept. 1913).
Flared composition head stitched to body, short composition arms. Right hand was molded into a fist with thumb turned in. Cloth body, arms, and bent legs, jointed with inside disks. Molded, painted blond hair with crimped top. Painted blue eyes, deep open/closed mouth.
Note: Left arm was stuffed with sawdust, as usual. Right arm was stuffed with cotton with a piece of wire imbedded that extends the length of the arm. When the right arm is bent and raised, the thumb knuckle fits into the mouth. $250.00.

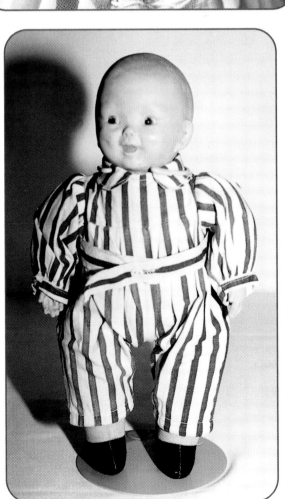

12". Marks: none (Playthings, July 1913).
Composition head and short lower arms. Cloth body and limbs, jointed at shoulders and hips with inside disks. Black cloth boots are part of the leg casing. Faintly molded hair and painted blue eyes. Open/clsoed mouth. All original. (May have had pointed harlequin hat). Robin Tickner collection. $150.00.

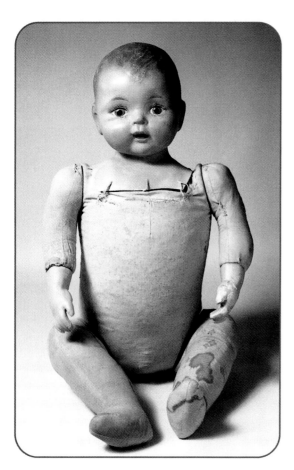

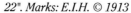

22". Marks: E.I.H. © 1913
Composition shoulder plate and lower arms. Cloth body, upper arms, and bent legs. Jointed with inside disks. Slightly molded and painted blond hair, painted eyes, open/closed mouth.
Note: This is a rare large size. Also unusual are the rays painted on the iris. $250.00.

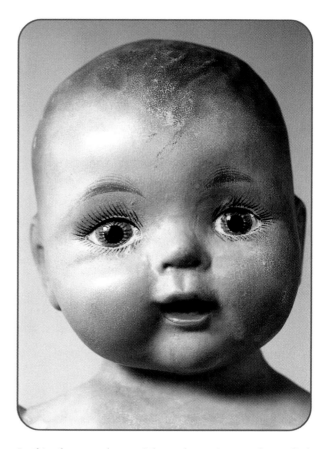

In this close-up, the special eye decoration can be studied. Painted eyelashes encircle the eye opening. Next to the black pupil, a light blue line has been painted on top of the blue iris. Dark blue "rays" are painted on top of the iris. This special treatment has not been seen on any of the other early Horsman babies.

15". Marks: EIH © 19(illegible). (Playthings, July 1913 School Boy). Flared composition head sewed into body, short composition arms. Cloth body, upper arms, and legs, jointed at shoulders and hips with inside disks. Additional knee joints have outside rivets. Molded, painted blond hair and painted blue eyes, closed mouth. All original, except for shoes and tie. $250.00.

12". Marks: none (Playthings, Jan. 1914).
Cloth label sewn to kimono: Trade Mark // "Baby Butterfly" // E.I. Horsman Co. New York (third line not legible)
Flared composition head and short arms. Cloth body, upper arms, and bent legs, jointed with inside disks. Faintly molded, painted black hair and painted brown eyes, closed mouth. Original kimono. Head and arms have been restored. $250.00.

15" Baby Butterfly. Marks: EIH © 1915
Cloth tag on kimono: Baby Butterfly // E.I. Horsman Co., New York // produced Dec. 12, 1913
Composition shoulder head and lower arms. Cloth body, upper arms, and bent legs, jointed at shoulders and hips. Molded, painted black hair and painted brown eyes. Closed mouth. All origianl, except for lavender ribbon.
Note: This Baby Butterfly is of a different mold as the one seen in the previous illustration. Sherryl Shirran collection. $350.00.

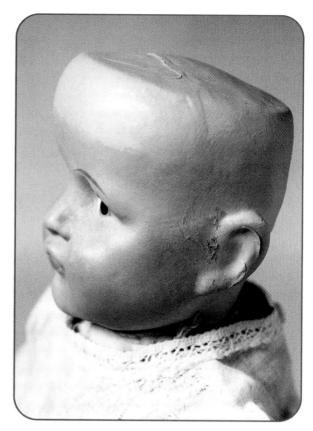

Side view without wig shows treatment of crown.

12". Marks: none.

Flared composition heads sewn to the cloth body. Short com-position arms. Cloth bodies, upper arms, and legs, jointed at shoulders and hips with inside disks. The girl has her original blond mohair wig with wig-cap. The boy's is a replacement. Painted, blue side-glancing eyes (one to the right, the other to the left). Closed mouth. Top of the head is closed off flat (see separate illustration). Appropriate old clothes, original felt shoes.

Note: The heads for these dolls were copied from a German bisque head by the firm of Kaemmer and Reinhardt (#114 Hans). $350.00.

14". Marks: none.

Cotton Joe with real hair (short black mohair glued directly to the head) and molded hair. (For molded hair Cotton Joe, see 1914 Marshall Fields catalog.)

Composition heads sewn to bodies, composition arms to above the wrist. Cloth bodies, upper arms, and legs, jointed with inside disks. Painted brown eyes, open/closed mouths.

Left: All original, Cynthia Whittaker collection. Right: Only the shirt is original. $250.00 each.

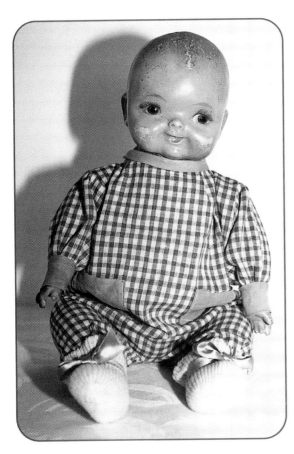

14". Marks: none. Ca. 1915.
Composition flange head and short arms. Cloth body, upper arms, and bent legs, jointed at shoulders and hips with inside disks. Slightly molded blond hair, painted eyes, open/closed mouth. Original romper. Cynthia Whittaker collection. $150.00.

13". Marks: E.I.H. © 1916 (Playthings, June 1915)
Sleeve tag: Gene Carr Kids // From New York World's Lady Bountiful comic series // MF'D. by E.I. Horsman Co., N.Y.
Composition heads are sewn to body. Short composition arms. Cloth body, upper arms, and legs, jointed at shoulders and hips with inside disks. Molded, painted, brown hair and painted blue eyes (one closed eyes). Open/closed mouth with molded teeth. All original. Left: Cynthia Whittaker collection. $350.00 each.

Group of three Horsman dolls with identical heads (one with glass eyes and mohair wig, two with painted eyes and painted hair).
15½" and 18". Marks: E. I. H. © 1916
20". Marks: E.I.H. © 1914
Composition shoulder heads stitched to bodies. Composition lower arms. Cloth bodies, upper arms, and legs, jointed at shoulders and hips with inside disks. Open/closed mouths with molded, painted upper teeth. Smallest doll all original, medium size re-dressed, large doll with clothes made for him. Molded hair dolls have wire staples for insertion of hair bows. 15½", $250.00. 18", $150.00. 20", $500.00.

16" Topsy. Marks: EIH © 1914

Brown composition shoulder head and lower arms. Cloth body, upper arms, and legs, jointed with inside disks. Molded, painted black hair and painted brown eyes. Open/closed mouth with two upper molded, painted teeth. All original, except hair bow (stick pin into head for attachment of bow).

Note: No knee joints. Only the cloth legs are brown. Upper arms and body are made of white cloth. White versions of doll seen in previous illustration. $250.00.

18". Marks: E.I.H. 1914 // ©

Compostion shoulder head and short lower arms. Cloth body, upper arms, and legs, jointed at shulders and hips with inside disks. Molded painted light brown hair and painted blue eyes. Open/closed mouth with four painted upper teeth. All original.

Note: Hair bow is held in place with a stick pin into the head. Cynthia Whittaker collection. $350.00.

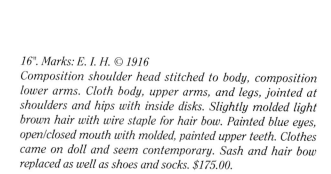

16". Marks: E. I. H. © 1916

Composition shoulder head stitched to body, composition lower arms. Cloth body, upper arms, and legs, jointed at shoulders and hips with inside disks. Slightly molded light brown hair with wire staple for hair bow. Painted blue eyes, open/closed mouth with molded, painted upper teeth. Clothes came on doll and seem contemporary. Sash and hair bow replaced as well as shoes and socks. $175.00.

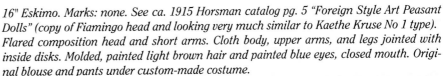

16" Eskimo. Marks: none. See ca. 1915 Horsman catalog pg. 5 "Foreign Style Art Peasant Dolls" (copy of Fiamingo head and looking very much similar to Kaethe Kruse No 1 type). Flared composition head and short arms. Cloth body, upper arms, and legs jointed with inside disks. Molded, painted light brown hair and painted blue eyes, closed mouth. Original blouse and pants under custom-made costume.
Note: Doll is wearing handmade all leather Eskimo outfit consisting of trousers, jacket, boots, cap, and mittens. Mittens are attached to a cord made of wool with two cross bars and decorated with pompons. Boots are seal skin and suit, boots, and mittens are decorated with beads. One wonders if this beautifully handmade outfit was a souvenir doll from Alaska; i.e., that Alaskan Eskimo women dessed it. $150.00 (doll in poor condition).

11". Marks: none. This is Peterkin. (See ca. 1915 Horsman catalog).
Composition head stitched to cloth body, full composition arms that are rather flat. Legs and lower torso are one piece and cloth body is glued to the composition lower torso section. Jointed at shoulders with elastic. Molded, painted light brown hair, painted blue eyes, closed mouth. Old clothes came on doll and seem contemporary. $150.00.

13". Marks: none. (Gene Carr Kid, outfitted and sold as Carnival Kid), ca. 1915. Composition flange head and hands. Cloth body and limbs, jointed at shoulders and hips with inside disks. Head was painted white, including the molded hair. Eyes are closed, open/closed wide grin. All original. Cynthia Whittaker collection. $350.00.

249

11½". Marks: none. This is Fifi (Horsman catalog ca. 1915, pg. 1, #215).
Composition shoulder head, arms, and legs with part of lower torso, cloth body.
Jointed only at shoulders. Medium brown mohair wig and stationary, blue glass
eyes, closed mouth. Clothes are old but may not be original.
Note: While the head probably was intended to be turned slightly to the left, it
seems to have sagged a little in the drying stage. Madeline B. Klein collection.
$250.00.

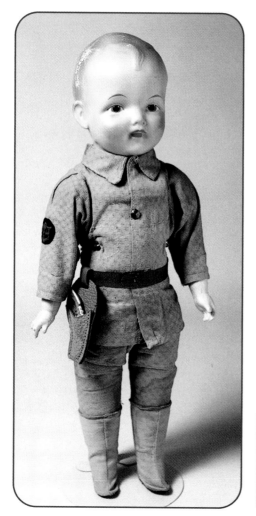

16". Marks: none (made by E.I. Horsman) WWI era.
Composition shoulder head stitched to body, short composition arms.
Cloth body, upper arms, and legs, jointed with inside disks. Molded,
painted light brown hair, painted blue eyes, open/closed mouth with
molded upper teeth. All original, with belt, holster, and metal gun.
Arm patch marked K C. $250.00.

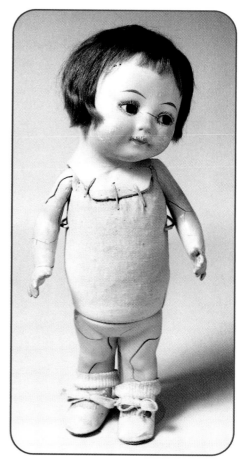

Fifi seen in the illustration above, undressed.
Note: While her head is of a different mold, she was constucted in the same fashion
as the early Peterkins and was advertised with them in the ca. 1915 Horsman cata-
log as follows: "Super Grade Peterkins w/Mohair Wigs. - #215 Fifi, a sweet-faced lit-
tle tot in crip, spotless lawn, silk sash and hair ribbon." (Sash at hip level.) Madeline
B. Klein collection.

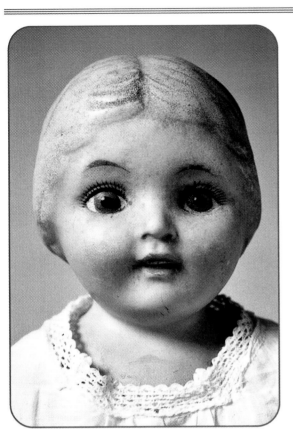

16". Marked: E.I.H. © Co. 1916
Composition shoulder head and full arms. Cloth body and legs, jointed at shoulders and hips. Also jointed at knees. Molded, painted hair with middle part. Painted blue eyes and open/closed mouth with four molded, upper teeth. Re-dressed. Cynthia Whittaker collection. $250.00.

14". Marks: none.
Composition shoulder head and short arms, cloth body, upper arms, and bent legs, jointed at shoulders and hips (head is stitched to body). Molded, painted blond hair and painted blue eyes. Open/closed mouth with white line between lips to indicate teeth. Cap and long gown probably original.
Note: Doll is in original and mint condition with no surface dirt on the matte finish. It confirms what had always been suspected, that Horsman was trying to imitate the look of bisque. An old hand-written paper tag remains at the wrist; "Our Baby // 1.50." No original advertising was located for this baby. $300.00.

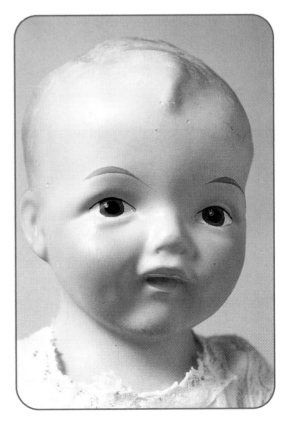

16". Marks: E.I.H. © 1917 (Rookie, Toys and Novelties, May 1917).
Composition shoulder head and arms. Cloth body, upper arms, and full legs, jointed with inside disks. Molded, painted light brown hair and blue eyes, open/closed mouth. All original.
Note: Baby and Rookie were produced with identical heads. $250.00.

Horsman's Blue Bird Dolls

In an illustrated advertisement in the trade journal *Playthings* of March 1920, the E. I. Horsman advertised a Blue Bird Doll, the latest sensation in the doll world. Elsewhere it was stated that these dolls had been created to commemorate the visit to America of the Belgian author Maurice Maeterlinck, who wrote the play *The Blue Bird*.

Maurice Maerterlinck (1862–1949), famous dramatist, essayist, poet, translator, and short story writer, was considered the major dramatist of the Symbolist movement in Europe. He was awarded the Nobel Prize for Literature in 1911. One of his greatest theatrical successes was the play *The Blue Bird*.

Mr. Maeterlinck's works must have been quite popular in this country for some time, as, seven years earlier in 1913, the *Ladies' Home Journal* published in serial form a Blue Bird version adapted for children, entitled *The Children's Blue Bird, the Wonderful Adventures of Tyltyl and Mytyl in Search of Happiness. A Story Version of Maurice Maeterlinck's Famous Play,* by Madame Maurice Maeterlinck.

The main characters, Tyltyl and Mytyl, were a young boy and girl. In the play, Mytyl, the girl is wearing a similar cape as featured by Horsman on the dolls.

Mytyl or Mr. Maeterling's play were not mentioned in the Horsman ad. While dollmakers sometimes had licensing arrangements with authors or actors, on other occasions they did not and would only infer a connection to the famous play or person.

Two Blue Bird dolls.
Left: 13½". Marks: E.I.H. Co. 1914
Cloth label on sleeve: Design // Pat. Applied for
Composition shoulder head and short arms. Cloth body, upper arms, and legs, jointed at shoulders and hips with inside disks. Blond mohair wig, no wig cap. Painted blue eyes, closed mouth. Original dress, old shoes and socks. Cape is a replacement. Cynthia Whittaker collection.
Note: Dress has long sleeves and deep pleats from the shoulders.
Right: 8" Peek-A-Boo dressed as Blue Bird Doll.
Marks: E.I.H. // ©
All composition, jointed only at shoulders. Molded, painted blond hair and painted black eyes, closed mouth. All original except for shoes and socks. Left: $150.00. Right: $250.00.

Full page ad Playthings, *December 1920.*
The dolls seen above, dressed as Blue Bird dolls, were also sold with other identitiies. When found without their original clothes, particularly the trademark blue cape, they should not be called Blue Bird Dolls.
Note: The dolls in the upper row are shown with painted hair and in the lower row with wigs.

Shown here is a 12" Peterkin on the left and two 14" and 16" so-called "dolly face" dolls. As can be seen in the previous ad, besides Peek-A-Boo, these three types were also sold in Blue Bird costumes $200.00, $150.00, $150.00.

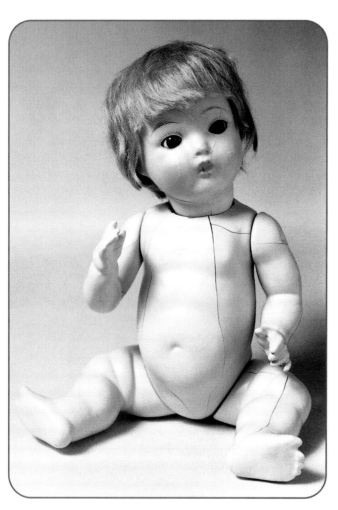

14". Marks: E.I.H. © Co. ca. 1918.

All composition, fully jointed. Original, blond mohair wig, blue real glass sleep eyes, closed mouth.

Note: The real glass eyes were not set with plaster plugs, but are mounted on a steel frame. Deep cracks can be seen on the doll throughout. At this early time, Horsman was trying to produce composition dolls whose surface resembled that of German bisques. They were not oil painted but some other medium was used to achieve the rather matte finish. Apparently, this was not sufficient to protect the intermediate composition layer, which is not impervious to moisture. This intermediate layer may also have been applied too thick. Apparently, because of this handicap, these beautiful, early all-composition babies with glass eyes are rarely seen. $75.00 poor condition.

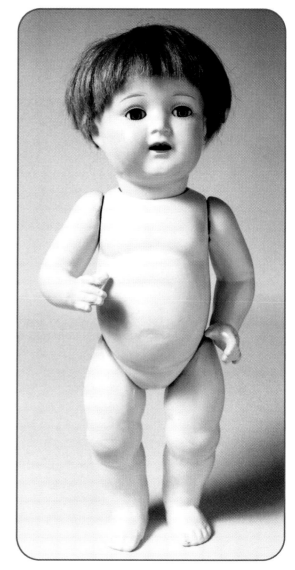

14". Marks: E.I.H. © Co. Ca. 1919.

All composition, fully jointed. Replaced human hair wig, blue celluloid over metal eyes, open mouth with two upper teeth.

Note: Unlike the doll in the previous illustration, this doll's composition parts were finished with oil paint and have held up beautifully. (The head was probably copied from a German bisque head.) Cynthia Whittaker collection. $250.00.

24". Marks: E.I. © H. Co. Baby Horsman 1923, designed by Edith Hitchcock, see Coleman I, page 305.
Composition flange head and hands, cloth body and limbs. Molded, painted blond hair, blue sleep eyes, closed mouth. All original. Cynthia Whittaker collection. $400.00.
Baby Horsman was also available with painted eyes.

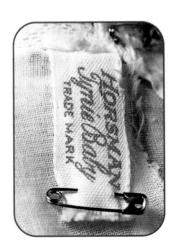

11" Tynie Baby Twins. Marks: © 1924 // E.I.H. Co. Inc. (dress tag see separate illustration).
Composition flange heads and hands, cloth bodies and limbs, stitched hip joints (straight legs). Molded, painted blond hair, gray tin sleep eyes, closed mouths. All original, taged clothes.
Note: Original clothes have been enhanced with additional lace and ribbons by previous owner. Center front decoration is not original. $250.00 each.

HEbee SHEbees
Created by Illustrator Charles Twelvetrees
(*Playthings*, April 1926)

Charles Twelvetrees drew these characters for the children's section of the lady's magazine *Pictorial Review*. In the October 1917 issue of this journal it was claimed that Twelvetrees was doing the Baby Pictures exclusively for their publication.

The E. I. Horsman Company secured HEbee SHEbee as a trademark in 1926. A Horsman ad in a *Pictorial Review* issue of 1926 announced: "At last they (the HEbee SHEbees) have come to life! Those lovable magazine cover characters of Charles Twelvetrees."

Regarding the German SHEbee pictured, it is interesting to note that even in 1926, close ties existed between German and American toy manufacturers and that some American designed items intended for the American market were made in Germany.

10½" HEbee. Marks: none.
Cartoon character created by Charles Twelvetrees (also see Playthings *April 1926).*
All composition, fully jointed. Molded and painted white shirt. Molded booties have loop for attaching real bow. All original cowboy outfit, consisting of large hat, brown neck scarf with black and white polka dots. Attached tag reads "Horsman Doll." Leather belt with holster and painted red metal gun. Green cord lasso. Sharon Jorgensen collection. $450.00.

Left and rear: Pair of 10½" HEbee SHEbees.
Marks: none.
All composition, fully jointed. Painted blue eyes, closed mouth. Molded, painted shirts and booties. A metal loop on top of the booties allows for the insertion of a bow.
Front: 8½" SHEbee.
Marks: Ink stamp on sole of shoe — GERMANY
Made of German composition, jointed only at shoulders. Painted blue eyes, closed mouth. Molded booties have painted bows, and the real shirt is original. 10½", 350.00. 8½", $100.00.

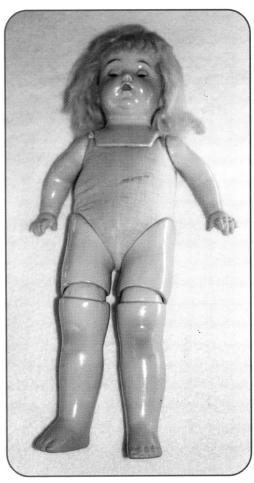

18". Marks: E.I. © H. Co.//e.I. Horsman Co. Inc. (Playthings, August 1926). Composition shoulder head and limbs, jointed at shoulders and hips. Additional above the knee joints. The balls of these special joints have been molded to the lower legs. Cloth body. Blond mohair wig, blue tin sleep eyes, closed mouth. All original, except for shoes.
Note: American Character was also selling a doll with above the knee joints at this time. Arlene and Don Jensen collection. $300.00.

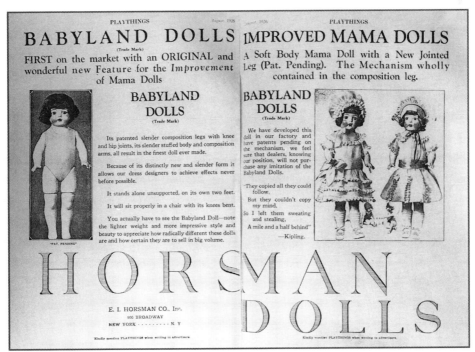

Double page ad dated August 1926, announcing "A Soft Body Mama Doll with a New Jointed leg (Pat. Pending)," as seen in the previous illustration.
Note: Horsman is still calling these dolls mama dolls even though they now have tightly jointed hips rather then the original stitched hip joints which allow the legs to swing back and forth.

13". Marks: E. I. Horsman // Co., Inc.
Dress tag: Horsman // Doll // M'F' D'. In U.S.A.
Composition shoulder head, arms, and legs to above the knee. Cloth body and upper legs, jointed at shoulders and hips. Blond mohair wig, tin sleep eyes, closed mouth. All original. $275.00.

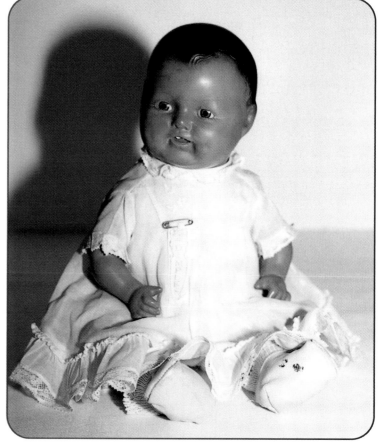

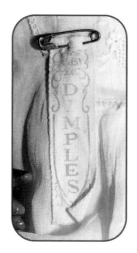

13" Brown Baby Dimples. Marks: E.I.H. Co.
Dress label: Baby Dimples (Toys and Novelties, Sept. 1927).
Composition flange head, full arms, and lower bent legs. Cloth body and upper legs. Jointed at shoulders, stitched hip joints. Molded, painted black hair, brown tin sleep eyes, open mouth with two upper teeth. All original. Patricia N. Schoonmaker collection. $400.00.

13½" Marks: E.I.H. Co. Inc.
Composition shoulder head, full arms, and legs, jointed at shoulders and hips. Cloth body. Molded, painted blond hair, painted blue eyes, closed mouth. All original. Cynthia Whittaker collection. $125.00.

19". Marks: E.I.H. Co. Inc. Composition flange head, full arms, and legs. cloth body, jointed at shoulders and hips. Brown mohair wig, blue sleep eyes, open mouth with four upper teeth. All original.
Note: Though a "Rosebud" head was used for this doll, this name is not indicated on the head. Cynthia Whittaker collection. $250.00.

19" Boy. Marks: © // E.I.H. Co. Inc.
Sewn in cloth tag: Horsman // Doll // MR'D In U.S.A.
Composition flange head, full arms, and legs, jointed at shoulders and hips. Cloth body. Brown mohair wig, blue tin sleep eyes, open mouth with two upper teeth. All original, including small hankie in chest pocket. Anita Maxwell collection. $375.00.

19". Marks: E.I.H. Co. Inc.
Composition flange head, full arms, and legs, joined at shoulders and hips. Cloth body. Blond human hair wig, blue sleep eyes, open mouth with four upper teeth. All original.
Note: Though a "Rosebud" head was used here, the name was not indicated on the head. Cynthia Whittaker collection. $200.00.

21". Marks: E.I.H. Co. Inc. Late 20s – early 30s.
Dress tagged: Horsman Doll // MFD. In U.S.A.
Composition flange head, full arms and legs to above the knee, cloth body, jointed at shoulders, stitiched hip joints. Blond human hair wig, blue tin sleep eyes, open mouth with four upper teeth. All original. Cynthia Whittaker collection. $250.00.

11". Marks: E.I.H. © Inc. Ca. 1928.
Composition shoulder head and full arms, cloth body and bent legs, jointed with inside disks. Molded, painted blond hair and painted blue eyes. Closed mouth. Original romper. $175.00.

260

14" Peterkin. Marks: E.I.H. Co. Inc. Ca. 1928. Composition flange head, full arms, and legs, jointed at shoulders and hips. Cloth body. Molded, painted blond hair, painted blue eyes, closed mouth. All original. Cynthia Whittaker collection. $250.00.

13" Peterkin. Marks. E. I. H. Co. Inc. (Toys and Novelties, June 1929).
Cloth tag on blouse: Horsman // Doll // M'fd. U.S.A. plus Horsman symbol (same as girl).
Composition flange head and limbs, cloth body, fully jointed. Molded, painted blond hair and painted blue eyes, closed mouth. Original blouse and pants, old shoes. $250.00.

Group of three identical all-original Horsman Rosebuds. $350.00 each.

20". Head marked: Rosebud. Ca. 1930.
Dress tag: Horsman Doll // MF'D. In USA
Composition swivel head, shoulder plate and limbs. Cloth body. Human hair wig, gray tin sleep eyes, open mouth with four upper teeth. All original, including shoes and socks. $350.00.

Horsman's Peggy

This doll has caused collectors great confusion.

She was originally sold by Louis Amberg & Son as "It" (in reference to famous actress Clara Bow, who was known as the "It" girl). The Amberg composition doll line was sold to Horsman in 1930, including It. The Amberg marking on the shoulder plate was left in place by Horsman, and the doll advertised and sold as Peggy. The only thing that Horsman did change was to drill a hole into the doll's head. A stickpin was pushed through this hole, and it held a hair bow in place.

An often-used name for this doll is Edwina. Coleman II states: "Edwina 1928, Trade name of composition doll made by Amberg, Ht. 13." – Comment: No "twist waist" is mentioned by the Coleman's. In 1928, Amberg had several dolls of similar height. No primary information has been found to confirm that this name was meant for the doll in question.

Some collectors use the name "Sue" for this doll. This could have come from the 1930 Sears catalog, where it says: "Skating Sue the Body Twist Dolly, 15" Horsman quality." This is accompanied by a drawing resembling the doll in question (with hair bow). It is felt that the doll should be called Sue only if somebody found it in its original Sears box.

14" Horsman's Peggy.
Marks: Amber // Pat. Pend. // L.A. & S. c 1928
All composition, fully jointed with additional waist joint. Molded, painted blond hair with drill hole into the head to accommodate a stickpin holding a hair bow. Painted brown eyes, closed mouth. Contemporary clothes. $300.00.

11½", 14", 17", and 19". Marks: none (Babs, Sue, Jane, and Nan (Playthings, April 1931).
All composition, fully jointed. Molded, painted brown hair, blue tin sleep eyes (14" Sue has painted eyes), closed mouths. All four have a dimple in their chins. Only 11½" Babs is all original and includes a same fabric bonnet (bonnet not shown).
Note: These four Horsman dolls were obviously designed to compete with Effanbee's Patsyette, Patsy, Patsy Joan, and Patsy Ann. $250.00, $150.00, $250.00, and $300.00.

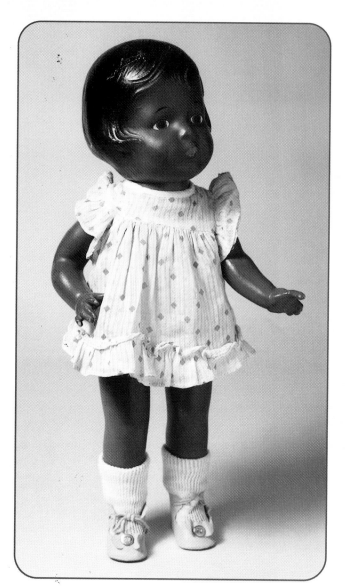

14". Marks: none (Black version of Sue).
All composition, fully jointed. Molded, painted black hair and painted brown eyes, closed mouth. Dress may be original, old shoes and socks. Note: She too has a dimple in her chin. $350.00.

13" and 17". Marks: none on dolls (Sue and Jane).
Cloth label on dresses: Horsman // Doll // M'FD. In U.S.A.
Both are all composition and fully jointed. Molded, painted brown hair, blue tin sleep eyes, closed mouths. All original. 13", $200.00, 17", $280.00.

19". Marks: none.
Dress tag: Horsman // Doll // MFD U.S.A.
All composition, fully jointed. Molded, painted brown hair, gray tin sleep eyes, closed mouth. All original. Faye S. Wetherhold collection.
Note: This is Nan, the largest in a set of four dolls designed to compete with Effanbee's Patsy Jr., Patsy, Patsy Joan, and Patsy Ann, as advertised in the 1931 Sears Roebuck catalog. Their names were Babs, Sue, Jane, and Nan. $400.00.

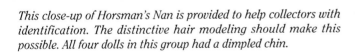

This close-up of Horsman's Nan is provided to help collectors with identification. The distinctive hair modeling should make this possible. All four dolls in this group had a dimpled chin.

"Win-A-Doll-A-Day" Joint Radio Advertising Campaign

In September of 1931, the E. I. Horsman Co., Inc. and the Averill Co., Inc. announced their joint advertising campaign in the trade journals.

An October 1931 ad in *Playthings* stated: "First to sell dolls for your store via radio."

At first, the Win-A-Doll-A-Day ads were illustrated with Mme. Hendren's Peaches and Horsman's Dimples etc. In subsequent ads, things were more specific. A Gold Medal Baby was offered as the prize to contestants. Entry blanks could be picked up at toy stores and department stores. (Madame Hendren Dolls was the tradename for the Averill's line of dolls.)

A *Playthings* ad from November 1931 stated as follows: "What is the Win-A-Doll-A-Day Radio Contest? Every day, over powerful Radio Stations, a favorite Children's character like Uncle Don or Uncle Bob or Uncle Wip announces the award of a Gold Medal Baby to the child who writes best the HORSMAN-HENDREN slogan. The children will come to your store for contest blanks! Your name is mentioned on the air when the child wins the prize!"

All Gold Medal Baby prizes were equipped with a golden good luck coin, as seen in the *Toys and Novelties* ad of September 1931, pictured on the right. In addition, see Lillian McClure's Gold Medal Baby and coin, also illustrated in this section.)

It is furthermore possible, that the Averill's Baby Hendren was also used in this campaign. See the Baby Hendren pictured in the Averill section dressed in tagged Horsman clothes.

The Sears Roebuck catalog of 1931 and 1932 also carried a Gold Medal Baby in the Horsman section, showing the good luck coin pinned to its dress. The description seems to confirm that this too is the doll like Lillian McClure's (swivel shoulder plate, straight legs). There is no mention of the radio advertising campaign in the Sears catalog.

It will be of interest to mention in this connection that the good luck medal was created by the Averills and used throughout the twenties on all their mama dolls. For the joint radio campaign, this medal was adapted for the Horsmans. The back side of the coin remained identical. On the front side, of course, the name was changed to Horsman, and a sitting image of a baby used instead of a standing one, as for the Averill's.

Toys and Novelties *ad dated September 1931, showing the Gold Medal Baby and the good luck coin as it was adapted for the Horsman firm.*

266

November 1931, Playthings *ad, showing three sizes of the Gold Medal Baby used in the radio advertising campaign. (It would be interesting to know if various size dolls were given away.)*

19" Gold Medal Baby.
Marks: none on doll (see separate illustrations of coin).
Composition head, swivel shoulder plate, straight legs to above the knee, and arms to above the elbow. Cloth body and upper limbs. No shoulder joints, stitched hip joints. Molded, painted blond hair, sleep eyes and open mouth with two upper teeth. Dress and bonnet are replicas of the original. Original underwear, booties, and socks.
Note: Gold Medal Baby was created for the Horsman-Hendren radio advertising campaign in 1931. Lillian McClure collection. $250.00.

Front and back views of the Horsman coin used with the Gold Medal Baby in the joint radio advertising campaign. Lillian McClure collection.

Horsman's Baby Buttercup

In the 1930s, all major American doll companies endeavored to produce more life-like dolls. At first, babies with rubber limbs and compsition heads were introduced, shortly followed by all rubber babies that did not yet have a drink and wet feature. In 1934, Effanbee introduced Dy-Dee, the all rubber drink and wet doll, which became immensely successful.

Horsman's Baby Buttercup with composition head and cloth body and limbs seems to have been affected by this development and may have been sold only for a relatively short time. Apparently introduced in 1931, by 1932, an all rubber Baby Buttercup was on the market. By 1938, Horsman was offering an all rubber Baby Buttercup with drink and wet mechanism.

Advertising and the original box label of a baby Buttercup with composition head and limbs and a cloth body illustrated in this section makes reference to a very popular refrain: "I'm call'd Little Buttercup..." These lines were sung by the main character in the well known Gilbert and Sullivan operetta *H.M.S. Pinafore*. No official tie-in could be documented.

12". Marks: H © C.
Original box label: "I'm call'd Little Buttercup // Dear Little Buttercup // Sweet Little Buttercup I" // BUTTERCUP // Trade Mark // The Horsman Corp. // New York // Made in U.S.A.
Composition flange head, full arms and bent legs. Cloth body, jointed at shoulders and hips. Molded, painted blond hair, glassine sleep eyes, open mouth. All original, with pillow.
Note: The outside of the original box was covered with a paper decorated with stylized little buttercup flowers. Cynthia Whittaker collection. $300.00.

16" (40.6cm). Marks: E. I. H. Co. (Playthings, Jan. 1932).
Dress tag: Buttercup // The Horsman Corp. // MF'D. in U.S.A.
Composition flange head and limbs (bent legs), jointed at shoulders
and hips. Cloth body is lightly stuffed, mama voice box. Molded,
painted blond hair and green celluloid sleep eyes, open mouth, metal
tongue, no teeth. $250.00.

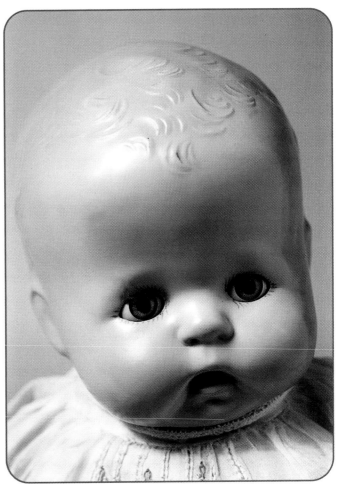

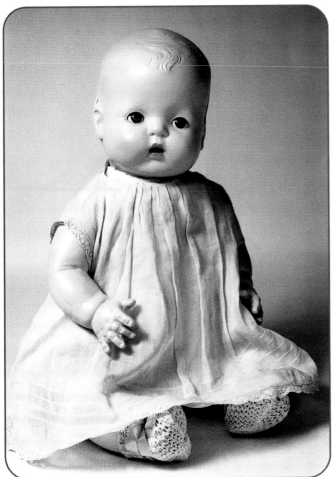

19". Marks: H. c Co. Late 1920s – early 1930s.
Composition flange head, full arms, and bent legs. Cloth body, joint-
ed at shoulders and hips. Molded, painted blond hair, blue tin sleep
eyes, open mouth, no teeth. All original.
Note: Very similar to Buttercup, but different hair modeling in front.
Cynthia Whittaker collection. $125.00.

11". Marks: © // Horsman.
Box lid: Baby Buttercup // Kantbreak // Hard Rubber Head
All rubber, fully jointed. Molded, painted dark brown hair, gray tin sleep eyes, open mouth with round hole and drink and wet mechanism. Original clothes and box.
Note: Though this doll has a hard rubber head (not composition), it is included here for completeness sake. ca. 18" version of this baby has been seen marked: 1938. $250.00.

25" Baby Darling (Blue Ribbon Baby). Marks: none (see separate illustration of tags). Early 1930s.

Compositon flange head, full arms and legs to above the knee, jointed at shoulders, stitched hip joints. Cloth body. Molded, painted blond hair, brown sleep eyes, open mouth with two upper and two lower teeth and molded tongue. All original.

Note: The head used for this doll was a very popular one and was used by several manufacturers, such as the Averill Company. Sometimes, makers would change the hair molding a little when using a very similar face. In this case, they used identical head molds. Therefore, if the doll is not marked, a producer can only be known if original labels are still in place. $250.00.

This doll, obviously, resembles Effanbee's very popular Lovums.

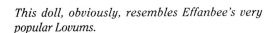

271

16". Marks: none. Ca. 1939.
Paper tag: Gold Medal Baby // Horsman // Super
Quality
All composition, fully jointed. Blond mohair wig over
molded hair, brown sleep eyes, open mouth with two
upper teeth. All original. $250.00.

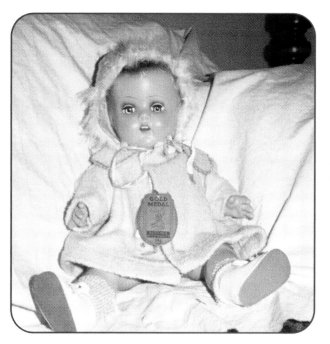

17" Gold Medal Baby. Marks: none (paper hang
tag identical to previous illustration, but molded,
painted hair).
All composition, fully jointed. Molded, painted
brown hair and blue sleep eyes. Open mouth with
two upper teeth. All original. Elizabeth Mizerck
collection. $250.00.

14" Bright Star. Marks: none (see illustration of original tag).
All composition, fully jointed. Blond mohair wig, blue tin sleep eyes,
open mouth with two upper teeth. All original.
Note: The doll shown in this illustration seems the most often seen
face of Bright Star. However, there were others. See Collector's
Guide to Horsman Dolls, 1865–1950, page 147 and 187–88, by Don
Jensen. Also see Pat Schoonmaker's "Compo Corner" in the February 2000 issue of Doll Reader. The "Compo Corner" of September
1995 even show a toddler by that name. $200.00.

11". Marks: none.
Paper tag: Horsman's // Bright Star
// With Eyes That Shine // And Hair
So Fine (see close-up of tag in next
illustration).
All composition, fully jointed,
blond mohair wig, blue tin sleep
eyes, open mouth with four upper
teeth. All original, with trunk and
four sets of extra clothes $300.00.

23" and 18". Marks: Sister // c 1937 Horsman
Composition flange heads, full arms, and straight legs to above the knee. Cloth body, jointed at shoulders, stitched hip joints. Large doll has brown tin sleep eyes and smaller one celluloid eyes that have been oiled. Closed mouths. Both have been re-dressed. 23", $350.00. 18", $150.00.

13". Marks on head: Horsman
Paper tag: A // Genuine // Horsman // Art Doll
All composition, fully jointed. Blond mohair wig with wig cap but stapled to head. Brown tin sleep eyes, closed mouth. All original with original box. Alice Toovey collection. $350.00.

19" Marks: none.
Paper tag: A // Genuine // Horsman // Art Doll (see close-up of tag on doll in previous illustration). 1940s.
All composition, fully jointed. Blond mohair wig, blue sleep eyes (plastic), open mouth with six upper teeth. All original. Cotton dress features sewn-on, short panties of dress material. $200.00.

24". Marks: none. Box: Horsman // Genuine Art Doll // Made In USA // Trenton NJ #35028. 1940s.
Composition flange head, arms to above the elbow, and legs to above the knee. Cloth body, no shoulder joints, stitched hip joints. Molded, painted dark brown hair, blue sleep eyes, open mouth with two uppert teeth. All original. $250.00.

Close-up of doll in previous illustration. The well defined molded curls in this close-up should be helpful in the identification of an unmarked doll.

24". Marks: A // Horsman // Doll. 1940s.
Composition flange head, arms to above the elbows, and bent legs to above the knees. Cloth body with stitched hip joints. Molded, painted brown hair and blue sleep eyes. Open mouth with two upper teeth. All original including labeled box. Anita Maxwell collection. $250.00.

21". Marks: A // Horsman // Doll. 1940s.
Paper tag: Horsman's // Baby Prescious // A Horsman // Super Quality // Doll
Composition flange head, wired on arms and legs to above the knee. Cloth body, stitched hip joints. Light brown mohair wig, blue sleep eyes, closed mouth. All original. $250.00.

21" Baby Prescious without coat.

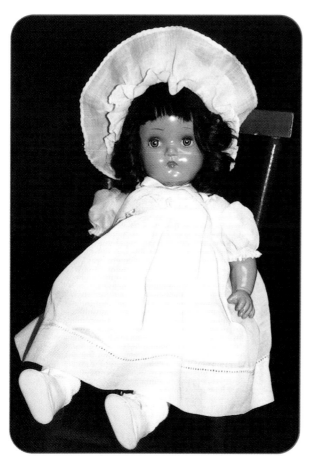

18". Marks: A // Horsman // Doll. Montgomery Ward catalog, 1944. Composition flange head, arms to above the elbow, and legs to above the knee. Cloth body and upper limbs, stitched hip joints. Black mohair wig, brown tin sleep eyes, closed mouth. All original. Arlene and Don Jensen collection. $300.00.

15". Marks: A // Horsman // Doll. 1940s.
Paper tag: See separate illustration.
Composition flange head, full arms, and legs above the knee. Cloth body with disk joints at shoulders, stitched hip joints. Molded, painted dark brown hair, sleep eyes that also move from side to side, closed mouth. All original. Cynthia Whittaker collection. $150.00.

Notice the distinctive hair modeling for this Enchanting Eyes toddler.

16". Enchanting Eyes. Marks: A // Horsman // Doll (See tag of doll previous illustration). Late 1940s.
Composition flange head, arms to above the elbow, and legs to above the knee. Cloth body, upper arms and legs, stitched hip joints. Molded, painted brown hair and sleep eyes that also move from side to side, so called "flirty" eyes, closed mouth. All original. $150.00.

16". Marks: A // Horsman // Doll Composition flange head, lower arms, and legs to above the knee. Cloth body, stitched hip joints. Molded, painted brown hair, blue sleep eyes, closed mouth. All original (original shipping carton).
Note: The head mold is identical to the previous two examples, but this doll has metal eyes that do not move from side to side (previous two have plastic eyes). Cynthia Whittaker collection. $150.00.

12" Campbells Kid. Marks: none (made by E.I. Horsman). 1948.
All composition, fully jointed. Molded, painted, brown hair and black eyes, closed mouth. Molded, painted shoes and socks. All original. $500.00 (mint in box).

House of Puzzy

15". Marks: Puzzy c // H.OF.P. USA
All composition, fully jointed. Molded, painted brown hair, black eyes. Open/closed mouth with white line between lips to simulate teeth. Redressed.
Puzzy has a compaion girl named Sizzy (see next illustration showing a pair of banks).
Note: Copyright 1948 by Herman Cohn, Baltimore, MD. These characters were known as the Good Habit kids. Their images appeared on soap, hairbrushes, toothbrushes, and dozens of other grooming items for children, decorated with decals produced by the Meyercord Co. of Chicago. (More 20th Century Dolls, J. G. Anderton). $250.00.

8½" Puzzy and Sizzy banks.
Both marked in front with their names.
One-piece construction with slits in back of their heads and openings at the bottom for removal of coins. Molded, painted clothes, hair, and features. All original. Also see note with 15" Puzzy, previous illustration. Gayle and Jerry Reilly collection. $100.00 pair.

Mary Hoyer Dolls
Reading, Pennsylvania

Mary Hoyer started her career as a designer of children's knitted fashions in the early 1930s, working for several major yarn companies. Eventually, the Hoyers' started their own publishing company. In 1937, a 14" slim bodied doll was added to their offerings for which Mrs. Hoyer designed knit and crochet patterns. Ready made doll clothes and accessories were also sold. The Hoyer Company is still in existence today, headed by Mrs. Hoyer's granddaughter. (For more information see *Mary Hoyer and Her Dolls*, by Mary Hoyer, Hobby House Press Inc.)

Special Costumes Sold by the Hoyers

The following was submitted by long-time collector of Hoyer dolls, Venice E. Loder, who gained this information through personal contact with the Hoyers.

"Mr. Hoyer was in charge of the business part of the company. Many people approached him with ideas for clothes and related items. Unknown to Mrs. Hoyer, her husband contracted for a small amount of three costumes: A reversible Cinderella dress, a Pilgrim outfit, and a costume for a Centennial Queen. None are tagged. When Mrs. Hoyer saw the items chosen by her husband, she wasn't pleased with the fabric or workmanship. Consequently, very few were sold.

"I (Mrs. Loder) doubted the Pilgrim outfit the first time I saw it because of the fabric. I didn't think Mrs. Hoyer would use that type of material. I later learned it was one of the three contracted outfits.

"I have never been able to purchase the Centennial Queen. It appears on the price list dated September 1, 1950, on page 22, of *Mary Hoyer and Her Dolls*. I was finally able to get an ad showing a picture of the costume and it isn't anything like I imagined it."

The following illustrations show two Cinderella dolls in reversible dresses in Mrs. Loder's collection, one of them a blond and the other one a brunette plus a Hoyer doll in Pilgrim costume. A picture of the ad in which the Centennial Queen is advertised, is also shown.

15" Poor Cinderella and Rich Cinderella. Marks: none.
Created and sold by Mary Hoyer.
Cinderella with reversible dress.
All composition, fully jointed. Blond mohair wig, brown sleep eyes, closed mouth. All orignial except for flower wreath. Venice E. Loder collection. (Authenticity verified by Mary Hoyer.) $500.00 +.

*15". Marks: none.
Cinderella with reversible dress.
Identiacl to previous doll, except
dark hair. All original. Venice E.
Loder collection. $500.00 +.*

*Illustrated ad of Centennial Queen costume. Also mentioned
in their price list dated September 1, 1950, on page 22, of
Mary Hoyer and Her Dolls.*

*14" Mary Hoyer in Pilgrim Costume
All composition, fully jointed. Brown mohair wig and brown sleep eyes, closed
mouth. All original. Venice E. Loder collection. $500.00 +.*

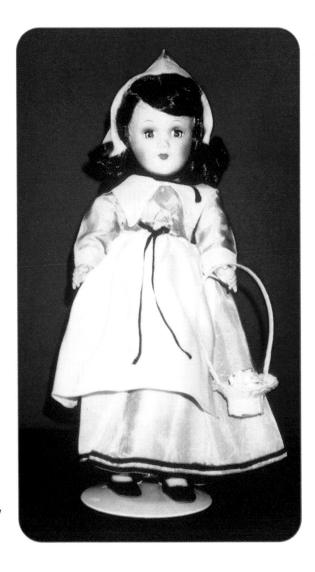

14". Marks: The // Mary Hoyer // Doll
All composition, fully jointed. Red mohair with brown sleep eyes,
closed mouth. All original, including shipping box. $700.00.

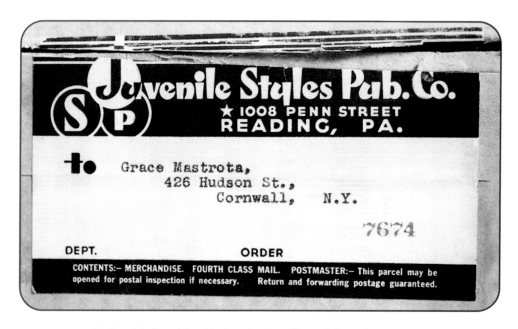

Mailing label used for shipping the Mary Hoyer dolls and accessories.

14" Mary Hoyer. Marks: none.
All composition, fully jointed. Blond mohair wig, painted blue eyes, closed mouth. Dressed in all original, complete ski outfit Juliana.
Note: Doll has the early, painted eyes (not sleep eyes). Anita Maxwell collection. $400.00.

14". Marks: Mary Hoyer in circle
All composition, fully jointed. Red mohair wig, blue sleep eyes, closed mouth. Dressed in knitted outift made from Mary Hoyer pattern. Anita Maxwell collection. $450.00.

14". Marks: Mary Hoyer in circle
All composition, fully jointed. Blond mohair wig, sleep eyes, closed mouth. In original shipping box from Reading, Pennsylvania, dressed in outfit Arlene. Anita Maxwell collection. $450.00.

283

Ideal Novelty & Toy Co.
Established 1906 –

Many dolls not seen before have been discovered and researched. They are presented in the following section. As a group, they document Ideal's considerable contribution to dollmaking throughout the composition era.

In the early days, heads were copied from German bisque dolls, a group collectors might enjoy seeking out. These dolls are still affordable, compared to the German originals.

When one studies early production lists, one is intimidated by their length, thinking that many of the faces and names have never been seen. When studying Three Dolls – Heads from the Same Mold, with Slight Variations, on page 286, one realizes that manufacturers had a few basic heads that were outfitted in various ways that made them look different from one another. Therefore, the list of unknown doll faces might not be as long as we thought.

Sanitary Baby and others listed illustrate that Ideal was experimenting early on with new body styles and ways of constructing dolls.

Individually rocking sleep eyes that winked and blinked and could be set through the neck opening, even for 12" and 14" dolls, were a new invention in American dollmaking. Ideal had a patent on those.

When, in the early twenties competing companies had one mechanical walking doll, Ideal introduced four with individual faces and in varying sizes, though using heads that had been seen previously on some of their dolls. Untold numbers of walking mama dolls with their stitched hip joints were sold in the twenties and thirties.

Ideal had been very successful with their Uneeda Bisquit Boy in 1915. Ideal produced additional dolls that tied in with some product or other. See the Zu Zu Kid, for example, that originally carried a small Zu Zu Cracker box under its arm. This item was another product of the National Bisquit Company.

The Genuine Twinkie Doll is pictured with a book of *Twinkie Town Tales*, and the connection to the Hamilton Brown Shoe Co. is explained. Then, there is Mr. Peanut, surely familiar to everyone.

Not always is the product tie-in very clear, as with the all original Buster Brown illustrated in this section. No authorization was found for the use of that name.

In the 1920s, Ideal pioneered the use of rubber limbs with much success. See the section on New Models of Tickletoes and Flossie Flirt on page 297. Snoozie from the early thirties is also noteworthy with its special eye mechanism, rubber limbs and oil cloth body. As can be seen in the illustrated ad from 1939, Deanna Durbin and Shirley Temple were featured stars, besides Princess Beatrix.

The events of WW II and its effect on the availability of raw materials, influenced Ideal's doll production. During the forties, they continued to produce dolly-faced babies and children made of composition. By the middle of the decade, some dolls with magic skin (thin rubber) and hard plastic heads were offered. By 1950, stars like Sparkle Plenty with hard plastic head and magic skin body and the all hard plastic Toni had been introduced. Composition as a material for making dolls was fazed out.

13". Marks: none. (Playthings, Oct. 1912, ad shows this doll dressed in a Russian suit.)
Flared composition head and short arms. Cloth body, upper arms, and legs, jointed with outside disks. Leg casing serve as striped stockings and black boots. Molded, painted light brown and striated hair, painted blue eyes, closed mouth. Face has been touched up. Old clothes.
Note: This seems to be a copy of Heubach #7622. Also see next illustration. $150.00.

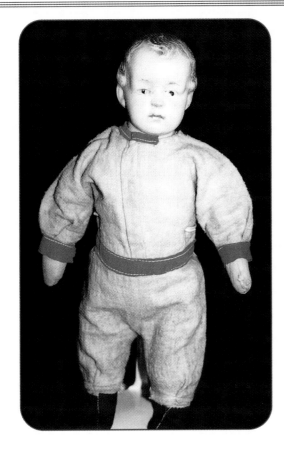

11". Marks: none. (Playthings Oct. 1912 ad shows identical doll dressed in Russian suit. This may be their Ty Cobb, as seen in another ad illustration, Playthings, June 1911.)
Flared composition head, cloth body and limbs jointed with outside disks (stump hands). Molded, painted, and striated brown hair, painted blue eyes, closed mouth. All original. Arlene and Don Jensen collection. $250.00.

16". Marks: none. (Playthings, March 1913, Country Cousin.)
Flared composition head, short arms, and bare legs to the knee. Cloth body and upper limbs, jointed with inside disks. Molded, painted light brown hair and painted blue eyes, closed mouth. Original hat and blouse. Overalls are exact copy of the original ones. Cynthia Whittaker collection. $250.00.

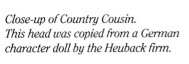

Close-up of Country Cousin.
This head was copied from a German character doll by the Heuback firm.

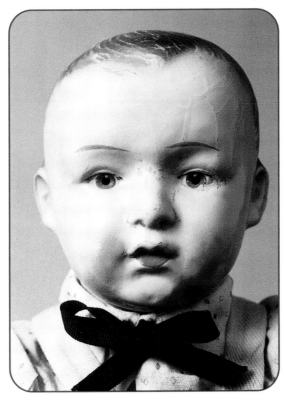

Three Dolls — Heads from the Same Mold, with Slight Variations
Ca. 15". Marks: none on dolls.
Tagged sailor dress on left: Ideal Novelty & Toy // Moving eyes // Trad Mark, Pat. August 10 -15
Rear and right: Painted eyes
Two dolls have molded white boots, one has real shoes.
All feature flared composition heads with molded hair and short composition arms, cloth bodies, upper arms, and legs, jointed with inside disks. Back: $150.00. Front: $250.00, $225.00.

16" Zu Zu Kid. Marks: none.
A 1916 Ideal ad in Playthings *stated: "Under license from Nathional Bisquit Co."*
Flared composition head, short arms, and molded, painted blond hair, painted blue eyes. Open/closed mouth with four painted teeth. Original outfit. Originally, doll came with same fabric pointed cap and a cracker box. $150.00.

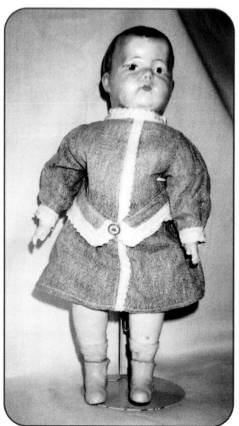

16". Marks: none.
Flared composition head, short arms, and molded boots, Cloth body and limbs, jointed with inside disks. Molded, painted blond hair, painted blue eyes. Closed mouth. All original.
Note: Same style outfit as doll in the previous picture (right), including identical button decoration. Also, same head as used on Uneeda Bisquit Kid. Sharon Aikins collection. $250.00.

286

15" Our Pet.
Marks: none (Playthings, July 1915).
Flared composition head and lower arms. Cloth body, upper arms, and bent legs, jointed iwth inside disks. Molded, painted blond hair, painted blue eyes, closed mouth. Lower garment may be original.
Note: In the ad, the doll is shown in knitted leggings, sweater, and stocking cap with tassel. $125.00.

13". Marks: none. Ca. 1915.
Flared composition head, short arms, and molded, painted boots. Molded, painted blond hair, blue sleep eyes that also rock back and forth individually, closed mouth. Cloth body, upper arms, and legs. Striped stockings are part of the leg casing. jointed at shoulders and hips with outside disks. All original. $80.00.

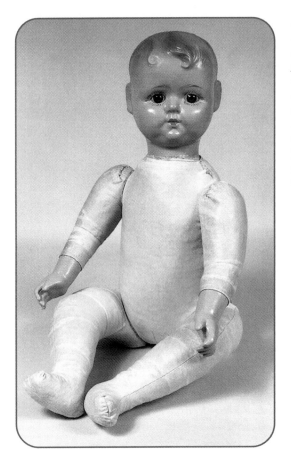

22" Marks: none. This is Sanitary Baby (Made of) Imitation Kid, Stronger Than Kid, Washable" — Playthings, *July 1915).*

Flared composition head and short arms. Oil cloth body, upper arms, and legs, jointed at shoulders and hips. Molded, painted blond hair (repaired) with two distinctive locks of hair in front. Inset real glass eyes, closed mouth (was also advertised with painted eyes). From the ad it is not clear how long Sanitary Baby was sold, as pictures were not always identified.

Note: An identical head was used for the doll called Peggy, in the next illustration. (1918, dressed in short baby dress).

This head was also used for Baby Talc (in soft sleeper with hood) and advertised from 1915 to 1917. No mention as to what type eyes were used. This head was also used for one of their early 20s walkers, see page 294. $150.00.

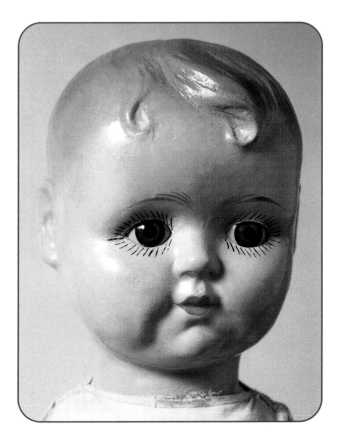

This close-up shows the original black eyelashes and multi-stroke brows. Hair has been repainted.

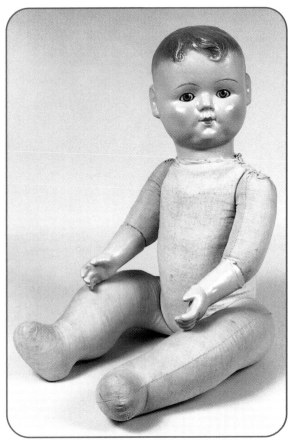

22". Marks: none.

This is Peggy (see Playthings, *January, 1918).*

Flared composition head and lower arms. Cloth body, upper arms, and bent legs, jointed at shoulders and hips with inside disks. Molded, painted blond hair with two distinctive locks in front, gray tin sleep eyes that rock individually, closed mouth. Head and arms have been repainted.

Note: Identical head mold as doll in the previous illustration. In this case tin sleep eyes were used instead of stationary glass eyes. The high (original) coloring of the other doll also makes it look very different from this example. $100.00 (repainted).

Full page ad, Playthings, *January 1918, showing the Baby Peggy doll with its distinctive two curls on the forehead in the lower right corner. In the close-up, these two distinctive curls can be seen even more clearly, thus helping to identify this umarked doll as produced by the Ideal Novelty & Toy Co. Individually rocking eyes are further proof.*

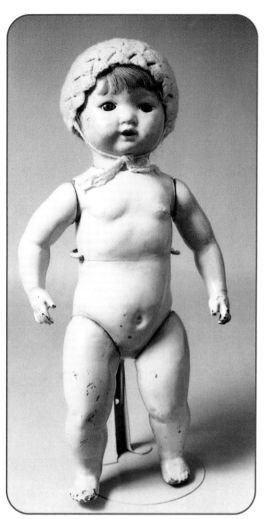

16". Marks: Ideal, underneath Compo Baby (see close-up of this mark and another of special constuction inside head).

All composition, fully jointed with steel springs. Replaced blond wig. Blue tin sleep eyes that rock individually. Open mouth, no teeth. Indented line at waist level.

Note: A thorough check of the Ideal ads for this doll in Playthings from 1916 to 1918 did not result in more information on the special construction inside the head. Apparently, it served only to hold the steel spring stringing. No explanation was found for the line across the torso. The doll was introduced in 1916 and frequently featured in their full-page ads. It was stressed that the doll was made of all composition and had flawlessly functioning sleep eyes. Further emphasized was that it could stand unaided, and a standing doll in profile was shown. (Actually, the doll cannot stand by itself.) The baby was available with painted or sleep eyes and with painted hair or wig. $150.00.

This illustration shows the special constuction inside Compo Baby's head. A cardboard cylinder was glued in place. Two disks are visible further down. The button in the middle seems to hold the stringing hook. All of this is located above the eye mechanism and does allow movement of the eyes in the usual manner.

Further note: This is not an ordinary socket head with rounded lower neck and socket. The head is flat at its lower end and so is the socket. In other words, the head can move only from side to side but not swivel.

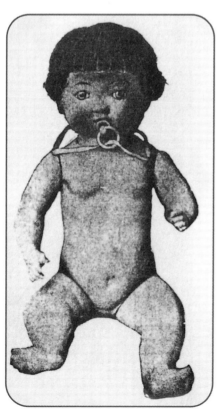

Close-up of mark of Compo Baby.

Close-up of Compo Baby as seen in a full-page ad in Toys and Novelties, *dated February 1918. The name Compo Baby was used in the ad. It also shows the very low placement of the navel.*

13". Marks: none (have individually rocking sleep eyes patented by Ideal.) Ca. 1919.
Flared composition head, short arms, and brown boots. Cloth body, upper arms, and legs, jointed with outside metal disks. Molded, painted light brown hair, blue tin sleep eyes, closed mouths. All original. Striped stockings serve as leg casings. $250.00 each.

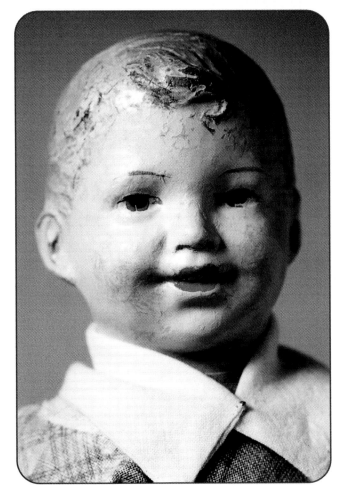

13". Marks: none. Doll is assumed to have been produced by Ideal. Same molded cap as their Farmer Boy.
Flared composition head, short arms, and molded light brown boots. Cloth body, upper arms, and legs, jointed with outside disks. Molded painted blond hair and molded cap painted the same color as the hair. Painted blue eyes. Open/closed mouth with four molded, painted upper teeth. Re-dressed. $125.00.

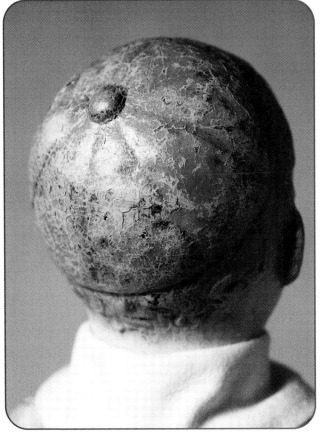

15". Marks: none. 1915 – 1920.
Composition flange head, hands, and molded brown boots. Cloth body and limbs, jointed with outside disks. Brown mohair wig, painted blue eyes, closed mouth. All original. Cynthia Whittaker collection. $150.00.

12½". Marks: Ideal // US of A
Composition flange head, short lower arms, and molded brown boots, cloth body and limbs jointed at shoulders and hips with outside disks. Molded, painted blond hair, blue tin sleep eyes, closed mouth. All original. Robin Tickner collection. $200.00.

13" Baby Mine. Marks: Ca. 1915.
Paper tag: See separate illustrations (front and back).
Flared composition head, short lower arms, and molded, brown boots. Cloth body, upper arms, and legs, jointed with pin and outside disks. Molded, painted blond hair, blue, individually rocking sleep eyes, open/cloesd mouth with four upper painted teeth. All original. Don and Arlene Jensen collection. $250.00.

Front and back side of Baby Mine label.
Note: Configuration of "Ideal" and "Baby Mine" on front tag is identical to that seen embossed on the back of the Baby Mine baby pictured in Collector's Encyclopedia of American Composition Dolls, Volume I. *The baby was advertised in* Playthings *in 1911.*

14". Marks: none (assumed to be Naughty Marietta). Ca. 1915. Flared composition head, short lower arms, and brown boots. Cloth body, upper arms, and legs, jointed with outside disks. Molded, painted light brown hair, painted blue eyes, open/closed mouth with four upper painted teeth. Original, except for hair ribbon. $150.00.

Ideal's Walking Dolls from the Early 1920s

In 1918, Georgene Averill of Averill Manufacturing Co., had introduced the Walking Life Like dolls (mama dolls). The early twenties saw a flurry of activity by various manufacturers with mechanical walking dolls. The next two illustrations show four examples of this type in four different sizes produced by Ideal. Note that four different head molds were used.

13". Marks: none (clue to identification: doll feautres the individually rocking sleep eyes that were patented by the Ideal Co.).
Flared composition head and short arms. Cloth body with walker mechanism at hips, cloth upper arms and legs. Dark brown mohair wig over molded hair, blue sleep eyes that rock individually, closed mouth. Socks seem to have been sown on when the leg was fashioned, but they are on top of the leg casing. Original shoes, old dress.
Note: A larger size Ideal walker of this type was sold by Sears Roebuck & Co. in 1923. $125.00.

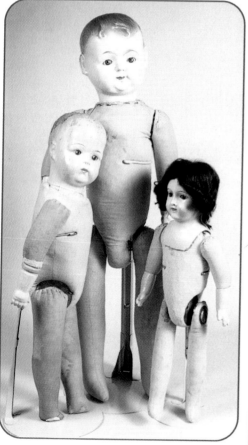

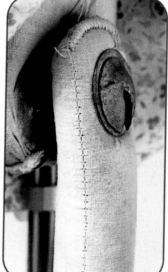

Close-up of walker mechanism of dolls seen in previous illustration.

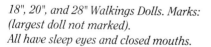

18", 20", and 28" Walkings Dolls. Marks:
(largest doll not marked).
All have sleep eyes and closed mouths.
Walker mechanism operation: When one foot is put down and pressure applied in a forward motion, the other automatically moves forward.
Note: Head of doll on the left is identical to that used for the Uneeda Bisquit Boy, except for the sleep eyes. The head of the 20" doll was previously used for Sanitary Baby and Peggy, also a baby (both illustrated). $100.00, $150.00, $125.00.

13½". Marks: Genuine // Twinkie Doll // copyr. 1916 // Eyes Pat //. Twikies Specialty. (The 1916 date refers only to the patent issued to Ideal for their special rocking eye).

Flared composition head, celluloid hands, cloth body and limbs, jointed at shoulders and hips with inside disks. Vest and shoes are removeable. Lower edge of vest is decorated with tiny bells. Molded, painted brown hair. Rocking sleep eyes, that in addition move from side to side. Closed mouth.

Measurements of hard cover book: 6 x 8½" Twinkie Town Tales. *Story in Rhyme by Carlyle Emery, Illustrations by Arthur Henderson. Copyright 1926 Hamilton-Brown Shoe Co.*

Note: Doll and book were promotional items used by the Hamilton-Brown Shoe Co. in the twenties and early thirties. Head was made by Ideal. Doll was probably assembled and sold by the Quaker Doll Co. of Philadelphia. (See Coleman II). A 2½" all bisque Twinkie was also available. Doll $350.00. Book $45.00.

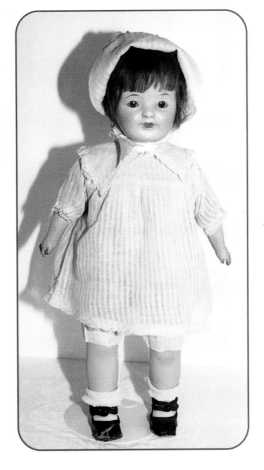

17". Marks: Ideal US of A Composition flange head, short arms, and legs to above the knee. Cloth body stuffed with excelsior, no shoulder joints, stitched hip joints. Brown mohair wig, blue sleep eyes, open/closed mouth with four painted upper teeth. All original. Cynthia Whittaker collection. $100.00.

22". Marks: Ideal (in diamond)

Paper label: Vanity Flossy Flirt

Composition flange head and lower legs. Rubber lower arms with curled fingers on right hand. Cloth body, upper arms, and legs. Jointed at shoulders, stitched hip joints. Blond mohair wig over molded hair. Gray tin sleep eyes that also move from side to side. Closed, smiling mouth. All original. Cynthia Whittaker collection.

Note: Ideal used the identical head for their Peter Pan, advertised in 1929. At the time, dolls with rubber limbs were an exciting novelty. In an ad, Vanity Flossy was seen holding a mirror in the curled fingers of her right hand and glancing into it with her "flirty" eyes. $200.00.

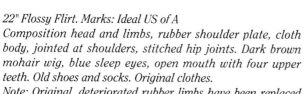

19" Flossy Flirt. Marks: Ideal (in diamond)
Compositon flange head and lower arms. Cloth body,
upper arms and legs, stitched hip joints. Brown mohair
wig, gray tin sleep eyes that also move from side to side,
closed mouth. All original. Cynthia Whittaker collection.
$200.00.

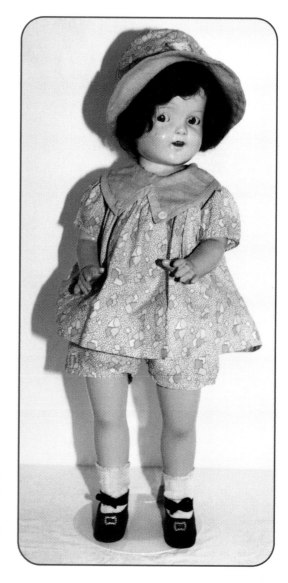

22" Flossy Flirt. Marks: Ideal US of A
Composition head and limbs, rubber shoulder plate, cloth
body, jointed at shoulders, stitched hip joints. Dark brown
mohair wig, blue sleep eyes, open mouth with four upper
teeth. Old shoes and socks. Original clothes.
Note: Original, deteriorated rubber limbs have been replaced
with compositon arms and legs. Cynthia Whittaker collection.
$125.00.

New Models of Tickletoes and Flossie Flirt

A full-page ad in the trade journal *Playthings*, dated January 1930, announced "New Models with rubber arms and legs – New Tickletoes and Flossie Flirt Dolls."

Both dolls had proven very popular with the toy buying public during the mid- and late twenties. Usually, "new models" meant that new clothes had been designed or last year's dolls had been outfitted with new wigs. Apparently, in this case, Ideal thought it worth their while to create new, more up-to-date heads for these two very popular models.

For this reason and to facilitate a better comparison study, the following illustrations have been marked Old Tickletoes and New Tickletoes. The same was done for the New and Old Flossie Flirt.

Although by 1939, Ideal's all rubber Betsy Wetsy had been a great success, their 1939 catalog still offered a Tickletoes baby with those "soft flesh-like rubber arms and legs" and a composition head. However, Tickletoes again had a new face (not illustrated). This time a so called dolly face.

16" Old Tickletoes. Marks: Ideal// Us of A in diamond (Playthings, *June 1930).*
Composition flange head, rubber arms and legs to above the knee, cloth body, jointed at shoulders, stitched hip joints, Faintly molded, paitned blond hair, blue sleep eyes that also move from side to side. Open mouth with two upper painted teeth. All original. $350.00.

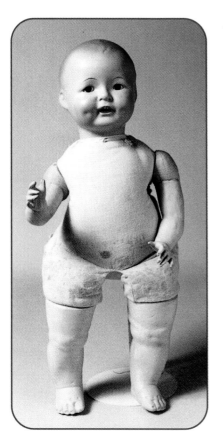

16" Old Tickletoes, undressed.
Though produced later, the 21" Tickletoes pictured in this section shows identical construction.

Close-up of 16" Old Tickletoes.
Note different treatment of molded hair and open mouth from the later, 21" Tickletoes seen in this section. A new mold was created for the later Tickletoes, though identical hang tags were used for both.

21" New Tickletoes. Marks: Ideal // US of A (in diamond)
Rectangular tag: " I Say Ma-Ma"
Tag with doll picture: See separate illustration.
Streamer: "Second Prize // prettiest doll // Canton (Ohio) Play-ground 1934 // Waterworks"
Composition flange head, rubber arms and legs to above the knee, cloth body. Jointed at shoulders, stitched hip joints. Mold-ed, painted blond hair, blue sleep eyes which also move from side to side. Open mouth with two upper, inset teeth. All original. Cynthia Whittaker collection. $350.00.

Close-up of 21" New Tickletoes.
Compare with 16" Old Tickletoes. A newly created head mold was used for the doll shown here.

Front panel of original box of 21" New Tickletoes.

Note the original price tag. The doll was sold by Hearn and cost $4.94, a considerable sum in 1934.

Front and back panel of package insert for 21" New Tickletoes.

Note the copyright date listed there of 1928 (for Tickletoes). Cynthia Whittaker collection.

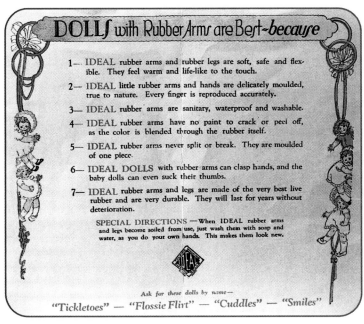

Inside page of package insert for 21" New Tickletoes. Cynthia Whittaker collection.

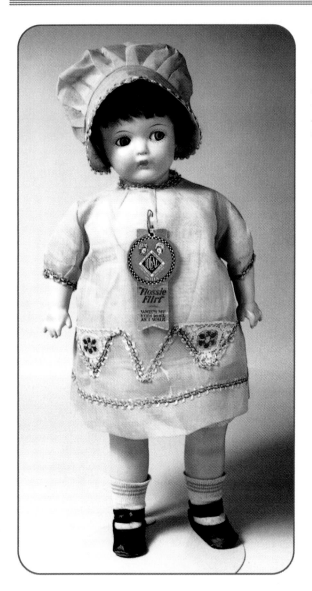

19" Old Flossie Flirt. Marks: US of A (in diamond). Late twenties. Composition flange head, lower arms and legs to above the knee. Cloth body, upper arms and legs, stitiched hip joints. Brown mohair wig was glued directly to the head (no wig cap). Individually rocking blue sleep eyes that also move from side to side. Open/closed mouth with two painted upper teeth. All original, including two-sided paper tag (see separate illustration).

Note: Some Flossie Flirt dolls were produced with composition limbs. Fewer examples with rubber limbs have survived in excellent condition. $600.00 mint.

Front and back of Flossie Flirt doll tag.

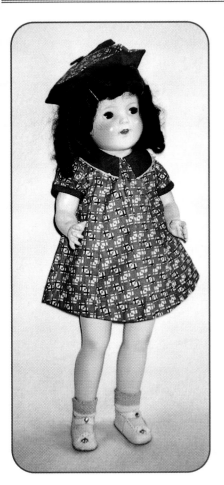

22" New Flossy Flirt. Marks: US of A (in diamond). 1930 – 1934.

Composition swivel head and full legs, rubber shoulder plate and arms to above the elbow, cloth body and upper arms. Dark brown mohair wig, brown sleep eyes, that also move from side to side. Open mouth with two upper teeth. Dimple in chin. Original underwear, shoes, and socks. Original box. Dress and beret added. Though the doll was found in unplayed with condition in the original box, her dress is believed not to be a factory original. It is handmade of silk and hand embroidered.

Note: Though very popular at the time, because of the rubber arms the attrition rate for this doll was high. Examples are difficult to locate today. The 1934 Sears catalog carried the new Flossie Flirt in 16" , 19", and 20". It was also offered in the 1933 – 34 Butler Brother's catalog (Anderston II, pg. 846). Anita Maxwell collection. $350.00 up.

New Flossie Flirt has a slightly smiling, open mouth with two teeth. Her arm construction is the same as on the Old Flossy Flirt. Instead of lower rubber or composition legs with stitched hip joints, she features full composition legs with disk hip joints.

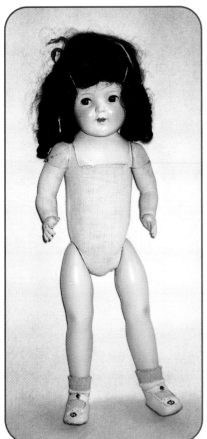

For completeness sake, a picture of the "as found in the original box" handmade dress is included.

301

17" Buster Brown. Marks: Ideal U.S. of A. (in diamond). Ca. 1929 –. Composition flange head and very short lower arms, and legs to above the knee. No shoulder joints, stitched hip joints. Cloth body, upper arms and legs. Body and upper arms stuffed with excelsior, upper legs stuffed with cotton. Molded, painted blong hair, blue sleep eyes that also rock individually. Closed mouth. All original, including fragile silk bow. Brass buttons are attached to jacket front by two prongs each.

Note: Buster Brown was a cartoon character created by Richard F. Outcault in 1902. No Ideal advertising was located for this doll. $350.00.

15" Kandy Kid (1928 Sears Roebuck catalog). Marks: US of A (in diamond)

Composition flange head and legs to above the knee. Rubber arms. Cloth body, upper arms, and legs, jointed at shoulders and hips. Molded, painted blond hair and blue tin sleep eyes that also move from side to side. Closed, smiling mouth. Redressed in appropriate old clothes.

Note: Same head mold as Buster Brown seen in previous illustration. $150.00.

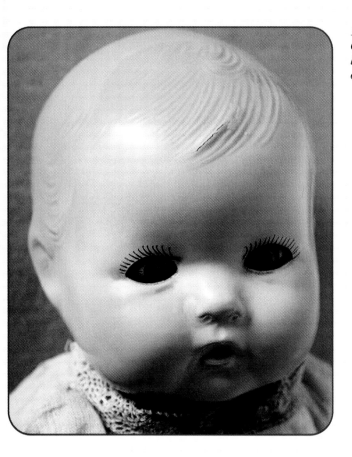

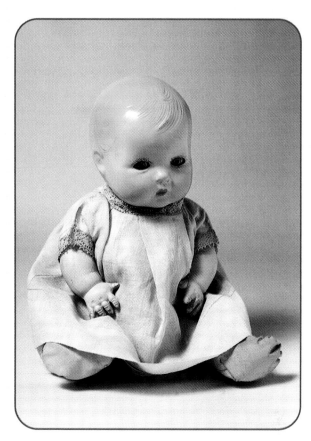

11". Marks: none (has individually rocking Ideal eyes). Early 1930s. Composition head, heavy rubber body and limbs, fully jointed, bent legs. Individually rocking, blue tin sleep eyes, closed mouth. All original, including socks and booties. $85.00.

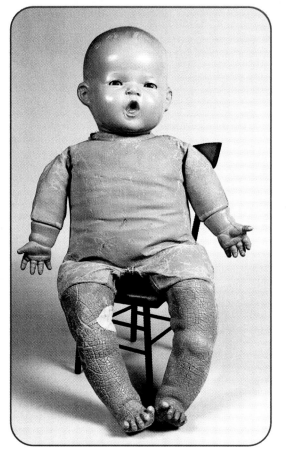

22". Marks: © by B. Lipfert. This is Snoozie (Playthings, November 1933). *Composition flange head, rubberized cloth body, upper arms, and legs. Rubber hands and slightly bent legs, stitched joints at shoulders and hips. Molded, painted blond hair, sleep eyes and open/closed mouth. Special eye mechanism. The 1933 ad stated: "Snoozie lies on her back wide awake, with her baby-like glass (actually celluloid) eyes wide open. But lay her on her right side and she goes to sleep peacefully."*

Note: For additional info on Snoozie see Doll Reader *March/April 1998 and September 1999, "American Doll Showcase" column. An open mouth version of Snoozie with regular sleep eyes was also produced. $85.00 (poor condition, no clothes).*

Shirley Temple, Ideal's Biggest Hit

Ideal's biggest success was the Shirley Temple doll, produced under license from Fox Film Corp., and created by famous doll sculptor, Bernard Lipfert. Introduced in 1934, she was still listed in their 1939 catalog. She was made in seven sizes and dressed in copies of the costumes Shirley wore in the movies in which she starred.

18". Marks on head: Shirley Temple // Ideal N. & T. C
On back: Shirley Temple
Dress tag: A Genuine // Shirley Temple // Doll Dress // Reliable Toy Co., Ltd. // Made in Canada
All composition, fully jointed. Blond mohair wig, hazel sleep eyes, open mouth with six upper teeth. All original including metal pin.
Note: This costume is a copy of the one worn by Shirley Temple in the film The Little Colonel. *$2,300.00.*

18". Marks: Shirley Temple (on head and body)
Pin: Genuine Shirley Temple Doll // The World's Darling
All composition, fully jointed. Blond mohair wig, sleep eyes, open mouth with six upper teeth. All original. $1,000.00.

13". Marks: Shirley Temple (on head and body)
Pin: Genuine Shirley Temple Doll // The World's Darling
All composition, fully jointed. Blond mohair wig, sleep eyes, open mouth with six upper teeth. All original. $900.00.

8½" Mr. Peanut. Marks: none. 1935.
All wood, including his top hat. Jointed at shoulders and hips. In addition, ball joints at elbows, wrists, knees, and ankles. Drill holes in both hands. Note: See Dolls Created by Joseph Kallus, Dorothy S. Coleman, Spinning Wheel's Complete Book of Dolls, *1975. Mrs. Coleman states that Mr. Peanut was designed by Mr. Kallus for Ideal Toy & Novelty Co. Though Mr. Peanut is made of all wood, he is included here for completeness sake. $190.00.*

12" Charlie McCarthy hand puppet. Marks on head: Charlie McCarthy. (Playthings, April 1939).
Marks front: Edgar Bergen's // Charlie McCarthy // Made in USA
Composition head with molded on hat, brown painted eyes, closed mouth. Wire monocle. Cloth mitten imprinted in front to look like pants, jacket, vest, and tie. $95.00.

20" Princess Beatrix (1939 Ideal catalog, pgs. 8 – 9).
Compostion flange head, full arms, and bent legs to above the knees. Cloth body and upper legs, stitched hip joints, jointed at shoulders. Molded, painted, curly dark brown hair, brown sleep eyes that also move from side to side. They were advertised as "Magic eyes." Closed mouth. Redressed.
Note: This head was used by other companies as well. It is Princess Beatrix when the doll has the clenched fists with full compositon arms which are wired on at the shoulders and can rotate. (These arms were also used on "Baby Georgene" by the Averills.) $100.00.

306

12" Sunny Sue (see 1939 Ideal catalog). Marks: Ideal Doll
Composition head is mounted on a wooden neck joint which is nailed
to the wooden body. Composition hands, wooden shoes. Arms and legs
are made of a woven, flexible wire rod, neck is jointed. Molded, painted
brown hair, painted blue eyes, closed mouth. All original. $250.00.

12" Sunny Sam (see 1939 Ideal catalog).
Same construction as Sunny Sue. All original.
Note: Was also offered in military uniforms, and as a black-skinned
version. $250.00.

Front panel of Snow White's original box.

21" Snow White. Marks on back: Shirley Temple // 22
Marks on head: US of A in diamond. Early 1940s.
All compostion, fully jointed. Black mohair wig,
brown sleep eyes that also move from side to side.
Open mouth with four upper teeth. All original,
including box. Caryl Silber collection. $500.00.

14". Marks on chest: S. Late 1940s.
Marks at waist: Des. & Copyright by Superman // Made by
Ideal Novelty & Toy Co.
Composition head and upper torso molded as one piece.
Lower torso and limbs segmented wood. Molded, painted
dark hair and painted brown eyes. Open/closed mouth with
white line between lips to indicate teeth. Real cloth cape. All
original. Susan Ackerman collection. $1,500.00 +.

20". Marks: none on doll. Ca. 1950.

Double-sided paper hang tag: An Ultrafine Product // An // Ideal Doll // Made in U.S.A. By // Ideal Novelty & Toy Co. // Hollis 7 // New York

All composition, fully jointed. Blond mohair wig with long braids, blue sleep eyes, closed mouth. All original.

Note: This is obviously a forerunner of the very popular all hard plastic Toni doll produced by Ideal in the 1950s. $2,300.00, rare in original box.

Jointed Waist Doll

10". Marks: none.
All composition, jointed only at shoulders and lower torso (leg and lower torso one piece). Molded, painted blond hair with molded ridge over the crown to help hold a real hair ribbon. Painted blue eyes, closed mouth. Molded, painted pink shoe. Clothes are old and seem to have been made for her. Also see black dolls under Lu Jon. $200.00.

Joy Doll Corporation
New York, New York

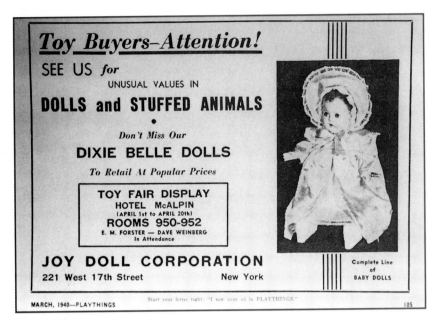

Half-page ad, Playthings, *March 1940.*
As can be seen from this ad, mama dolls were still being actively promoted in the forties. It aslo indicates that the Joy Doll Corporation offered dolls in the medium price range.

Full-page ad placed by the Joy Doll Corporation of New York in 1939, showing: Girl of To-Morrow, Mother of All Nations, Maid of America, Dandy Goodwill.
Text with illustration seen in the middle of the ad:
"This official seal on each unit is your assurance of authentic World's Fair design. Our N. Y. W. F. License No. 2441.
New York World's Fair 1939, Inc. certifies that our organization is licensed to produce and distribute Dolls and Stuffed Toys incorporating its name, copyright, and license. It is unlawful to use New York World's Fair Designs without such license."

"Two Favorites in the Joy Doll Company's Line of Licensed New York World's Fair Dolls," caption and illustration, Playthings, *June 1939.*

12". Marks: none.
Metal pin front: Baby Joyce // The Children's Favorite
Metal pin rim: Joy Doll Corp. // 30 Division Street // Brooklyn NY
All composition, fully jointed. Molded, painted brown hair, painted blue eyes, closed mouth. All original.
Note: Came with unpainted hair and remnants of glue, indication that the doll originally had a wig. $125.00.

Since the doll itself is unmarked, this close-up illustration, showing the very distinctive curl on top of her head, should be helpful with identifying other unmarked dolls.

Close-up of pin.
As can be seen in the picture, Baby Joyce was also sold wigged.

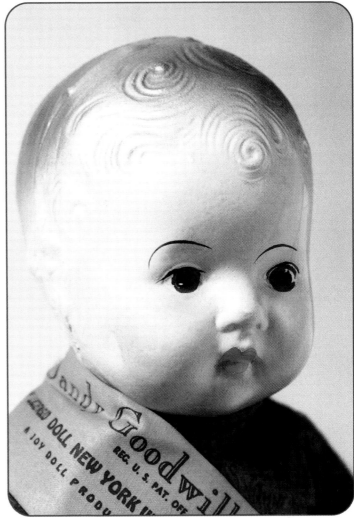

13". Marks: none.

Decal on belt: New York // World's Fair // 1939

Orange shoulder band: Dandy Goodwill // Reg. U.S. Pat. Off. // Officially Licensed Doll New York World's Fair 1939 // A Joy Doll Product

All composition, fully jointed. Molded, painted blond hair, painted brown eyes, closed mouth. Feet painted black to simulate shoes. Symbol of Trylon and Perisphere on cap and belt. All original. For further, extensive information see "Dolls of the New York World's Fair," Don Jensen, Doll Reader, November 1992.

Note: Joy Doll Corp. had an exclusive license to produce World's Fair souvenir dolls. Margo Delaughter collection. $250.00 up.

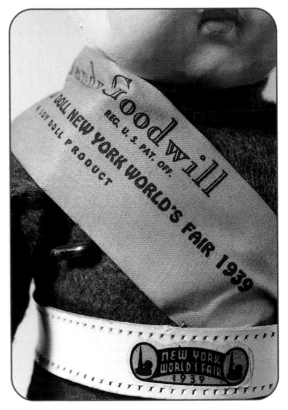

Note the World's Fair symbol on belt (and cap). Quote from contempaorary souvenir booklet: "The Trylon and Perisphere is the Center of the Fair. It arrests the attention for miles around: The Trylon piercing the sky 700 feet above the earth, symbol of the Fair's lofty purpose and the Perisphere, a huge hollow globe 200 feet in diameter." Close-up of unmarked head with unusual modeling will help identify bare dolls.

Kewpie Type

17" Kewpie Type. Marks: none.
Composition flange head, cloth body and limbs with sewn in pink booties.
Molded, painted brown whisps of hair, with a very pronounced curl on fore-
head. Painted blue eyes, closed mouth. Original rayon dress. $75.00.

Knickerbocker Toy Co., Inc.

10". Marks on head: Jiminey Cricket // W.D. PR. KN.T. Co. // USA // © (produced under license from Walt Disney Productions)
All composition, jointed at shoulders and neck, only four fingers, feet molded together at heels. Painted features, black felt hat, yellow felt vest and black tail coat. Gayle and Jerry Reilly collection. $550.00.

17" Pinocchio. Marks on head: Pinocchio // Knickerbocker Toy Co. // © // Made in USA // Walt Disney Toy Product. (Playthings, *August 1939).*
Paper tag front: Walt Disney's Pinocchio
Paper tag back: Made Under Sanitary Laws // Trade Mark // Knickerbocker // Toy Co. Inc. // New York
All compostion, fully jointed. While there are molded indications of hinges at elbows and knees, there are no actual hinges. Molded, painted black hair and painted blue eyes, closed mouth. All original. Caryl Silber collection. $500.00.

Blondie

In the next three illustrations we see characters from the comic strip Blondie (Blondie, Dagwood, and Baby Dumplings). This perennially popular strip was created by Chic Young (1901 – 1973) and can still be found in today's newspapers country wide. It is now created by Denis LeBrun.

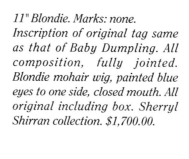

11" Blondie. Marks: none. Inscription of original tag same as that of Baby Dumpling. All composition, fully jointed. Blondie mohair wig, painted blue eyes to one side, closed mouth. All original including box. Sherryl Shirran collection. $1,700.00.

14" Dagwood. Marks: Knickerbocker Toy (no "c")
Tag on pants: "A Sanitary Toy // Makers // Knickerbocker Toy Co. Inc, // New York
Composition flange head and hands, cloth body, arms, and legs with sewn on oil cloth shoes. Molded, painted brown hair and black eyes, closed mouth. All original. Sherryl Shirran collection. $750.00.

9½" Baby Dumplings. Marks: Knickerbocker Toy.
Tag front: Columbia Pictures Corp. // Blondie // with // Baby Dumpling // Dagwood // and // Daisy // C. King Features Syndicate.
Tag back: (Inside shape of horseshoe) Made under sanitary laws (picture of a man) Trademark // Knickerbocker Toy Co. Inc. N.Y.
Cloth tag in back: A Sanitary Toy // Makers // Knickerbocker Toy Co. Inc. // New York
All composition, jointed at neck and shoulders. Body and legs one piece, molded shoes and socks. Hands have only four fingers. Molded, painted borwn hair, painted black eyes, closed mouth. Tagged original clothes. Hazel Coons collection. $450.00 up.

L.D. Co.

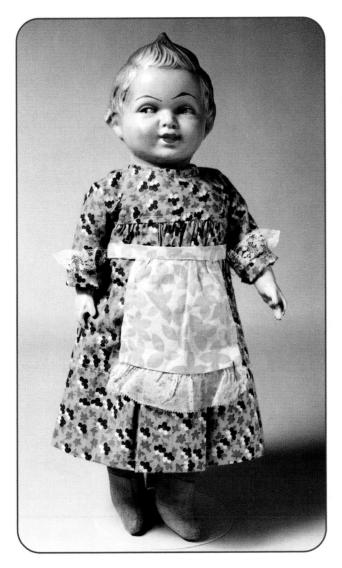

15". Marks: L.D. Co. // 1915
Flaired composition head and short arms. Cloth body, upper arms, and legs. White casing for feet also serves as boots. Jointed at shoulders and hips with outside metal disks. Molded, painted light brown hair with top knot. Painted blue eyes, open/closed mouth. Re-dressed. $175.00.

L.Q.D. Co.

18". Marks: L.Q.D. (before 1920)
Composition flange head and short arms. Cloth body, upper arms, and full legs, jointed at shoulders with inside disks and at hips with outside disks. Molded, painted blond hair and painted blue eyes, open/closed mouth. All original. $150.00.

Lu Jon
Colored Doll Co.
36 West 32nd Street
New York

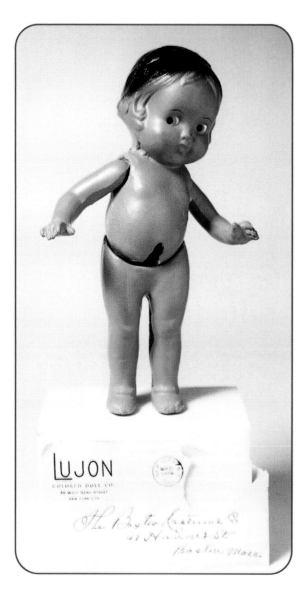

10". Marks: none.
All composition, jointed at shoulders and hip area. Molded, painted black hair, painted brown eyes, closed mouth. Molded shoes are not painted.
Note: Doll is in unplayed with condition and was accompanied by a letter sent by LU JON, dated May 20, 1941, and addressed to The Baxter Costume Co., 47 Hanover St., Boston Mass. In it, receipt of payment for sample dolls is acknowledged. The letter further stated, that Lu Jon manufactured colored dolls exclusively. $150.00 up. Janet Shiely collection.

10". Marks: none.
All composition, jointed only at shoulders and hip area. Molded, painted black hair with three drill holes and three black cotton yarn pigtails glued in place. Painted brown eyes, closed mouth. Molded, painted shoes. Re-dressed.
Note: See white version of this doll under Jointed Waist Doll. $150.00.

318

Madame Louise Doll Co., Inc.
405 Denison Bldg.
Syracuse, New York
1939 – 1947

19". Marks: none.
Box label: Madame Louise Doll Co. Inc. // 405 Division Street //
Syracuse NY // Madame Louise
All composition, fully jointed. Blond mohair wig, brown sleep eyes,
open mouth with four upper teeth. All original. $200.00.

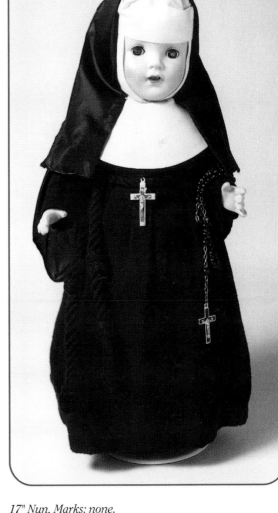

17" Nun. Marks: none.
Box label: See separate illustration.
All composition, fully jointed. Sleep eyes, open mouth
with two upper teeth. All original, including cross and
rosary. $275.00.

9" Magic Light Doll (Magic Light Products Co., New York). Marks: none, Patsy type.

All composition, fully jointed. Lightly molded, painted brown hair and painted blue eyes, closed mouth. All original including box.

Note: Instructions were given to hold the doll to a light for a few seconds for it to glow, also assuring that no phosphorus or aluminum was used in production and that the doll was perfectly harmless. Collection Barbara's Dolls. $150.00 up.

Maxine Doll Company
New York City
1926 – 1930+

Made mama dolls, baby dolls, and all-composition child dolls (Coleman 11, pg 821).

Original outfit for Gloria Lou.

20". Marks: none.
Paper tag: Gloria Lou. See separate illustration of tag.
Composition shoulder head, full arms, and legs to above the knee. Cloth body and upper legs, jointed at shoulders, stitched hip joints. Dark brown human hair wig, blue sleep eyes, open mouth with four upper teeth. Replaced dress. See separate illustration of the very fragile, original organdy dress and bonnet. Elizabeth Conde collection. $175.00.

Maiden America Toy Mfg. Company, Inc.
New York City

Little is known about the Maiden America Toy Mfg. Company, and they have come to doll collectors' attention only as the manufacturers of the Maiden America doll. As the following two ads show, the company produced addtional dolls. Unfortunately, little information is given. Pictured seems to be one type of doll dressed in various costumes. They seem made of all compostion, but may have been jointed only at the shoulders. None of them have ever been seen. It is hoped that by including these illustrations some of the dolls might come to light. Particularly the ones dressed as service personnel might have survived in their original clothes.

Full-page ad, Playthings, *May 1919.*

Full-page ad, Toys and Novelties, *August 1919.*

8". Marks: none.
Paper label front: Maiden America // Reg. US Pat.Off. // The National Doll
Paper label foot: Des. Pat. // 8-24-15 // © 1915 // Kate Silverman
All composition, jointed only at shoulders. Molded, painted brown hair with top knot. Painted blue eyes, closed mouth. All original.
$300.00.

Mama Dolls
Manufacturers/Sellers Unknown

Mama dolls, first introduced by Georgene Averill of Averill Manfacturing, featured mama voice boxes in their stuffed cloth bodies. Stitched hip joints allowed them to "walk" freely (legs swinging back and forth). They were offered in various price ranges, as the examples shown here reflect.

Over time, dolls with new attributes were introduced by all makers with steady regularity, but the mama dolls remained popular during the twenties, thirties, and into the forties.

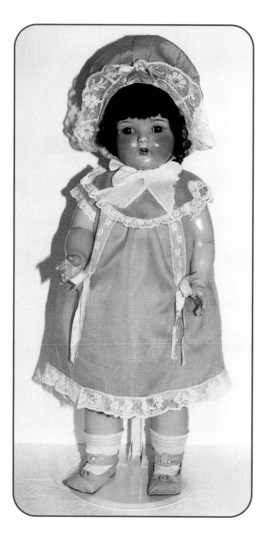

27½". Marks: none. Mid-1920s (seee 1925 Sears catalog). Composition shoulder head, full arms, and legs to above the knee, jointed at shoulders, stitched hip joints. Dark brown mohair wig, blue tin sleep eyes, open mouth with two upper teeth, all original. Cynthia Whittaker collection. $350.00.

16". Marks: none. 1920s. Composition shoulder head, short arms, and legs to above the knee. Cloth body stuffed with excelsior. Stitched hip joints, no shoulder joints. Molded, painted blond hair, painted blue eyes, closed mouth. All original. $75.00.

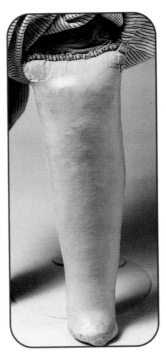

20" mama doll. Marks: none. 1920s.
Composition shoulder head and short arms. Cloth body, upper arms, and legs. Cloth legs and feet were dipped into composition right up to the hip joint and painted. No shoulder joints, stitched hip joints. Molded, painted light brown hair and painted blue eyes. Open/closed mouth, re-dressed.
Note: The dipped legs are a very unusual feature that has never been seen before. $80.00.

14". Marks: none.
Composition shoulder head, arms, and legs to above the knee. Cloth body and upper legs. Pin-jointed arms, stitched hip joints. Brown mohair wig, gray tin sleep eyes, closed mouth. All original except for shoes and socks. Cynthia Whittaker collection. $100.00.

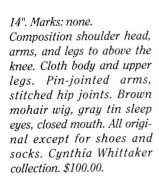

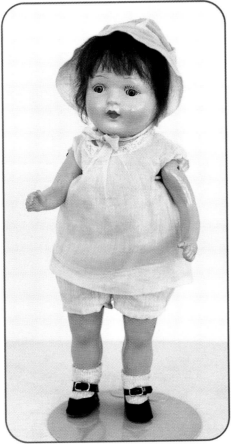

18" Toddler. Marks: none. 1940s.
Composition flange head and lower limbs, cloth body and upper limbs, stitched hip joints. Molded, painted hair. Stationary eyes consist of plastic pupil and iris set directly into composition, closed mouth. All original. (Eyes may be a case of war shortages, this type is rarely seen.) $100.00.

22". Marks: none.
Composition flange head lower arms and sturdy toddler legs. Cloth body, upper arms, and legs. Stitched hip joints. Molded, painted brown hair, sleep eyes and open mouth with two upper teeth. All original. Michelle Brusic collection. $250.00.

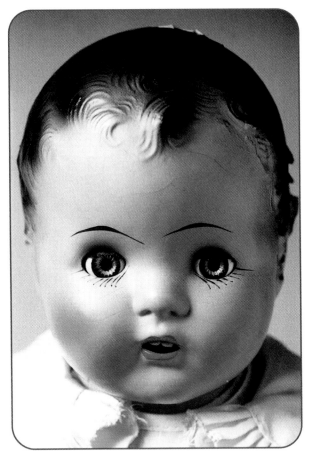

20". Marks: none. 1940s.
Compostion flange head, arms to above the elbow, and legs to above the knees, titched hip joints. Molded, painted brown hair, blue sleep eyes, open mouth with two upper teeth. All original, except the booties. $150.00.

19". Marks: none.
Composition flange head, full composition arms and legs to above the knee. Cloth body, jointed at shoulders, stitched hip joints. Red mohair wig over molded hair, blue sleep eyes, that also move from side to side (so called flirty eyes), closed mouth. All original except for booties.
Note: The head used for this doll seems to be identical to that of Ideal's Princess Beatrix, as seen in Ideal's 1939 catalog, including the flirting eyes. An identical head has been seen on a doll produced by Sayco and on one additional unmarked example. Therefore, if a doll has no identification marks, she cannot be called a Princess Beatrix doll. $175.00.

Metropolitan Doll Co.

12" Pair. Marks: Metropolitan // Doll Co.
Cloth streamers: TERCENTARY CELEBRATION // 1630 – 1930
Composition heads, cloth bodies and limbs and celluloid shoes. Molded, painted blond hair
with molded hair loop, painted blue eyes, open/closed mouths. All original.
Note: These dolls were obviously produced on special order for a special event. Shoulder plates
on the heads were cut off, so that they could be tied into the bodies. The material used for the
bodies and limbs is a knitted jersey, similar to that used by the Nelke Doll Company for their
all cloth dolls. The possibility exists that these dolls were produced by the Nelke Company.
The city of Boston, Massachusetts, was founded in 1630. The dolls may have been sold on the
occsaion of Boston's three hundredth birthday.

Mitred Box Co.
New York City
1911 – 1917

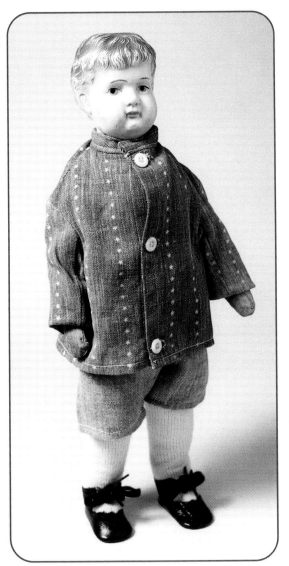

15". Marks: none. Ca. 1912.
Head is a copy of an early German celluloid doll by the Turtle Mark firm.
Flared composition head, cloth body and limbs, jointed with outside disks (stumb hands). Molded, painted light brown hair and painted blue eyes. Closed mouth, re-dressed.
Note: An all-composition doll with this identical head had previously been identified (on the basis of an illustrated ad) as having been sold by the Mitred Box Co. For this reason, the doll in question is listed here.

On the right is the all-composition doll and in the back the celluloid original. Left to right: $125.00, $175.00, $250.00.

Modern Toy Co.
Brooklyn, New York
1914 – 1926

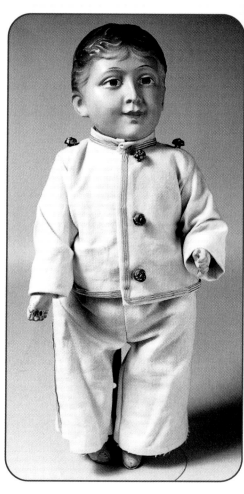

15" Babbitt Cleanser Boy. Marks: none (Playthings ad February, 1916 — see next illustration).
Flared composition head, short lower arms, and molded, white boots. Cloth body, upper arms (one bent), and legs, jointed with outside disks. Molded, painted light brown hair, painted brown eyes, closed mouth. Re-dressed.
Note: Left arm is bent so that the doll could hold a box of Babbitt Cleanser. $150.00.

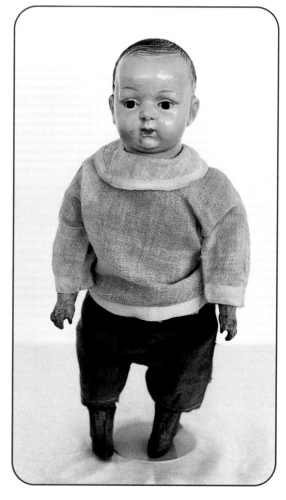

13". Marks: M.T. Co. Ca. 1915.
Flared composition head, short arms, and molded boots. Cloth body, upper arms, and legs, jointed with outside disks. Molded, painted brown hair and eyes, closed mouth. Old clothes. Cynthia Whittaker collection. $150.00.

Full-page ad, Playthings, *February 1916.*

Natural Doll Company
New York City
Established 1915

1927, Member of the American Doll Manufacturing Association.
1931, Advertised that they made doll parts for leading American doll manufacturers since 1917.
Trade names: Just Lyk and Ritzi (Coleman II, pg. 879).

12". Marks: none.
Paper Tag: "It's a Natural" Ritzy Chubby Baby Dolls // Natural Doll Co., Inc. // Est. 1915 // Made In U.S.A.
All composition, jointed only at shoulders and hips. Molded, painted light brown hair, painted blue eyes, open/closed mouth. All original (dress stapled on in back). $95.00.

New Era Toy and Novelty Co.

9". Marks: none (See Playthings, *June 1921, New Era Toy and Novelty Co. Newark, NJ — next illustration).*

The Kimball Boy (pictured also was a Kimball Girl, with ball in left hand), "Dolls With A Punch, The Kimball Kids."

All composition, jointed only at shoulders with steel springs. Molded, painted brown hair, painted black eyes, closed mouth. Molded boxing gloves, shoes, and socks. Costumes came in six different colors. $150.00.

Nun

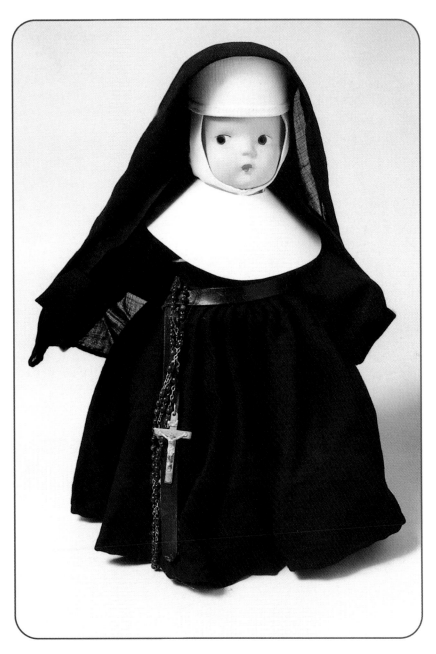

12". Marks: none.
All composition, jointed at shoulders and hips only with steel springs. Painted blue eyes, closed mouth. Nun's habit seems authentic. It is well sewn and made of excellent fabrics (fine wool skirt etc.). $80.00.

Oriental Men

16" Oriental Man. Marks: none.
Composition flange head with molded cap, molded, drooping mustache and goatee. Cloth body and limbs, stitched shoulder and hip joints. Sewn in black cloth boots. Molded, painted black hair and painted black eyes, closed mouth. All original. $125.00.

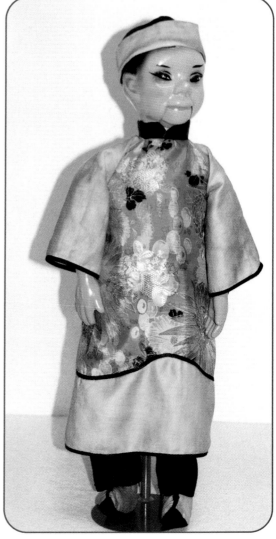

21". Marked: K. S.
Composition flange head and hands, cloth body, upper arms, and legs. Molded, painted black hair and painted black eyes, jointed lower jaw. String at back of neck to operate the jointed jaw. All original with matching cap and cloth shoes. Don and Arlene Jensen collection. $250.00.

Patsy Look-Alike Dolls

The Effanbee Company had introduced their Patsy doll in 1928. Her modern, up-to-date look was very appealing. She met with instant success and was imitated and copied outright by small as well as large doll manufactures. Following are some examples of those look-alikes. Their sellers are not known.

14" (without cap). Marks: none.
Composition shoulder head, cloth body (soft flannel) and limbs. No joints. Molded, painted blond hair, painted blue eyes, closed mouth. Cloth cap came glued on. Separate vest, belt, and tie.
Note: Though it is a shoulder head, the modeling is identical to that of Effanbee's Patsy. This fact does not guarantee that the toy was produced by Effanbee. $40.00.

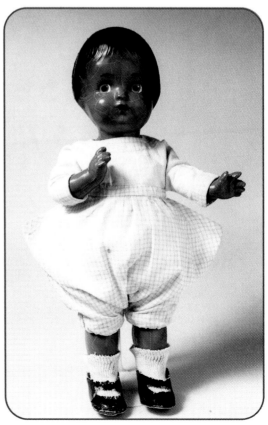

9". Marks: none.
All composition, jointed at shoulders and hips only. Molded shoes and socks are not painted. Molded, painted blond hair, painted black eyes, closed mouth. Original teddy and dress. $40.00.

13". Marks: none.
All composition, fully jointed. Molded, painted reddish brown hair with molded hair loop, painted blue eyes, closed mouth. Re-dressed. $85.00.

13½". Marked: Phyllis (low on her back)
All composition, jointed only at the shoulders. Molded, painted black hair, painted brown eyes, closed mouth. All original. Janet Shiely collection. $85.00.

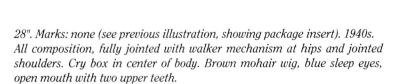

Paris Doll Company
New York, New York

Original, illustrated package insert for the Peggy walking doll. The small print on the left reads: "In order to make Peggy walk, stand in back of her, holding her by the shoulder as you would a baby learning to walk. With her feet on the floor, keep her erect and then walk gently behind her, giving a light push. You will see her make forward steps, just like a baby. To make the Peggy cry, first hold her face downward and then tilt her over her back.

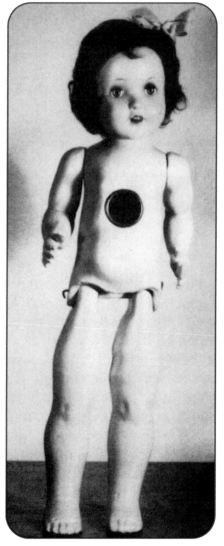

28". Marks: none (see previous illustration, showing package insert). 1940s. All composition, fully jointed with walker mechanism at hips and jointed shoulders. Cry box in center of body. Brown mohair wig, blue sleep eyes, open mouth with two upper teeth.
Note: This doll was also produced of hard plastic. $50.00.

Perfect Toy Manufacturing
New York City

18". Marks: Perfect. 1930s.
Composition shoulder head, arms, and legs to above the knee. Cloth
body and upper legs. Jointed at shoulders, stitched hip joints. Original
brown mohair wig, blue tin sleep eyes, open/closed mouth with three
painted teeth. All original. Cynthia Whittaker collection. $150.00.

Personality

29". Marks: none.

Composition shoulder head and hands, cloth body and limbs, no hip joints. Slightly molded brown hair and two-tone painted eyes. Open/closed mouth with six painted, upper teeth, painted brown mustache. All original except for scarf and boots.

Note: This doll has the same leg construction as the Charles Lindbergh doll — no evidence of ever having had feet. Therefore, he was restored with similar oilcloth boots as Lindy, that have been stuffed and attached.

Further note: This doll was sold as representing John Barrymore. So far, nothing has been found (advertising etc.) to substantiate this claim. $400.00.

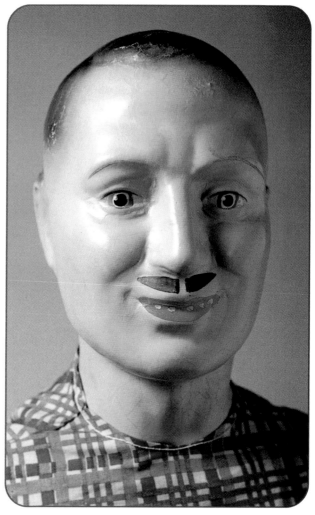

Peter Puppet Playthings, Inc.

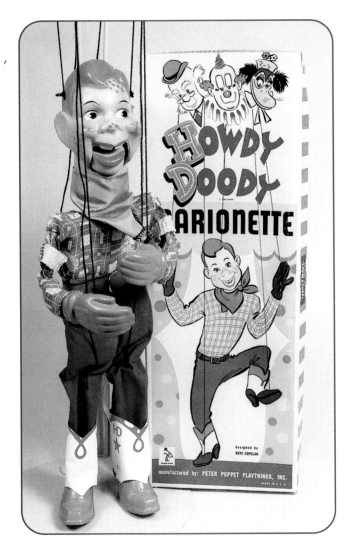

16" Howdy Doody Marionette. Marks: none.
On Box: Designed by Raye Copelan, manufacyured by: Peter Puppet Playthings, Inc. Made in U.S.A., ©Bob Smith, 'Unitrol' pat. No. 2,509,135
Composition head with jointed jaw, composition hands and molded brown boots. Boots mounted on wooden sticks. Body consists of two separate, rectangular pieces of wood. Neck hardware stapled to upper wooden body. All original including string mechanism and oilcloth spats which are marked HD and box. $275.00.

Inside cover of the Howdy Doody box, giving operating instructions for the marionette.

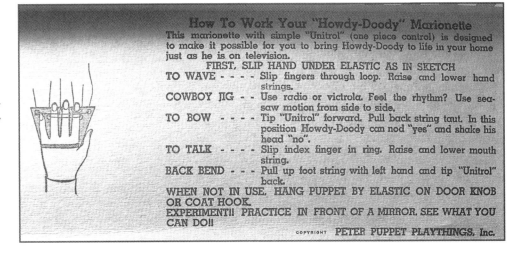

Ca. 15" Clarabell Clown. Marks: none. See Howdy Doody. (Clarabell was a member of the Howdy Doody team.) Ca. 1950.
Composition head, hands, and red shoes. Molded, painted red tufts of hair, red nose, black eyes, moveable jaw. All original red clown suit with blue striped collar. $150.00+.

Ca. 15" Princess Summerfall-Winterspring. Marked: ©P.P.P. (see pictures on dress).
Character from Howdy Doody show.
Composition head and shoes. Painted black hair, real cotton yarn pig tails. Painted brown eyes, moveable jaw, yellow plastic gloves. All original. $175.00 and up.

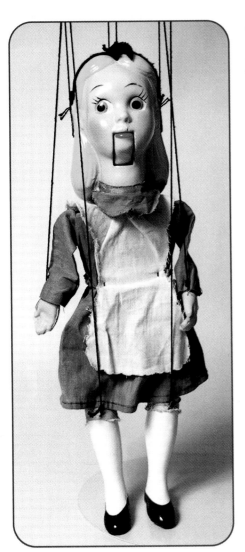

15" Alice in Wonderland. Marks: ©P.P.P. (inside of hair).
Composition head, hands, and legs to the knee. Block of wood for body. Molded, painted yellow hair and painted blue eyes, moveable jaw, molded, painted black slippers and white stockings. All original including black hair ribbon. $125.00.

Ca. 15" Marks: ©P.P.P. Ca. 1950.
Composition head, hands, and red shoes. Molded, painted white hair and painted black eyes, moveable jaw, two painted upper teeth, block of wood for body, all original. $100.00.

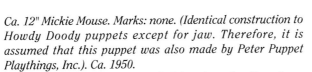

Ca. 12" Mickie Mouse. Marks: none. (Identical construction to Howdy Doody puppets except for jaw. Therefore, it is assumed that this puppet was also made by Peter Puppet Playthings, Inc.). Ca. 1950.
Composition head, white hands (gloves), and yellow shoes, block of wood for body. Molded, big black ears, painted black eyes (no moveable jaw). $250.00.

Pinocchio

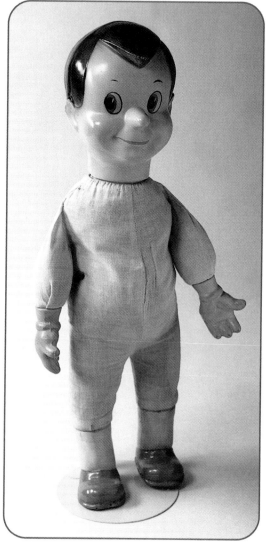

21". Marks: none (Pinocchio).
Composition flange head, short arms (gloves), and short legs with molded shoes. Molded, painted dark brown hair and painted blue eyes, closed mouth. Cloth body and upper legs one piece (no stitching at hip level). Cloth upper arms, stitched joints at shoulders. All original, including felt hat. $150.00.

Plush Body Dolls

Three 14" Plush body dolls. Marks: none. 1930s.
Flared composition heads, plush body and limbs with contrasting color mitten type velvet
hands and sewn in boots. Caps are removable. Stitched shoulder and hip joints. Molded,
painted blond hair and painted blue eyes, closed mouth.
Note: Heads mostly repainted. (Squeakers in body don't work anymore.) $75.00 each.

Priest

Ca. 20" Priest. Marks: none (but seems to be Toddling Sue doll seen in 1939 Ideal catalog). All composition, fully jointed. Molded, painted dark brown hair, blue sleep eyes. Open mouth with two upper teeth. Outfit consists of well sewn white men's shirt, black pants, cassock and black tie belt, black shoes, cap. $150.00.

Priest with Original Vestments

10¾". Marks: none.
All composition, jointed at shoulders and hips only. Molded, painted brown hair, painted blue eyes, closed mouth. Original black tuxedo and shoes. Tailored black wool cassock has snaps and covered buttons, opens in front. Beautifully sewn (finished seams) white shirt trimmed with double row of lace and white apron that is worn over the white shirt and tied crosswise. Five 3-piece vestments (one piece missing on gold one), and handmade white cloth (altar cover?), embroidered, edged with button hole stitch.
Note: Vestments are all handmade, embroidered, and lined. Workmanship varies from excellent to barely adequate (on the black one), which seems to indicate that several people worked on this project. $200.00.

Puss 'N Boots

14" Puss 'N Boots. Marks: none. Ca. 1910.
Flared composition head and long black boots. Velour covered body, arms, and upper legs, jointed at shoulders and hips with inside disks. Painted green eyes, open/closed mouth with two white lines inside lower jaw to indicate teeth. Original belt. Piece of velour pinned on at waist level to give the impression of a jacket. May originally have had a collar to further give that impression and to hide the stitching at the neck.
Note: The molded black boots were originally intended to resemble ribbed socks and high lace boots. By painting all black, the impression of long boots was created. $650.00.

Quaker Doll Company
Philadelphia, Pennsylvania
1915 – 1930 and later

The Quaker Doll Company were importers and wholesale distributors of dolls. They specialized in supplies for doll hospitals (Coleman II – Also see "Quaker Catalog Reference," by Loraine Burdick, *Doll Reader*, May 1986. Included with it was the reproduction of a Quaker Co. catalog from the late twenties.)

The Quaker Doll Co. distributed a broad range of popular German bisque and American composition dolls. Not many of the composition dolls sold by them apparently were identified with the "Quaker Quality" symbol. Dolls so marked are rarely seen.

21". Marks: Quaker Quality (for configuration of mark, see 5½" shoulder head seen in the next illustration). Ca. 1920.
Composition shoulder head and short arms. Cloth body, upper arms, and legs, jointed at shoulders and hips with inside disks. Original brown mohair wig, painted blue eyes, multi-stroke brows. Open/closed mouth with two painted teeth. Simple, white dress may be original. Cynthia Whittaker collection. $125.00.

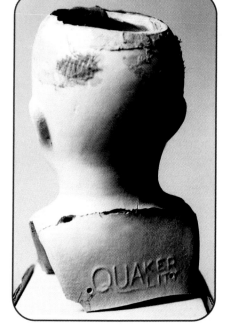

5½" shoulder head only. Marks: Quaker Quality
Woodpulp composition, open crown. Celluloid covered metal sleep eyes, open/closed mouth with two upper molded, painted teeth. Four sew holes in corners of shoulder plate.

Jessie McCutchen Raleigh
Chicago
1916 – 1920

Jessie McCutchen Raleigh, a successful businesswoman and entrepeneur, operated a novelty and doll business from 1916 to 1920. She had made an effort to offer dolls with artistic merit. They looked like real children (later, some dolly faces were added) and were created with beautifully modeled limbs and correct body proportions.

Unfortunately, the company did not survive increased competition after World War II.

Also see: "Raleigh Dolls" by Margaret Whitton, *Doll Reader*, Feb./March 1988.

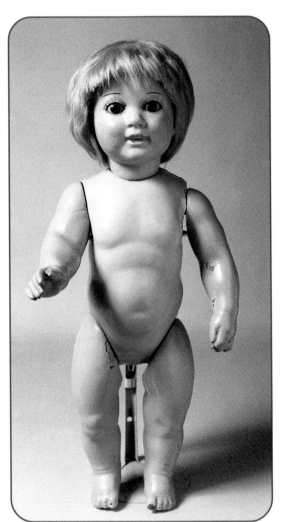

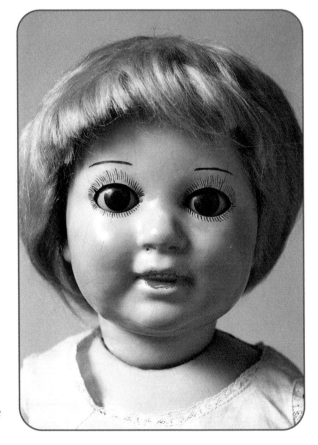

18". Marks: none.
All composition, fully jointed with steel springs. Old mohair wig, brown sleep eyes, rimmed by vertically painted eyelashes, open/closed mouth with four upper, painted teeth.
Note: The same style dolly face head can be seen in the next illustration. Instead of the slimmer body used there, this example shows the chunkier toddler body, identical to the one used by Raleigh for an 18" character girl with molded hair and barrette. $275.00.

Note the vertical eyelashes and dark brown eyebrows seen only on Raleigh dolls.

22". Marks: none. Ca., 1919.
Composition shoulder head, lower arms, and legs. Cloth body, upper arms, and upper legs, jointed at shoulders and hips with inside disks. Blond human hair wig is original. Blue sleep eyes, open/closed mouth with four upper painted teeth. Re-dressed. $250.00.

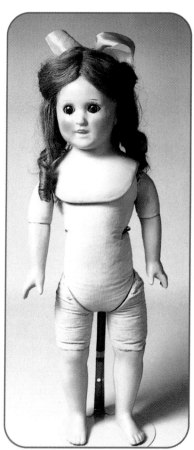

Raleigh dolly face doll seen in the previous illustration, shown here undressed. These dolls were also produced with all-compostion body and limbs or with all cloth legs.

22". Raleigh doll. Marks: none.
Composition shoulder head and lower arms, cloth body, upper arms, and legs. Dark brown human hair wig, sleep eyes, open/closed mouth with four upper molded and painted teeth, dimples in cheeks. Original underwear, shoes, and stockings, old dress.
Note: Note eyelashes and brows painted in unusual manner, but typical of Raleigh dolls. Unusual construction of shoes found on Raleigh dolls: Outer soles are made of canvas type fabric, inner soles of cardboard, and uppers have a vertical middle seam in front. Cynthia Whittaker collection. $300.00.

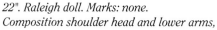

Rattle Baby

11" Rattle Baby. Marks: none. 1930s.
Composition flange head has pebbles inside. Plush body and limbs. Cap is removable.
Molded, painted blond hair, painted blue eyes, closed mouth. All original.
Note: Has real pebbles inside its head and was, obviously, meant to be a baby toy. $50.00.

Regal Doll Manufacturing Company
New York City and Jersey City, New Jersey
1919 – 1930+

In 1933, Regal bought the E.I. Horsman Company. For more extensive information see "The Regal Years," in *Collector's Guide to Horman Dolls, 1865 – 1950*, by Don Jensen.

30" Our Lindy (Charles Lindbergh). Marks: 1928 © // Regal Doll Co. // Sculpt. E. Peruggi Composition shoulder head, cloth body and limbs. Molded, painted blond hair, painted blue eyes, open/closed mouth with six upper molded teeth. All original except for mittens. Note: This doll does not have hands or feet, but rather the oilcloth boots were stuffed and then glued on. The gloves were also stuffed and pinned in place with 2" long brass stick pins (two for each mitten). $500.00+.

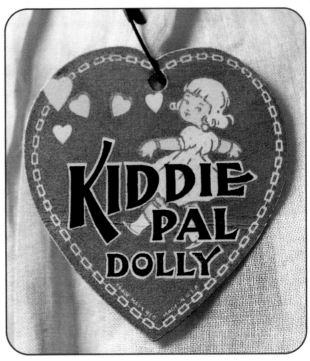

24". Marks: none.
Heart-shaped paper label: Kiddy Pal Dolly
Composition shoulder head, full arms, legs to above the knee, cloth body. Jointed at shoulders, stitched hip joints. Blond mohair wig, blue sleep eyes that also move from side to side. Open mouth with four upper teeth. All original. Cynthia Whittaker collection. $250.00.

16". Marks: Kiddie Pal Dolly
Composition shoulder head and lower arms. Cloth body, upper arms, and legs with black boots (leg casing serves as boots). No shoulder joints, stitched hip joints. Molded, painted blond hair with molded hair loop. Painted blue eyes, closed mouth. Re-dressed. Cynthia Whittaker collection. $95.00.

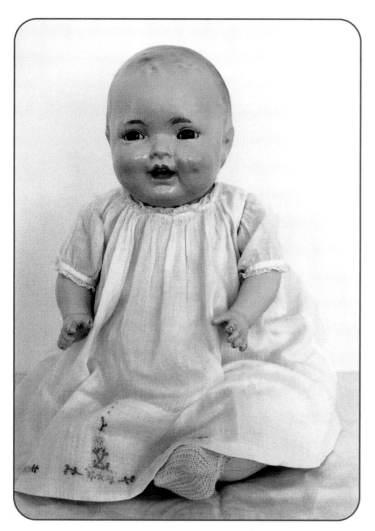

18". Marks: Kiddie Pale Baby // Regal Doll Mfg. Co. (note misspelling – see separate illustration of markings). Late 1920s. Full composition shoulder plate to under the arms, composition arms and bent legs. Cloth body, jointed at shoulders and hips. Molded, painted blond hair and blue tin sleep eyes. Open/closed mouth with two upper molded, painted teeth and molded tongue. Re-dressed. Cynthia Whittaker collection. $180.00.

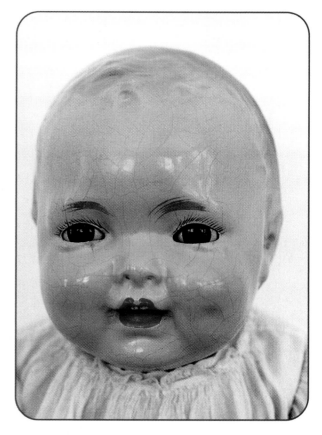

Close-up of Regal's Kiddie Pal Baby. Late 1920s. Note the multi-stroke eyebrows, dimples, and overall nice modeling on this chubby baby.

Close-up of Kiddie Pale Baby mark (note the mistake in "Pal").

19" The Judy Girl. Early 1930s.
Composition shoulder head, very short arms, and legs to above the knee. Cloth body with stitched hip joints. Molded, painted blond hair, blue tin sleep eyes, closed mouth. Re-dressed. $85.00.

12". Marks: none. Mid 1930s.
Heart-shaped paper tag: Bobby Anne // A Kiddie Pal // Dolly
All composition, fully jointed. Molded, painted blond hair, painted blue eyes, closed mouth. All original with additional clothes: one beach pajamas, one dress with matching bonnet, roller skates.
Note: Unusual shape of original carrying case.
Also Note: An identical set (including pink coat and tam and identical hang tag) has been seen where Regal used a Patsyette look-alike doll. $250.00+.

Since Bobby Anne is not marked, this close-up should be helpful to collectors in identifying dolls without marks.

13". Marks: none.
Paper tag: Bobby Anne // A Kiddie Pal // Dolly
All composition, fully jointed. Dark brown mohair wig over molded hair, blue tin sleep eyes, closed mouth. All original except hair bow.
Note: This doll is identical to Bobby Anne with carrying case and extra clothes. A mohair wig over molded hair and sleep eyes created a different looking doll. Note also the different shape for this tag. $150.00.

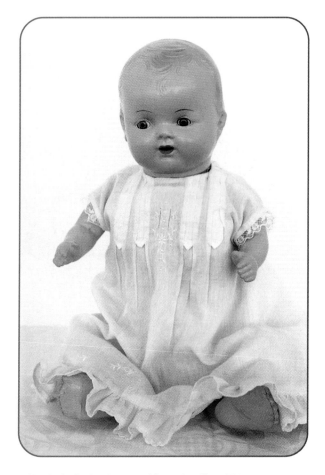

18". Marked: Hug Me // Kiddie Pal Dolly. 1930s.
Composition flange head, arms, and bent legs. Cloth body, jointed at shoulders and hips. Molded, painted blond hair and blue tin sleep eyes. Open mouth with two upper teeth. Re-dressed. Cynthia Whittaker collection. $125.00.

17". Marks: Hug Me // Kiddie Pal Dolly. 1930s.
Composition flange head and arms, cloth body and bent cloth legs, jointed at shoulders, stitched hip joints. Molded two upper painted teeth. All original. Cynthia Whittaker collection. $150.00.

Royal Blue Stores

15" Susie-Q. Marks: none.
All composition, fully jointed. Black mohair wig with bangs, blue sleep eyes, open/closed mouth. Re-dressed. $150.00.

15" Susie-Q for Royal Blue Stores. Marks: none.
Tag front: I'm Susie-Q // of // ROYAL BLUE // ©1948 // Royal Blue Stores.
Tag back: Hi Gals! Hi Fellas! // I'm Susie-Q // I'm scheming big Plans for // all of you // Keep in touch with me and // I'll tell you more // You can always find me // at the // ROYAL BLUE STORE. All composition, fully jointed. Black mohair with bangs, blue sleep eyes, open/closed mouth with white line between lips to indicate teeth. All original, including paper hang tag. Jenny Keaton collection. $250.00.

Royal Toy Manufacturing Co.
New York City
1913 – 1930+

16". Marks: none.
See Box: Spirit of America // Colonial Period // Civil War Period // A Royal Doll Product
All composition, fully jointed. Brown mohair wig, blue sleep eyes. Open mouth with four upper teeth. All original except for two panties, straw bonnet. 450.00+.

Spirit of America

Civil War Period

Colonial Period

Shaw Doll Co. Inc.

21". Marks: Shaw Doll Co. Inc.
Composition shoulder plate and pin-jointed arms. Cloth body and legs, stitched hip joints. Molded, painted blond hair and painted blue eyes, open/closed mouth. All original. Cynthia Whittaker collection. $125.00.

Close-up of doll revealing a beautifully modeled head.

Mrs. Putman David Smith (Mabel)
Santa Cruz, California
1913 – 1922

Mrs. P.D. Smith, a portrait painter, and her daughter Margaret modeled heads for dolls. Cloth or ball-jointed bodies were used. The dolls came in black as well as white and various sizes. Dolls distributed by George C. Salch Co. of San Francisco. Some dolls marked: Mrs. P.D. Smith. For more information check *The Collector's Encyclopedia of Dolls, Vol I.* and *II* by Dorothy S., Elizabeth A., and Evelyn J. Coleman.

20". Marks: none.
Composition socket head on shoulder plate to under the arms, composition limbs, cloth body. Blond human hair wig, glass sleep eyes that also move from side to side. Open/closed mouth with six painted teeth. Old clothes. Susan Foreman collection.
$2,500.00+.

20". Marks: none.
Composition socket head on ball-jointed body. Human hair wig, glass sleep eyes, open/closed mouth with six painted teeth. Three dimples. Old clothes. Susan Foreman collection.
$2,500.00+.

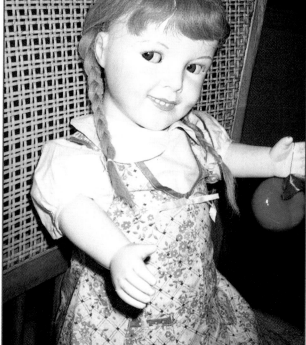

Snow White and Dwarfs

13" Snow White. Marks: none.
All composition, fully jointed (including neck). Molded, painted black hair with molded bow,
painted blue. Brown tin sleep eyes, closed mouth. All original.
8" Dwarfs. Marks: none.
All composition with molded-on tools (shovel, pick). No joints, painted features.
Snow White: $250.00. Dwarfs: $75.00 each.

Standard Specialty Company

14". Marked: 353 (Playthings January 1916).
Sticker on back of jacket: Flicks Kids // Trade Mark Registered // Des. Patent No. 1.059.178 // Copyr. 1915 // Standard Specialty Co. NY. // made under exclusive license // From the Girandelli Co. // San Francisco, Cal.
Flared composition head and short arms. Cloth body, upper arms and legs. Arms jointed with inside disks and legs jointed with outside disks.
Molded painted light brown hair and painted blue eyes, closed mouth. All original outfit made of felt. Brown cloth boots are part of leg casing.
Note: On checking the above mentioned patent, it was found that it was not relevant to this doll or the Girandelli Company. It was issued for a multi-face doll. $150.00.

Full page ad placed by the Standard Specialty Company in the January 1916 issue of Playthings. *Doll to the very left is wearing an identical outfit to the previously illustrated actual Flicks Kid. Though Flicks Kids is the big headline in this ad, nothing further is mentioned as to the identity of these dolls.*

Taiyo Trading Co., Inc.
New York and Chicago

16". Marks on both: H.B. Co. (Playthings, June 1919 and February 1920).
Left: Geisha
Right: Ming Toy
Composition shoulder heads and full arms, wood bodies and legs. Jointed at shoulders, special walking mechanism. Black mohair wigs over molded hair. Painted eyes, closed mouth. All original.
Note: The 1919 ad pictured here shows Ming Toy in a pants suit. The 1920 ad (not illustrated here) mentioned among several dolls Ming Toy and Geisha. The ad further stated: Ming Toy is delightfully dressed as a little Chinese kiddie. Geisha is attractively dressed as a Japanese geisha girl. (The ad did not illustrate either.) It is, therefore, assumed that the doll on the left is Geisha. $250.00 each.

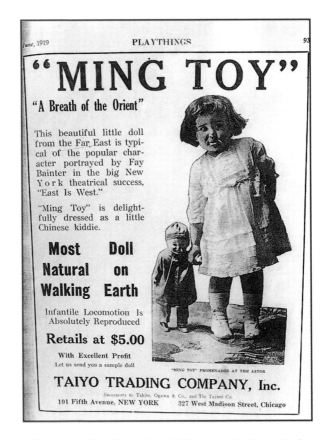

Full-page ad, Playthings, June 1919, placed by Taiyo Trading Company, Inc. The ad stated: This beautiful little doll from the Far East is typical of the popular character portrayed by Fay bainter in the big New York theatrical success, East Is West. For further information see "Ming Toy A Breath of the Orient" by Ursula Mertz, Doll News [UFDC] Spring 2001.)

Both Ming Toy and Geisha feature this walking mechanism.

Teddy Roosevelt

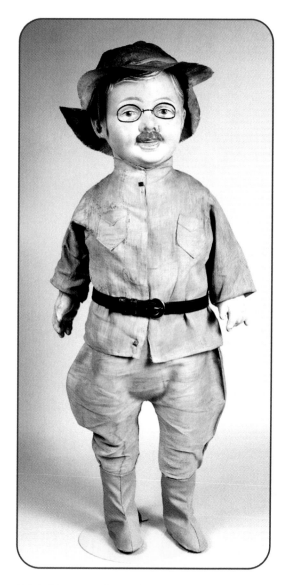
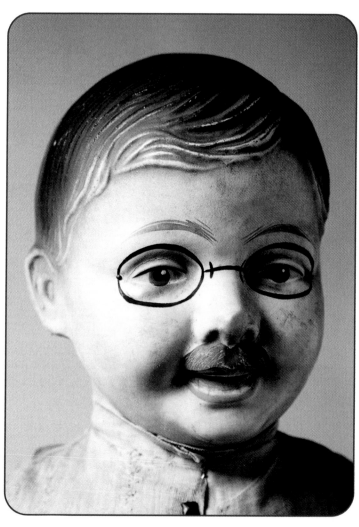

30" Teddy Roosevelt. Marks: none.
Composition flange head and short arms. Cloth body, upper arms, and legs are stuffed with exclsior, jointed with outside disks.
Molded, painted, and streated light brown hair and painted brown eyes, painted mustache. Open/closed mouth with two rows of
molded, painted teeth, painted pince-nez (eyeglasses clipped to nose by spring). Original uniform and hat. Boots are replace-
ments but copies of the originals, replaced belt.
Note: An ordinary so-called carnival doll was changed to Teddy Roosevelt by cleverly adding his trademark features: Pince-nez,
mustache, and protruding teeth. Also note the pin hole by the rim of the glasses on his right side. Pinned into it was probably a
string, just as it would have been for a real pince-nez. $250.00.

3-In-1 Doll Corporation
74 Laight St., New York

A full-page ad in *Toys and Novelties* of August 6, 1947, announced the three-face Trudy as "The Most Amazing Doll Creation in a Decade." Trudy's head was mounted on a wooden dowel that extended into the body. A knob on top permitted the turning of the head to make the different faces appear. Her hair was attached to the hood or bonnet.

An additional full-page ad by the 3-in-1 Doll Corp. has been located which supplies further information (see next illustration of ad). They offered five styles:

#1 dressed "in her soft, cuddly, year-round pink and blue costume, 14" tall"
#2 "In her cute party dress and bonnet. Unbreakable composition legs and arms."
#3 "Big sister edition of Trudy #2. Unbreakable composition legs and arms. Party dress, and bonnet. 20" tall."
#4 "Our newest Trudy for Easter in her bonny, bunny bonnet. Ears remove for year-round costume. 14" tall. Pink and blue. Green and yellow. Assorted."

In the above mentioned August 6, ad Trudy # 5 is shown with the following comment:
"Here's famous TRUDY ready for a shopping spree or a workout in the sandbox. Dressed in gaily colored felt overalls, with long sleeve felt blouse combination secured by handsome neck bow. Has a pert bonnet to match, and wears a modern shoulder strap utility bag. Head made of unbreakable composition. 14" Tall" In other words, it is the same costume and shoulder bag as for #4, just no ears.

For further study and additional copies of ads, see Patricia N. Schoonmaker's "Trudy … A Composition Collectible" in the October 1977 issue of *Doll Reader*.

Full page ad, Playthings, *February 1947, showing the five styles in which Trudy was produced.*

363

14" Trudy #1. Marks: none (see separate illustration of two-sided, round tag). Composition head with three faces is mounted on a dowel that extends into the cloth body. A molded knob on top of the head facilitates turning. Cloth body and limbs, stitched shoulder and hip joints. Painted features: awake and smiling, sleeping and crying. Three locks of mohair are sewn to the hood. All original overalls, short jacket and hood. $175.00.

14" Trudy #2. Marks: none.
Same construction as previous Trudy.
Trudy's all original cotton dress and bonnet are imprinted (in the shape of circles): "Smiley Trudy — Weepy Trudy — Sleepy Trudy," in pinks and blues. (No composition legs as mentioned in the ad.) Cynthia Whittaker collection. $200.00+.

14" Trudy #4. Marks: none (see separate illustration of tag, which is different from the two-sided, round tag of Trudy No. 2).
Same construction as Trudies #1 and #2 illustrated here. All original felt outfit consisting of overalls, short jacket tied in front and hood, includes a shoulder bag. The ends of a yellow felt strip are seen peeking out of the top of the bag which is probably meant to be the obligatory hankie. $300.00.

Tag: An Elise Gilbert Creation // Sleepy // Weepy // Smily // Trade mark of the Three In-One // Doll Corp. // Patents Pending Note: This is a copy and a "one side" tag only.

Toy Products Manufacturing Co.
New York City

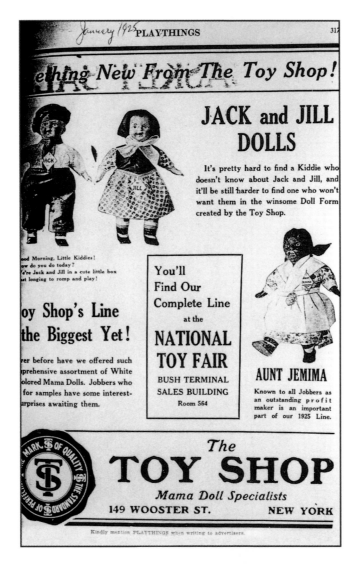

Full-page ad placed in the trade journal Playthings, *January 1925.*
Illustrated are three identical mama dolls outfitted as Aunt Jemima and
Jack and Jill. The latter would be recognizable only as the familiar story
book characters as long as they retain their pinned-on paper tags.

The Toy Shop
New York, New York
1920s – 1930s

22". Marks: Toy Products Mfg. Co. 1930s.
Composition flange head, lower arms, and legs to above the knee.
Cloth body, upper arms, and legs. No shoulder joints, stitched hip joints.
Molded, painted blond hair, painted blue eyes, open mouth with two upper
teeth and tongue. All original. Cynthia Whitaker collection. $125.00.

Trion Toy Co., Inc.
Brooklyn, New York
1911 – 1921

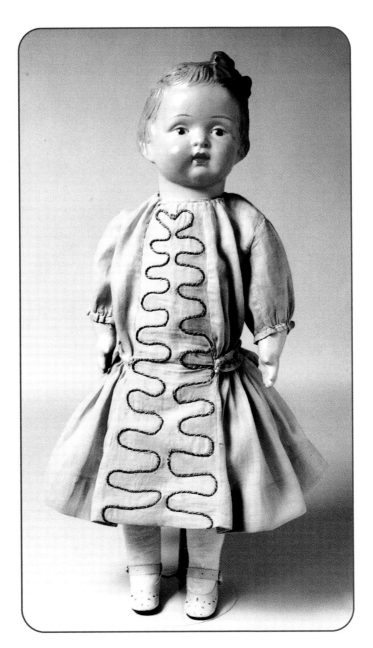

18". Marks: © // Trion Toy Co. (This is Sunny, Playthings, *August 1915).*
Flared composition head and arms to above elbow. Cloth body, upper arms, and legs, jointed with inside disks. Molded, painted blond hair with molded red bow. Blue eyes, closed mouth. Old clothes, new shoes.
Note: Some dolls marked "Trion" have been found dressed by Georgene Averill of Averill Mfg. Co. $175.00.

T.T. Co.

13". Marks: T.T. // Co.
Composition shoulder plate and full arms. Cloth body and legs. Arms are pin jointed, stitched hip joints. Large mama voice box. Original brown cotton yarn wig, painted blue eyes, closed mouth. Dress may be original. Old hat, shoes, and socks.
Note: Unusual yarn wig. Such yarn wigs are usually found only on dolls dating from WWII years. This doll seems much earlier. $150.00.

Uneeda Doll Co.
New York City
1917 – 1930+

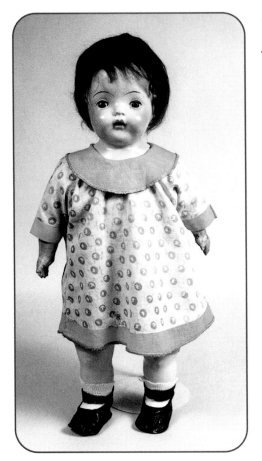

20". Marks: Uneeda. 1920s.
Composition shoulder plate, lower arms, and legs to above the knee. Cloth body, no shoulder joints, arms wired on. Dark brown mohair wig, gray sleep eyes, open mouth with two upper teeth. All original, old shoes. Cynthia Whittaker collection. $125.00.

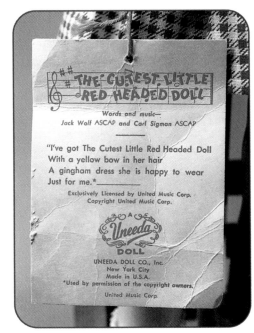

17". Marks: none on doll. See box label and hang tag. 1940s.
All composition, fully jointed. Red mohair wig, blue sleep eyes, open mouth with two upper teeth. All original. $175.00.

Unmarked Dolls of the Early Years

All dolls illustrated in this sction are from the period 1910 – 1920. It was a time of rapid development and change. Many small companies were at work producing dolls. Many of them were in existence only for a short time. Interesting character faces and a wide variety of molded hairdos were produced. Some dolls were copied from German bisque examples. Many can still be found in original clothes, as seen here. Never again would one see so much variety produced in so short a time span. Makers' names for these dolls are not available.

25". Marks: none. Ca. 1910. (The head is a copy of unspecified German bisque doll head.) Flared composition head, plush body and limbs, jointed with inside disks. Sewn in felt mitts. Molded, painted blond hair and painted blue eyes. Open/closed mouth with molded tongue and two painted upper teeth.

Note: This type doll usually came with some type of cap and removeable collar and short skirt that is open in front. Besides being pinned to the doll, that skirt is usually held in place with a belt. When all complete, collar, original cap and belt give the impression of a jacket. In the case of this doll, collar, original cap, and belt were missing. The skirt was converted (reversible) into a cap and a scarf substituted. Note also a blue hue at the hips where the skirt had been. When new, the plush actually was blue. $150.00.

17". Marks: H.B.P. Ca. 1910 – 1912. Flared composition head, plush body and limbs stuffed with excelsior, jointed at shoulders and hips with inside disks. Felt boots and mittens are part of limbs. Separate shirt and black oilcloth belt are held in place with nails. Molded, painted light brown hair with curls at sides and a molded braid laid around the head. Painted blue eyes, closed mouth. All original.

Note: This is a poured head made of American glue base composition. Obviously, the mold for this head was taken from a German dolly face porcelain doll. $150.00.

15½". Marks: none. Ca. 1910.
Flared head and short arms. Velvet body, upper arms, and legs. Velvet casings are also his suit. Jointed at shoulders and hips with inside disks. Detachable, trimmed collar and four metal buttons. Molded, painted brown hair and painted blue eyes, puckered mouth. $150.00.

24". Marks: none. (The head is a copy of an unspecified German bisque doll head.)
Flared composition head and short arms. Cloth body, upper arms, and bent legs, jointed with outside disks. Faintly molded brown hair, painted blue eyes, open/closed mouth. All original long half slip and long coat made of cheap cotton fabric and trimmed with narrow lace at sleeves and front, matching bonnet.
Note: This is an early doll (poured head). Cloth body and limbs are very clean. Rare originality for a doll that was initially of rather cheap quality. $175.00.

17". Marks: none.
Flared composition head and lower arms. Cloth body, upper arms, and legs. Arms jointed with inside disks, legs jointed with outside disks. Elaborately molded light brown hair and painted brown eyes, closed mouth. Re-dressed. $150.00.

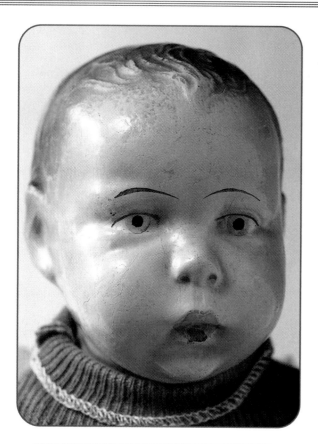

15". Marks: none.
Composition shoulder head on appropriate old body with short compo-sistion arms, jointed at shoulders with inside disks, at hips with outside disks. Molded, painted brown hair, painted blue eyes, small mouth. Re-dressed. $150.00.

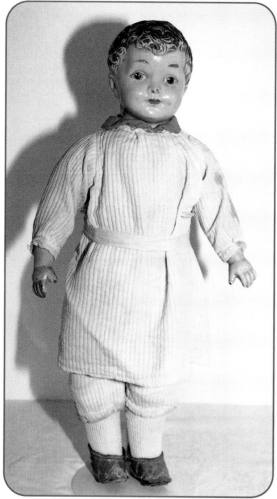

13". Marks: none. Ca. 1915.
Flared composition head and short arms. Cloth body, upper arms, and legs. Molded brown com-position boots are glued on. Jointed at shoulders and hips with outside disks. Molded, painted light brown hair, painted blue eyes to right. Open/closed mouth with three molded, painted upper teeth. Re-dressed. $175.00.

16". Marks: none. Ca. 1915.
Flared composition head and short arms. Cloth body, upper arms, and legs, jointed at shoulders and hips with inside disks. Molded, painted curly brown hair, painted blue eyes, closed mouth. All original. Cynthia Whitaker collection. $150.00.

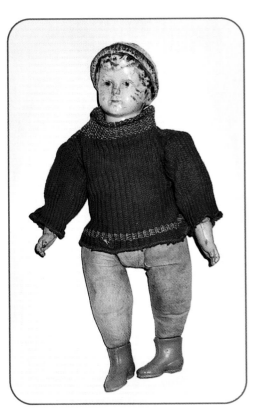

14". Marks: none.
Flared composition head with molded stocking cap, short arms and molded boots. Cloth body and limbs, jointed with inside disks. Molded stocking cap has a drill hole in back so that a real tassle can be attached. Molded blond hair and painted blue eyes, closed mouth. Maroon sweater is of the period. Kay Curtis collection. $250.00.

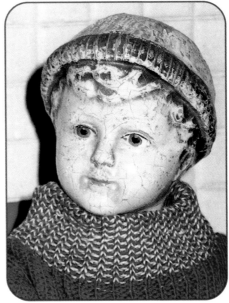

12". Marks: none.
Flared composition head, lower arms, and molded brown boots. Cloth body, jointed at shoulders and hips with outside disks. Molded, painted, striated hair, painted blue eyes and closed mouth. All original sailor suit. Cynthia Whittaker collection. $150.00.

15". Marks: none.
Flared composition head, short arms, and molded boots. Cloth body, upper arms, and legs, jointed at shoulders and hips with inside disks. Molded, painted light brown hair, painted blue eyes, closed mouth. All original except for belt. $150.00.

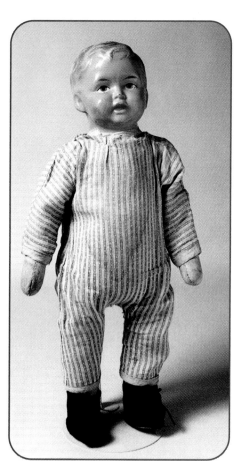

15" Boy. Marks: 302.
Flared composition head, cloth body and limbs (stump hands), jointed at shoulders and hips with outside disks. Molded, painted blond hair and painted blue eyes. Open/closed mouth. Original romper, old cloth shoes. Cynthia Whittaaker collection. $125.00.

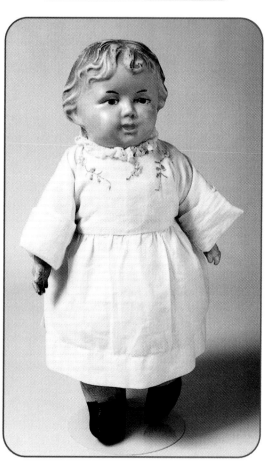

16". Marks: none. Ca. 1915.
Flared composition head and short lower arms. Cloth body, upper arms, and straight legs with light blue boots that double as foot casing. Jointed at shoulders and hips with outside disks. Molded, painted brown hair, painted blue eyes, closed mouth. Re-dressed. Cynthia Whitaker collection. $150.00.

14". Marks: none.
Composition flange head and short arms, cloth body, upper arms, and legs, jointed at shouldes and hips with outside disks, sewn in black cloth shoes. Molded, painted brown hair, painted blue eyes, closed mouth. Old clothes. $150.00.

Two dolls, identical head mold.
Left: 14". Marks: none.
Flared composition head and short arms. Cloth body, upper arms, and bent legs, jointed with inside disks. Molded, painted light brown hair and painted blue eyes, closed mouth. Old clothes.
Right: 15". Marks: none.
Identical to above except for staple in head to hold hair bow and straight legs. Re-dressed. $125.00 each.

11". Marks: none.
Composition flange head and short arms, cloth body, upper arms, and legs, jointed with outside disks. Red and white striped stockings and medium blue boots are actually the leg casings. Molded, painted blond hair and painted blue eyes. Closed mouth. Re-dressed. $75.00.

16". Marks: none.
Flared composition head and short arms. Cloth body, upper arms, and legs, jointed with inside disks. Molded, striated, painted brown hair, painted blue eyes, closed mouth. Old romper. Cynthia Whittaker collection. $150.00.

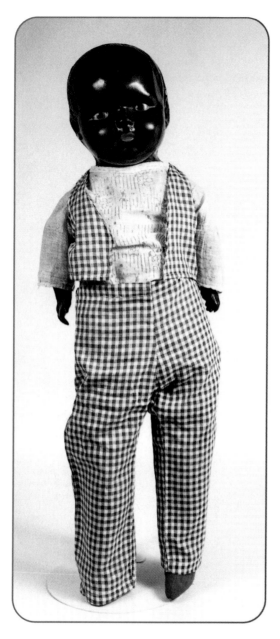

28". Marks: none.
Composition shoulder head and short arms. Cloth body and legs. Arms are tied on, no hip joints. Molded, painted black hair and painted brown eyes, open/closed mouth. All original. Cynthia Whittaker collection. $125.00.

13". Marks: 102.
Flared composition head, cloth body and limbs (stump hands), sewn in black cloth boots. Molded, painted blond hair, painted blue eyes, open/closed mouth. Old clothes.
Note: The hair modeling is almost identical to Effanbee's early Baby Grumpy. Cynthia Whittaker collection. $150.00.

15". Boy. Marks: none. Before 1920.
Compostion flange head and short arms. Cloth body, upper arms, and legs, jointed at shoulders and hips with inside disks. Original blond mohair wig is glued directly to head over molded hair. Painted blue eyes, closed mouth. Re-dressed. $150.00.

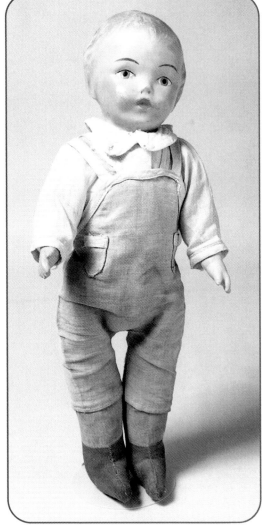

12½". Marks: none.
Flared composition head and short arms. Cloth body, upper arms, and legs with sewn in black boots, jointed at shoulders with inside disks, at hips with outside disks. Molded, painted light brown hair, painted blue eyes, closed mouth. Original overalls with two patch pockets, white blouse. $75.00.

17". Marks: none. 1918 – early 1920s.
Composition shoulder head and short arms. Cloth body, upper arms, and bent legs, jointed at shoulders and hips with inside disks. Brown mohair wig, painted blue eyes, open/closed mouth. Re-dressed.
Note: While the doll bears no identification marks, she is of excellent quality. The eyelashes are expertly painted. While the mohair is of good quality, there is no wig cap. The mohair has been directly glued to the head. Also, superior state of preservation for such an early doll. $160.00.

20". Marks: none.
Composition shoulder head and short arms, cloth body, upper arms, and bent legs, jointed with inside disks. Good quality, brown mohair wig, painted brown eyes, open mouth with two upper molded painted teeth. Three dimples. $85.00.

17". Marks: none.
Flared composition head and short arms. Molded, painted light brown hair and painted blue eyes, closed mouth. Cloth body, upper arms, and bent legs, jointed at shoulders and hips with outside disks. Original lace-trimmed panties, re-dressed.
Note: Doll has a one syllable crier in her straw stuffed body that works. Doll seems from before 1920 (glue base composition head), limbs stuffed hard with sawdust). Very nice quality doll. Mama dolls have a two-syllable crier. In other words, this doll is a forerunner of the mama dolls. $125.00.

Ventriloquist Dummy

40". Marks: none.
Composition flange head, short arms, and molded shoes. Cloth body,
upper arms, and legs. Stitched joints at shoulder, hips, and knees. Molded,
painted brown hair and painted brown eyes, hinged lower jaw. Re-dressed.
Note: Different head mold from Ralph Freundlich's Dummy Dan. $125.00.

Vogue Doll Inc.
Medford, Massachusetts
1922 – Present

8" head. Marks: Vogue. 1944.
Paper tag on pants: Vogue
Mark on right shoe sole: Chinese Boy
All composition, fully jointed, black mohair wig ending in one braid, hip length. Painted blue eyes, closed mouth. All original. $350.00.

5". Marks: Vogue
All composition, fully jointed, blond mohair wig, painted blue eyes, closed mouth. Dressed in Victory Gardner outfit with original hoe. Anita Maxwell collection. $425.00.

7½" Bunky and Binky. Marks on head and back: Vogue. 1947 – 1948.
All composition, fully jointed. Blond mohair wigs, painted blue eyes, closed mouths. All original, tagged clothes. Judy Johnson collection. $250.00 each.

19". Marks: none.

All composition, fully jointed. Good quality auburn mohair wig, brown sleep eyes, open mouth with four upper teeth. All original. Same fabric teddy has full cut and is also finished at neck and arms with brown seam binding. Could be worn alone as play suit.

Note: A member of these 19" dolls with identical face have been found unmarked but with Vogue tags attached to their garments. Quality and styling seem to indicate Vogue origin. $250.00.

Same fabric teddy can double as playsuit.

18". Marks: none.
All composition, fully jointed, blond mohair wig,
blue sleep eyes, open mouth with four upper teeth.
All original. $350.00.

13". Marks: (x)
Sticker on costume: Vogue
Bottom of shoe marked: Cynthia
All composition, fully jointed. Blond mohair wig, brown
sleep eyes, open mouth with four upper teeth. All original.
Anita Maxwell collection. $450.00.

13". Marks: none.
All composition, fully jointed. Blond mohair wig with braids, blue sleep eyes, closed mouth. All original. $160.00.

15". Marks: none. (Shoe soles on some examples marked: WAAC–ETTE.)
All composition, fully jointed. Blond mohair wig, painted blue eyes and closed mouth. All original, including shoulder bag.
Note: Unusual painted eyes and closed mouth version (versus identical head mold but sleep eyes and open mouth with teeth. Jean Grout collection. $250.00.

7". Marks: none. (This is Valerie see Collector's Encyclopedia of Vogue Dolls *by Judith Izen and Carol Stover). 1942. All composition fully jointed with molded shoes and socks. Blonde mohair wig and painted blue eyes, closed mouth. All original. Anita Maxwell collection. $250.00.*

8". Marks on back: Doll Co. (no "Vogue") Marks on shoe sole: John Alden All composition, fully jointed. Blond mohair wig, painted blue eyes, closed mouth. All oiginal. hat is open at crown. $150.00, fair condition.

Bibliography

General Reference Books/Periodicals

Anderton, Joanna Gast. *Twentieth Century Dolls from Bisque to Vinyl*. North Kansas City, MO: Trojan Press, 1971.
___. *More Twentieth Century Dolls* from Bisque to Vinyl. 1974.

Antique Doll World / Antique Doll Collector, 1993 – 2003.

Axe, John. *Collectible Patsy Dolls and Patsy Types*.
___. *Effanbee: A Collector's Encyclopedia, 1949 – 1983*. Cumberland, MD: Holly Hobby Press, 1983.
___. *The Encyclopedia of Celebrity Dolls*.
___. *Kewpies — Dolls and Art of Rose O'Neill & Joseph L. Kallus*. Cumberland, MO: Hobby House Press, 2001.

Blum, David. *A Pictorial History of the American Theater 1950 – 1960*.

Boardman, Gerald. *The Oxford Companion to American Theater*. 1984.

Burdick, Loraine. *Child Star Dolls and Toys*. New York: Macmillian, 1968.

Cochran, Dewees. *As If They Might Speak*. 1979.

Carlson, Nancy. *The Elegance of Efffanbee*.

Coleman, Dorothy S., Elizabeth A., and Evelyn J. *The Collector's Encyclopedia of Dolls, Vol. I and II*.

Corson, Carol. *Schoenhut Dolls: A Collector's Encyclopedia*. Cumberland, MD: Hobby House Press, 1993.

Doll News, United Federation of Doll Clubs, 1976 – 2003.

Doll Reader, 1976 – 2002.

Ellenburg, Kelly M. *Effanbee: The Dolls with the Golden Hearts*. North Kansas City, Mo: Trojan Press, 1973.

Foulke, Jan. *Blue Books, Vol. I – IV*.
___. *Focusing on # 1 – Effanbee Composition Dolls*.
___. *Focusing on # 2 – Treasury of Madame Alexander Dolls*.
___. *Focusing on # 3 – Gebrueder Heubach Dolls*.
___. *Kestner, King of Doll Makers*
___. *Simon & Halbig, The Artful Aspect*

Gale Research Co. *Something about the Author, Vol. 17 – 19*. Michigan, 1979.

Horn Maurice (ed.). *The World Encyclopedia of Comics*.

Hoyer, Mary. *Mary Hoyer and Her Dolls* Cumberland, MD: Hobby House Press, 1982.

Izen, Judith. *Collector's Guide to Ideal Dolls, Vol. I and II*. Paducah, KY: Collector Books, 1999.

Izen, Judith and Carol Stover. *Collector's Encyclopedia of Vogue Dolls* Paducah, KY: Collector Books, 1998.

Jensen, Don. *Collector's Guide to Horsman Dolls, 1865 – 1950.* Paducah, KY: Collector Books, 2002.

Judd, Polly and Pam. *Composition Dolls, Identification & Price Guide, Vol. I* and *II.*

Lackman, Ron. *Same Time…Same Station, an A – Z Guide to Radio.* New York, Facts on File, 1996.

McKeon, Barbara Jo. *Rare and Hard to Find Madame Alexander Dolls.*

Mandeville, Glenn A. *Alexander Dolls, Collector's Price Guide.* Grantsville, MD: Hobby House Press, 2000.
___. *Ginny … An American Toddler Doll.* Cumberland, MD: Hobby House Press, 1985.

Mertz, Ursula R. American Doll Showcase, *Doll Reader*, 1992–2002.

Moyer, Patsy. *Doll Values,* Vol. I–VI. Paducah, KY: Collector Books, 1997 – 2001.
___. *Modern Collectible Dolls*, Vol. I–IV. Paducah, KY: Collector Books, 1997 – 2002.
___. Patsy & Friends Newsletter

Pardella, Edward R. *Shirley Temple Dolls and Fashions.* Atglen, PA: Schiffer Publishing, 1999.

Schoonmaker, Particia N. *Effanbee Dolls, The Formative Years 1910–1929.*
___. *Patsy Family Encyclopedia, Vol. I* and *II.*
___. *The Effanbee Patsy Family and Related Types.* 1971.

Shoemaker, Rhoda. *Composition Dolls, Cute and Collectible, Vol. I – IV.*

The Antique Trader's Weekly, Book of Collectible Dolls (Reprints from four years)

Wiedman Casper, Peggy. *Fashionable Terry Lee Dolls.*

Articles and Catalogs

Adams, Margaret. *Collectible Dolls and Accessories of the Twenties and Thirties from Sears Roebuk & Co. Catalogs.*

Averill Manufacturing Co. catalog, ca. 1925 (Strong Museum, Rochester, NY)

The A. Schoenhut Company Catalog, 1930 (Reprinted by Schoenhut Coll. Club, 1996)

"The Development of the American Doll," *Toys and Novelties*, Jan. 1927, pg. 341.

E. I. Horsman catalog ca. 1915, (Strong Museum, Rochester, NY)

Fleischaker & Baum, Dolls Ancient & Modern 1915 catalog (Reprint)

Ideal Dolls, catalog from 1939, reprinted 1987 by Loraine Burdick

Jenson, Don. "Denivelle and His Deco Dolls," *Doll News*, Spring 1991.
___. "Effanbee's Unlikely Duo – W. C. Fields and Charlie," *Doll Reader*, Oct. 1990.
Old Catalogs and Reprints

Kringle Society of Dolls, Marshall Field & Company, 1914 (Reprint)

Playthings, 1900 – 1950, trade magazine (Library of Congress and New York City)

"Phenomenal Sale of American Walking and Talking Dolls," *Playthings*, Dec. 1936, pg. 103.

Tip Top Toy Co., catalog (Strong Museum, Rochester NY)

Toys and Novelties, 1900 – 1950, trade magazine (Library Congress and New York City)

U. S. Patents (N. Y. State Library, Albany N.Y.)

"What Type Doll Will Sell Best in 1927?" *Toys and Novelties*, Feb. 1927, pg. 131.

Index

About the Author

Ursula R. Mertz has been a doll collector since 1975. Composition dolls have become a full-time commitment. From 1976 to 1986, she had a repair business, specializing in partial restorations of composition and other painted surface dolls. Among her customers were collectors from throughout the United States. Her visual arts background and consequent knowledge of color theory and paint mixing enabled her to very successfully match her restorations to old painted surfaces, an art practiced by few.

It was this hands-on experience in doll repairs that gave Ursula an opportunity to study composition dolls inside out and develop proper maintenance procedures for them. It also was helpful in developing the technical information presented in this book.

At the same time, Ursula has been a dealer specializing in composition dolls and selling at various large doll shows. This has given her an opportunity to examine and evaluate great numbers of composition dolls.

Ursula has mounted doll exhibits on various themes at the local and national levels and she continues to lecture on various composition doll subjects. Throughout her career, she has written numerous articles for Doll News, Doll Reader and *Antique Doll Collector*. She is presently the author of the column "Learning About American Dolls," in *Antique Doll Collector*.

The author is a member of UFDC (United Federation of Doll Clubs) and has been very active in this organization for many years. At their annual convention in Anaheim, California, in July 1997, she was given their annual national Award of Excellence for Protection and Preservation of Dolls and in August of 2001, the Award of Excellence for Exhibit of Dolls.

Ursula is married to Otto J. Mertz, able photographer for the majority of photographs in this book. Otto and daughter Linda helped with the proofreading of the manuscript.

What are her plans for the future? "Much remains to be done in the area of composition doll research," she commented.

COLLECTOR BOOKS

informing today's collector

www.collectorbooks.com

For over two decades we have been keeping collectors informed on trends and values in all fields of antiques and collectibles.

DOLLS, FIGURES & TEDDY BEARS

6315 **American Character Dolls**, Izen $24.95
6317 **Arranbee Dolls**, The Dolls that Sell on Sight, DeMillar/Brevik $24.95
2079 **Barbie Doll** Fashion, Volume I, Eames $24.95
4846 **Barbie Doll** Fashion, Volume II, Eames $24.95
6319 **Barbie Doll** Fashion, Volume III, Eames $29.95
6022 The **Barbie Doll** Years, 5th Ed., Olds $19.95
5352 Collector's Ency. of **Barbie** Doll Exclusives & More, 2nd Ed., Augustyniak .$24.95
5904 Collector's Guide to **Celebrity Dolls**, Spurgeon $24.95
5599 Collector's Guide to **Dolls of the 1960s and 1970s**, Sabulis $24.95
6030 Collector's Guide to **Horsman Dolls**, Jensen $29.95
6224 **Doll Values**, Antique to Modern, 7th Ed., Moyer $12.95
6033 **Modern Collectible Dolls**, Volume VI, Moyer $24.95
5689 **Nippon Dolls** & Playthings, Van Patten/Lau $29.95
5365 **Peanuts Collectibles**, Podley/Bang $24.95
6336 Official **Precious Moments** Collector's Guide to Company **Dolls**, Bomm ...$19.95
6026 **Small Dolls of the 40s & 50s**, Stover $29.95
5253 Story of **Barbie**, 2nd Ed., Westenhouser $24.95
5277 **Talking Toys** of the 20th Century, Lewis $15.95
2084 **Teddy Bears, Annalee's & Steiff** Animals, 3rd Series, Mandel $19.95
4880 World of **Raggedy Ann** Collectibles, Avery $24.95

TOYS & MARBLES

2333 Antique & Collectible **Marbles**, 3rd Ed., Grist $9.95
5900 Collector's Guide to **Battery Toys**, 2nd Edition, Hultzman $24.95
4566 Collector's Guide to **Tootsietoys**, 2nd Ed., Richter $19.95
5169 Collector's Guide to **TV Toys** & Memorabilia, 2nd Ed., Davis/Morgan $24.95
5593 Grist's Big Book of **Marbles**, 2nd Ed. $24.95
3970 Grist's Machine-Made & Contemporary **Marbles**, 2nd Ed. $9.95
6128 **Hot Wheels**, The Ultimate Redline Guide, 1968 – 1977, Clark/Wicker $24.95
5830 **McDonald's** Collectibles, 2nd Edition, Henriques/DuVall $24.95
1540 Modern **Toys**, 1930–1980, Baker $19.95
6237 **Rubber Toy Vehicles**, Leopard $19.95
6340 **Schroeder's Collectible Toys**, Antique to Modern Price Guide, 9th Ed. $17.95
5908 **Toy Car** Collector's Guide, Johnson $19.95

FURNITURE

3716 American **Oak** Furniture, Book II, McNerney $12.95
1118 Antique **Oak** Furniture, Hill $7.95
3720 Collector's Encyclopedia of **American** Furniture, Vol. III, Swedberg $24.95
5359 Early **American** Furniture, Obbard $12.95
3906 **Heywood-Wakefield** Modern Furniture, Rouland $18.95
6338 **Roycroft** Furniture & Collectibles, Koon $24.95
6343 **Stickley Brothers** Furniture, Koon $24.95
1885 **Victorian** Furniture, Our American Heritage, McNerney $9.95
3829 **Victorian** Furniture, Our American Heritage, Book II, McNerney $9.95

JEWELRY, HATPINS, WATCHES & PURSES

4704 Antique & Collectible **Buttons**, Wisniewski $19.95
6323 **Christmas Pins**, Past & Present, 2nd Edition, Gallina $19.95
4850 Collectible **Costume Jewelry**, Simonds $24.95
5675 Collectible **Silver Jewelry**, Rezazadeh $24.95
3722 Collector's Ency. of **Compacts**, Carryalls & Face Powder Boxes, Mueller ...$24.95
4940 **Costume Jewelry**, A Practical Handbook & Value Guide, Rezazadeh $24.95
5812 Fifty Years of Collectible **Fashion Jewelry**, 1925 – 1975, Baker $24.95
6330 **Handkerchiefs**: A Collector's Guide, Guarnaccia/Guggenheim $24.95
1424 **Hatpins** & Hatpin Holders, Baker $9.95
5695 **Ladies' Vintage Accessories**, Bruton $24.95
1181 100 Years of Collectible **Jewelry**, 1850 – 1950, Baker $9.95
6337 **Purse Masterpieces**, Schwartz $29.95
4729 **Sewing Tools** & Trinkets, Thompson $24.95
6038 **Sewing Tools** & Trinkets, Volume 2, Thompson $24.95
6039 Signed Beauties of **Costume Jewelry**, Brown $24.95
6341 Signed Beauties of **Costume Jewelry**, Volume II, Brown $24.95
5620 Unsigned Beauties of **Costume Jewelry**, Brown $24.95
4878 Vintage & Contemporary **Purse Accessories**, Gerson $24.95
5696 Vintage & Vogue Ladies' **Compacts**, 2nd Edition, Gerson $29.95
5923 **Vintage Jewelry** for Investment & Casual Wear, Edeen $24.95

ARTIFACTS, GUNS, KNIVES, TOOLS, PRIMITIVES

6021 **Arrowheads** of the Central Great Plains, Fox $19.95
1868 Antique **Tools**, Our American Heritage, McNerney $9.95
5616 Big Book of **Pocket Knives**, Stewart $19.95
4943 Field Gde. to Flint **Arrowheads & Knives** of the N. American Indian, Tully ...$9.95
3885 **Indian Artifacts** of the Midwest, Book II, Hothem $16.95
4870 **Indian Artifacts** of the Midwest, Book III, Hothem $18.95
5685 **Indian Artifacts** of the Midwest, Book IV, Hothem $19.95
6132 **Modern Guns**, Identification & Values, 14th Ed., Quertermous $14.95
2164 **Primitives**, Our American Heritage, McNerney $9.95
1759 **Primitives**, Our American Heritage, 2nd Series, McNerney $14.95
6031 Standard **Knife** Collector's Guide, 4th Ed., Ritchie & Stewart $14.95
5999 **Wilderness Survivor's Guide**, Hamper $12.95

PAPER COLLECTIBLES & BOOKS

5902 **Boys' & Girls' Book** Series, Jones $19.95
5153 Collector's Guide to **Chldren's Books**, 1850 to 1950, Volume II, Jones $19.95
1441 Collector's Guide to **Post Cards**, Wood $9.95
5926 **Duck Stamps**, Chappell $9.95
2081 Guide to Collecting **Cookbooks**, Allen $14.95
2080 Price Guide to **Cookbooks & Recipe Leaflets**, Dickinson $9.95
3973 **Sheet Music** Reference & Price Guide, 2nd Ed., Pafik & Guiheen $19.95
6041 Vintage **Postcards for the Holidays**, Reed $24.95

GLASSWARE

5602 Anchor Hocking's **Fire-King** & More, 2nd Ed. $24.95
6321 **Carnival Glass**, The Best of the Best, Edwards/Carwile $29.95
5823 Collectible **Glass Shoes**, 2nd Edition, Wheatley $24.95
6325 Coll. **Glassware from the 40s, 50s & 60s**, 7th Ed., Florence $19.95
1810 Collector's Encyclopedia of **American Art Glass**, Shuman $29.95
6327 Collector's Encyclopedia of **Depression Glass**, 16th Ed., Florence $19.95
1961 Collector's Encyclopedia of **Fry Glassware**, Fry Glass Society $24.95
1664 Collector's Encyclopedia of **Heisey Glass**, 1925 – 1938, Bredehoft $24.95
3905 Collector's Encyclopedia of **Milk Glass**, Newbound $24.95
5820 Collector's Guide to **Glass Banks**, Reynolds $24.95
6454 **Crackle Glass** From Around the World, Weitman $24.95
6125 **Elegant Glassware** of the Depression Era, 10th Ed., Florence $24.95
6334 Encyclopedia of **Paden City Glass**, Domitz $24.95
3981 Evers' Standard **Cut Glass** Value Guide $12.95
6462 Florence's **Glass Kitchen Shakers**, 1930 – 1950s $19.95
5042 Florence's **Glassware Pattern Identification** Guide, Vol. I $18.95
5615 Florence's **Glassware Pattern Identification** Guide, Vol. II $19.95
6142 Florence's **Glassware Pattern Identification** Guide, Vol. III $19.95
4719 **Fostoria**, Etched, Carved & Cut Designs, Vol. II, Kerr $24.95
6226 **Fostoria** Value Guide, Long/Seate $19.95

Glass & Ceramic Baskets, White		$19.95

Glass & Ceramic Baskets, White $19.95
Glass Animals, Second Edition, Spencer $24.95
The Glass Candlestick Book, Volume 1, Akro Agate to Fenton, Felt/Stoer .$24.95
The Glass Candlestick Book, Volume 2, Fostoria to Jefferson, Felt/Stoer ..$24.95
The Glass Candlestick Book, Volume 3, Kanawha to Wright, Felt/Stoer $29.95
Glass Tumblers, 1860s to 1920s, Bredehoft $29.95
Imperial Carnival Glass, Burns $18.95
Kitchen Glassware of the Depression Years, 6th Ed., Florence $24.95
Much More Early American Pattern Glass, Metz $17.95
Mt. Washington Art Glass, Sisk $49.95
Pocket Guide to Depression Glass & More, 13th Ed., Florence $12.95
Standard Encyclopedia of Carnival Glass, 9th Ed., Edwards/Carwile $29.95
Standard Carnival Glass Price Guide, 14th Ed., Edwards/Carwile $9.95
Standard Encyclopedia of Opalescent Glass, 4th Ed., Edwards/Carwile $24.95
Treasures of Very Rare Depression Glass, Florence $39.95

POTTERY

American Art Pottery, Sigafoose $24.95
Blue & White Stoneware, McNerney $9.95
Collectible Cups & Saucers, Harran $18.95
Collectible Cups & Saucers, Book III, Harran $24.95
Collectible Vernon Kilns, 2nd Edition, Nelson $29.95
Collecting Head Vases, Barron $24.95
Collector's Encyclopedia of American Dinnerware, Cunningham $24.95
Collector's Encyclopedia of Bauer Pottery, Chipman $24.95
Collector's Encyclopedia of California Pottery, 2nd Ed., Chipman $24.95
Collector's Encyclopedia of Cookie Jars, Book II, Roerig $24.95
Collector's Encyclopedia of Cookie Jars, Book III, Roerig $24.95
Collector's Encyclopedia of Fiesta, 9th Ed., Huxford $24.95
Collector's Encyclopedia of Early Noritake, Alden $24.95
Collector's Encyclopedia of Flow Blue China, 2nd Ed., Gaston $24.95
Collector's Encyclopedia of Homer Laughlin China, Jasper $24.95
Collector's Encyclopedia of Hull Pottery, Roberts $19.95
Collector's Encyclopedia of Limoges Porcelain, 3rd Ed., Gaston $29.95
Collector's Encyclopedia of Majolica Pottery, Katz-Marks $19.95
Collector's Encyclopedia of McCoy Pottery, Huxford $19.95
Collector's Encyclopedia of Niloak, 2nd Edition, Gifford $29.95
Collector's Encyclopedia of Pickard China, Reed $29.95
Collector's Encyclopedia of Red Wing Art Pottery, Dollen $24.95
Collector's Encyclopedia of Rosemeade Pottery, Dommel $24.95
Collector's Encyclopedia of Roseville Pottery, Revised, Huxford/Nickel ... $24.95
Collector's Encyclopedia of Roseville Pottery, 2nd Series, Huxford/Nickel. $24.95
Collector's Encyclopedia of Russel Wright, 3rd Editon, Kerr $29.95
Collector's Encyclopedia of Stangl Artware, Lamps, and Birds, Runge $29.95
Collector's Encyclopedia of Van Briggle Art Pottery, Sasicki $24.95
Collector's Guide to Feather Edge Ware, McAllister $19.95
Collector's Guide to Made in Japan Ceramics, Book IV, White $24.95
Cookie Jars, Westfall $9.95
Cookie Jars, Book II, Westfall $19.95
Decorative American Pottery & Whiteware, Wilby $29.95
Dresden Porcelain Studios, Harran $29.95
Florence's Big Book of Salt & Pepper Shakers $24.95
Gaston's Blue Willow, 3rd Edition $19.95
Lehner's Ency. of U.S. Marks on Pottery, Porcelain & China $24.95
McCoy Pottery, Collector's Reference & Value Guide, Hanson/Nissen $19.95
McCoy Pottery, Volume III, Hanson & Nissen $24.95
McCoy Pottery Wall Pockets & Decorations, Nissen $24.95
North Carolina Art Pottery, 1900 – 1960, James/Leftwich $24.95
Pictorial Guide to Pottery & Porcelain Marks, Lage $29.95

5691 Post86 Fiesta, Identification & Value Guide, Racheter $19.95
1670 Red Wing Collectibles, DePasquale $9.95
1440 Red Wing Stoneware, DePasquale $9.95
6037 Rookwood Pottery, Nicholson & Thomas $24.95
6236 Rookwood Pottery, 10 Years of Auction Results, 1990 – 2002, Treadway $39.95
1632 Salt & Pepper Shakers, Guarnaccia $9.95
5091 Salt & Pepper Shakers II, Guarnaccia $18.95
3443 Salt & Pepper Shakers IV, Guarnaccia $18.95
3738 Shawnee Pottery, Mangus $24.95
4629 Turn of the Century American Dinnerware, 1880s–1920s, Jasper $24.95
5924 Zanesville Stoneware Company, Rans, Ralston & Russell $24.95

OTHER COLLECTIBLES

5916 Advertising Paperweights, Holiner & Kammerman $24.95
5838 Advertising Thermometers, Merritt $16.95
5898 Antique & Contemporary Advertising Memorabilia, Summers $24.95
5814 Antique Brass & Copper Collectibles, Gaston $24.95
1880 Antique Iron, McNerney $9.95
3872 Antique Tins, Dodge $24.95
4845 Antique Typewriters & Office Collectibles, Rehr $19.95
5607 Antiquing and Collecting on the Internet, Parry $12.95
1128 Bottle Pricing Guide, 3rd Ed., Cleveland $7.95
6345 Business & Tax Guide for Antiques & Collectibles, Kelly $14.95
6225 Captain John's Fishing Tackle Price Guide, Kolbeck/Lewis $19.95
3718 Collectible Aluminum, Grist $16.95
6342 Collectible Soda Pop Memorabilia, Summers $24.95
5060 Collectible Souvenir Spoons, Bednersh $19.95
5676 Collectible Souvenir Spoons, Book II, Bednersh $29.95
5666 Collector's Encyclopedia of Granite Ware, Book 2, Greguire $29.95
5836 Collector's Guide to Antique Radios, 5th Ed., Bunis $19.95
3966 Collector's Guide to Inkwells, Identification & Values, Badders $18.95
4947 Collector's Guide to Inkwells, Book II, Badders $19.95
5681 Collector's Guide to Lunchboxes, White $19.95
4864 Collector's Guide to Wallace Nutting Pictures, Ivankovich $18.95
5683 Fishing Lure Collectibles, Vol. 1, Murphy/Edmisten $29.95
6328 Flea Market Trader, 14th Ed., Huxford $12.95
6227 Garage Sale & Flea Market Annual, 11th Edition, Huxford $19.95
4945 G-Men and FBI Toys and Collectibles, Whitworth $18.95
3819 General Store Collectibles, Wilson $24.95
5912 The Heddon Legacy, A Century of Classic Lures, Roberts & Pavey $29.95
2216 Kitchen Antiques, 1790–1940, McNerney $14.95
5991 Lighting Devices & Accessories of the 17th – 19th Centuries, Hamper $9.95
5686 Lighting Fixtures of the Depression Era, Book I, Thomas $24.95
4950 The Lone Ranger, Collector's Reference & Value Guide, Felbinger $18.95
6028 Modern Fishing Lure Collectibles, Vol. 1, Lewis $24.95
6131 Modern Fishing Lure Collectibles, Vol. 2, Lewis $24.95
6322 Pictorial Guide to Christmas Ornaments & Collectibles, Johnson $29.95
2026 Railroad Collectibles, 4th Ed., Baker $14.95
5619 Roy Rogers and Dale Evans Toys & Memorabilia, Coyle $24.95
6339 Schroeder's Antiques Price Guide, 22nd Edition $14.95
5007 Silverplated Flatware, Revised 4th Edition, Hagan $18.95
6239 Star Wars Super Collector's Wish Book, 2nd Ed., Carlton $29.95
6139 Summers' Guide to Coca-Cola, 4th Ed. $24.95
6324 Summers' Pocket Guide to Coca-Cola, 4th Ed. $12.95
3977 Value Guide to Gas Station Memorabilia, Summers & Priddy $24.95
4877 Vintage Bar Ware, Visakay $24.95
5925 The Vintage Era of Golf Club Collectibles, John $29.95
6010 The Vintage Era of Golf Club Collectibles Collector's Log, John $9.95
6036 Vintage Quilts, Aug, Newman & Roy $24.95

This is only a partial listing of the books on antiques that are available from Collector Books. All books are well illustrated and contain current values. Most of these books are available from your local bookseller, antique dealer, or public library. If you are unable to locate certain titles in your area, you may order by mail from **COLLECTOR BOOKS**, P.O. Box 3009, Paducah, KY 42002-3009. Customers with Visa, Master Card, or Discover may phone in orders from 7:00a.m. to 5:00 p.m. CT, Monday – Friday, toll free **1-800-626-5420**, or online at **www.collectorbooks.com**. Add $3.00 for postage for the first book ordered and 50¢ for each additional book. Include item number, title, and price when ordering. Allow 14 to 21 days for delivery.

1-800-626-5420   Fax: 1-270-898-8890

www.collectorbooks.com

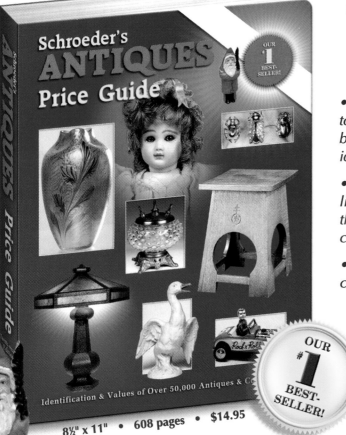